Parité!

CHICAGO STUDIES IN PRACTICES OF MEANING

Edited by

Jean Comaroff, Andreas Glaeser,

William H. Sewell Jr., and Lisa Wedeen

᪥

Also in the series:

Producing India: From Colonial Economy to National Space

by Manu Goswami

Logics of History: Social Theory and Social Transformation

by William H. Sewell Jr.

Parité!

SEXUAL EQUALITY AND THE CRISIS OF FRENCH UNIVERSALISM

Joan Wallach Scott

The University of Chicago Press
CHICAGO & LONDON

JOAN WALLACH SCOTT is professor of social science at the
Institute for Advanced Study. Her most recent book is *Only Paradoxes
to Offer: French Feminists and the Rights of Man.*

The University of Chicago Press, Chicago 60637
The University of Chicago Press, Ltd., London
© 2005 by The University of Chicago
All rights reserved. Published 2005
Printed in the United States of America

14 13 12 11 10 09 08 07 06 05   5 4 3 2 1

ISBN (cloth): 0-226-74107-9
ISBN (paper): 0-226-74108-7

Library of Congress Cataloging-In-Publication Data

Scott, Joan Wallach.
    Parité! : sexual equality and the crisis of French universalism /
Joan Wallach Scott.
        p.   cm. — (Chicago studies in practices of meaning)
    Includes bibliographical references and index.
    ISBN 0-226-74107-9 (cloth : acid-free paper) —
    ISBN 0-226-74108-7 (paper : acid-free paper)
    1. Women in politics—France.   2. Women political candidates—
France.   3. Equality—France.   4. Feminism—France.   I. Title.
II. Series.
    HQ1236.5.F8S36   2005
    320'.082'0944—dc22

                                                    2005050585

For Françoise and Claude

CONTENTS

ACKNOWLEDGMENTS

It is rare that a historian who has worked primarily in the nineteenth century gets to know the people she writes about beyond the traces they have left behind. For that reason, this study of the *parité* movement in France in the last decade of the twentieth century has presented new challenges for me. First among them has been to make sense of a political movement in process and to keep track of it as it faced new developments, forged new strategies, produced ever more quantities of documentation, and offered changing assessments of what it had or had not accomplished—how to keep a historian's distance, in other words, when time did not automatically provide it. Second has been to maintain the integrity of my interpretations, and to balance that against a strongly felt sense of responsibility to those who lent me their archives and their time and who did not (or might not) necessarily agree with my readings of their actions and words—how to be a historian of the present, and of a movement for whose members I had a certain sympathy, without losing the critical perspective so necessary to the task. Third has been to keep the focus on the issues that have seemed central for my ongoing preoccupation with the intellectual history of feminism, even as I was tempted to recount anecdotes I had heard or witnessed, delve at length into the biographies of some of the major players, or provide colorful details about personalities and their conflicts, commitments, and motives. This temptation, always there for historians of any period, who are, after all, professional storytellers, is particularly strong when one has experienced things firsthand.

If I have succeeded in meeting these challenges, it is at least in part due to the help I have received from friends and colleagues, as well as from some of the *paritaristes* who figure in this story. The critical advice of Elizabeth Weed was, as always, tremendously important for the conceptualization of my argument. Her clarity inevitably enables me to think more clearly. David Bell, Eric Fassin, Paul Friedland, Denise Riley, and William Sewell Jr. all read versions of the whole manuscript, and each offered different but equally valuable suggestions about how to improve it. I am grateful for their interest, their generosity, and their advice. As the book was developing, I tried out its material in a number of venues, where I was fortunate to get critical responses from Andrew Aisenberg, Homi Bhabha, John Borneman, John Bowen, Warren Breckman, T. David Brent, Wendy Brown, Judith Butler, Frances Ferguson, Susan Gal, Catherine Gallagher, Clifford Geertz, Andreas Glaeser, Rena Lederman, Patchen Markell, Miglena Nikolchina, Danilyn Rutherford, Jordan Stein, Tyler Stovall, Judith Surkis, and Lisa Weeden. Their comments moved the project forward and sometimes redirected parts of it in exactly the way academic exchanges are supposed to work. Thanks to Yves Sintomer for sharing his thesis with me, to Anne Le Gall for the hours of interview time she gave me, and to Debra Keates and James Swenson, who came to the rescue when I encountered difficulty translating some of the citations. Paula Cossart has been the ideal research assistant: savvy, knowledgeable, and amazingly quick in turning up sources. Her intelligent attention to substance and detail—in equal measure—has saved me from many mistakes, large and small. Gratitude is an inadequate word for my appreciation of the work she has done. At the University of Chicago Press, Margaret Mahan has been a terrific copyeditor. And David Brent has provided guidance and support from the outset. The staff at the Historical Studies/Social Science Library at the Institute for Advanced Study, especially the head librarian Marcia Tucker, has provided endless support. My secretary, Nancy Cotterman, has wrestled with various versions of the manuscript, mastered new electronic techniques, turned up elusive articles on the Internet or in libraries, and reacted to last-minute pressures with good will, good cheer, and impressive expertise. If there are limits to her patience and her abilities, I haven't yet discovered them.

Finally a word about some of the women who play such a big part in this story. Françoise Gaspard and Claude Servan-Schreiber shared their experience and their papers with me. (In fact, I had the good fortune to consult and organize Gaspard's papers before she deposited them in the Women's History archives at the University of Anger.) They answered my many questions patiently, directed me to sources and books I probably would not have found on my own, and told me frankly when they disagreed with my interpretations. Conversations with them enabled me to sharpen my analysis, sometimes in ways that diverged even more from their own accounts. I never felt obligated to conform to their views or to tell what they might have considered the official story of the movement. It was just the opposite: they knew I would tell the story as I understood it, which is what I have done. It is precisely because they have inspired and enabled the writing of a book that takes analytic distance from the movement they founded that I have dedicated this work to them. They are feminists who understand the critical power not only of theory and politics but of history.

INTRODUCTION

France today is in the throes of a crisis that began in the last decades of the twentieth century. It is a crisis defined through the rhetoric of universalism—a universalism taken to be uniquely French and therefore a defining trait of the system of republican democracy, its most enduring value, its most precious political asset. According to its defenders, French universalism has been, since the Revolution of 1789, the guarantee of equality before the law. It rests on a notion of politics that takes the abstract individual to be the representative not only of citizens but also of the nation. And it rests, as well, on the assumption that all citizens, whatever their origins, must assimilate to a singular standard in order to be fully French.

During the 1980s and 1990s, the rhetoric of universalism was offered in response to a series of challenges that involved claims for the recognition of the rights of different groups (women's right of access to elective office, the rights of North African immigrants and their children to be fully French, and the rights of cohabiting homosexual couples to enjoy the same benefits as heterosexual couples, including marriage) as the way to end discrimination against them. Discrimination that was not addressed—or was covered over—by invocations of universalism.

The debates have been furious. Defenders of the Republic have raised the flag of universalism, treating those who would recognize difference as, if not traitors, then as agents of American multiculturalism. The critics themselves have been divided. A few have insisted that the principle of universalism is itself the problem. But most have argued that they are not disputing the premises of universalism but realizing them in uncorrupted, purer form. Behind these debates lie much bigger questions, not only for France but for the systems of representative democracy born in the eighteenth century as alternatives to feudalism. Are these systems still relevant in the twenty-first century—the age of postcolonialism, postmodernity, and global capitalism? And what alternatives do we have?

This book is meant to open a discussion of these questions by looking at one of the movements that offered a challenge to French representative democracy in the 1990s by demanding a recognition of difference. The *mouvement pour la parité* was a feminist movement that sought to refigure the terms of French universalism in order to increase the numbers of women in elective office. The partial realization of that goal came with the law of June 6, 2000, which now requires that half of all candidates for almost all political offices be women.

The "*parité* law" (as it was popularly referred to), was unprecedented in France and, indeed, throughout the world. There are now many countries that have taken measures to increase the numbers of women in elective office, but France is generally considered to have been the first to insist that 50% of candidates for elective office be women.[1] This has astonished many observers, who wonder how the country that, all through the 1990s, ranked near the bottom of the list of European nations for the representation of women in the national parliament, managed to pass such a radical law. In its original conception, it was indeed radical. But even in its present form, the law not only expects political parties to drastically change their ways, it also challenges long-standing notions of republican representation premised on the universalism of a singular abstract individual. The new universalism, according to the proponents of parité, is that individuals are men *and* women. Parité's supporters (the *paritaristes*) deny that their law is an imposition of quotas (as many Americans who hear about it for the first time assume); it is rather the recognition of the universality of the physical difference of sex. Nor is it affirmative action as Americans have conceived it; it is not a program to remedy past discrimination by positively favoring an excluded group. Women are not a separate social category; according to advocates of parité, women are individuals. This is not multiculturalism (as we shall see in what follows, a much reviled concept in France), but a way of redefining who counts as an individual, a true realization of the principles of republican democracy.

When the law passed, it was hailed as a triumph in government publications. It was pathbreaking, a "rupture with the past." "For the first time in history," one pamphlet announced, "a country—France—has legislation that promotes equal numbers of women and men in elected assemblies."[2] This kind of self-congratulation could not have been predicted before the law passed. When the idea of a parité law was first introduced and during the campaign for its passage, it occasioned an enormous, often bitter controversy. Intellectuals and politicians argued at length about the implications of such a law for the future of feminism and of republicanism. The relation of sexual difference to republican citizenship was at the heart of this decade-long debate. How fundamental was sexual difference? Were the paritaristes making an essentialist argument about the connection between biology and politics, or were they insisting only that cultural constructions of gender be taken into account? If, as they charged, the supposedly neuter individual had always been coded masculine, would acknowledging that individuals come in two sexes perpetuate or end discrimination against women? And what was the nature of the discrimination?

Women had won the vote, after all, in 1944, so they were already designated citizens. The paritaristes were protesting women's systematic exclusion from the ranks of elected legislators by a party structure that functioned, they said, as a closed fraternity. It was not only unfair but undemocratic, the paritaristes claimed, for women to be denied access to decision-making. By undemocratic they meant unrepresentative, but the meaning of fair representation wasn't entirely clear. Did it simply require that women have access to the position of representative, a member of the body charged with formulating law in the name of the nation? Or did it signify something more: the explicit consideration of women's voices and women's interests by legislators who routinely ignored them? But were women's interests uniform and distinctive enough to require separate representation, and were women the only ones who could represent these interests? And was this a plausible political claim in a republican system that—in principle at least—rejected the notion that elected officials spoke for distinctive groups in society? Here the goal of increasing the numbers of women in power confronted the prevailing theory of representation: elected officials do not reflect specific constituencies but legislate in the name of the nation as a whole. Then what difference will it make if more women are elected? And how to make the case (can it be made?) for electing more women without calling into question the system of representation upon which French republicanism was based?

These were the questions that drew my interest as the campaign for parité developed in the course of the 1990s. I first learned about the parité movement in 1993, as I was working on a book about the history of French feminism. The *New York Times* carried a story in which one of the leaders of the movement, Claude Servan-Schreiber, acknowledged that while their goal might be "a bit utopian," the paritaristes' purpose was to secure fundamental change. "Exclusion of women has been part of France's political philosophy since the Revolution," she said; the point of parité was to alter that philosophy and the practices it countenanced.[3] In its desire to change both theory and practice, the parité movement resembled its feminist predecessors—the ones I was writing about—but there was a difference I needed to understand more fully. Unlike those earlier movements, which took French republicanism to be immutable, the parité movement sought to change the terms of republicanism by addressing the very problem I thought was intractable: the problem of sexual difference. If the activists I wrote about in *Only Paradoxes to Offer* got caught up in a logic of "sameness versus difference" while trying to argue for the equality of women and men, the paritaristes seemed to have figured a way out of the paradox I had described as one of feminism's constitutive contradictions.[4] Instead of saying either that women were the same as men (and therefore entitled to equal participation in politics), or that they were different (and therefore would provide something that was lacking in the political sphere), the paritaristes refused to deal in gender stereotypes at all. At the same time, they insisted that sex had to be included in any conception of abstract individualism for genuine equality to prevail. The abstract individual, that neutral figure upon which universalism depended—without religion, occupation, social position, race, or ethnicity—had to be reconceived of as sexed. Here was the innovation: unlike previous feminisms, women were no longer being made to fit a neutral figure (historically imagined as male), nor were they reaching for a separate incarnation of femininity; instead, the abstract individual itself was being refigured to accommodate women. If the human individual were understood to come in one of two sexes, the paritaristes reasoned, then the difference of sex could no longer be taken as the antithesis of universalism, and universalism's reach would be extended to women. But wasn't this a denial of abstraction? No, the paritaristes replied, because anatomical dualism could be distinguished from sexual difference, not as nature was from culture but as the abstract was from the concrete. The argument for parité was, at the outset, neither essentialist nor separatist; it was not about the particular qualities women would bring to politics or about the need to represent a special women's interest. Instead—and this is what has intrigued me since I began reading about it— the original argument for parité was rigorously universalist.

Initially, I found the distinction between anatomical dualism and sexual difference hard to follow, as I think many American readers will. Our ways of thinking about discrimination and democracy understand politics to be about conflicts of interests, about groups and their representatives. Although critics of affirmative action have taken to arguing about the rights of individuals and the dangers of thinking about individuals only as members of groups, the individual-versus-group distinction is not about abstraction in the United States. Rather it is about how we conceive—in concrete terms—of society and politics: as a collection of diverse individuals or as an amalgam of differently situated competing groups, as a pluralist mix or as a field of force marked by collective struggles for power. When we talk about political representation and the rights of citizens, it is specific individuals and groups we have in mind. For us, politics and society are interrelated institutions, the one is supposed to reflect and organize the other. "America" is the result of their interplay.[5]

In France, society and politics (often counterposed as "the social" and "the political") are considered separate entities in tension with one another. According to the prevailing interpretation of republican political philosophy, both the nation and the individual are abstractions, not reflections of social groups or persons. This, as I will explain in the chapters that follow, is the key to a claim for a distinctively French universalism, which takes abstraction to be the foundation of successful politics. The dilemma that confronted generations of feminists was how to make a case for the inclusion of women (as citizens, voters, elected representatives) when the difference of sex was considered an obstacle to abstraction, and when women were taken as the embodiment of the difference of sex. Embodiment, after all, was the opposite of abstraction; hence women could not be abstract individuals. While earlier feminist movements skirted the issues of abstraction and embodiment, either by insisting on the irrelevance of bodies or by attacking the requirements of abstraction, the parité movement tried to make the difference of sex amenable to abstraction. In a strikingly original and paradoxical move, the paritaristes sought to *unsex* the national representation by *sexing* the individual.

The difficulties they encountered in the process were enormous, not least because both critics and some supporters of the movement did not fully grasp its founding idea. Distinguishing between the abstraction of anatomical duality and the concrete cultural attributions of meaning to sexed bodies (what is usually referred to as "sexual difference") proved to be a complicated task, the more so because this was a political movement, consumed with the daily tasks of building a following and pressuring politicians. In addition, at a critical moment in the campaign the demand for parité coincided with the demands of homosexuals for political recognition, and the ensuing controversy changed the terms of the original appeal for a parité law. Still, parité managed to become a popular cause, endorsed not only by an extensive network of supporters but by an enthusiastic general public. And its champions succeeded in passing a law that, at the very least, now has the potential to constrain the behavior of politicians who for more than a century had contrived—in the name of universalism—to exclude women from full participation in representative democracy.

This book follows the parité movement, the controversies it provoked, and the constituencies it mobilized, over the course of its surprisingly brief history (1992–2000). It treats parité as a commentary on French political philosophy and French practical politics; the two are different, but the connections between them, in this case, are fascinating. Indeed, it is the connections between them that ultimately make sense of the movement and, beyond that, of some of the major questions raised by second-wave feminism (both in the United States and France): Is anatomical duality susceptible to abstraction? Is sexual difference (understood as the attribution of meaning—psychic, cultural, political) a fixed or a mutable phenomenon? Can the symbolics of sexual difference be stripped of their meaning—*de*symbolized—or is it only resymbolization that is possible? For many feminists (to say nothing of philosophers and psychoanalysts) those questions have required "an obligatory detour via philosophy."[6] My approach, following the hunch of the parité movement as well as my own disciplinary inclination, takes a different route, seeking its insights not so much in philosophy, as in history.

⚙

By "history" I do not mean a narrative account of the movement as a chapter in a self-contained women's history. Of course, the movement for parité was a feminist campaign, even though it occasioned serious disagreement among those who consider themselves advocates of women's rights. But it would be a mistake to treat it only in those terms. Instead, the movement for parité has to be understood (as does any such movement) as a development within the larger scheme of French politics and, beyond that, within the context of major changes faced by Western democracies in the late twentieth century.

The demand for equalizing women's access to elective office emerged at a moment when both the notion and the practice of representation were perceived to be in crisis. Although (as we shall see in what follows) it took a particular form in France, the crisis was, or is, a more general phenomenon evident in many Western democracies. Even as democracy was being heralded as the normative form of political organization after the fall of communism in 1989, the problem of dealing with exclusions based on social differences has come to the fore, and these exclusions often focus on or allude to the status and treatment of women. The system of democratic representation designed in the eighteenth century has not been able to accommodate the emergence of new forms of corporatism; racial, ethnic, religious, and other differences pose troubling political challenges to once unified national projects. Clifford Geertz has tellingly referred to a "world in pieces," characterized by massive migrations and in which lines of affiliation and identification cross national boundaries such that nations no longer command the primary allegiance of large sectors of their populations. "Heterogeneity is the norm," he writes, "conflict the ordering force."[7]

The internal pressures undermining a sense of cultural, hence of national, solidarity are compounded by external pressures: global markets, which don't always operate in terms of national interests; international institutions (the World Court, the World Bank, the International Monetary Fund, the United Nations), whose rulings and policies challenge the very notion of state sovereignty even as they formally respect it; and—in Europe—the emergence of the European Union, which has begun to dismantle the boundaries (border police, passports, fiscal policy, currency) and the social policies (the welfare state, labor market regulation, gender relations) that long distinguished one nation from another. Although official rhetoric and popular opinion have usually equated European unification, as well as the expansion of the European Community beyond the original member nations, with progress, there is also evidence of deep anxiety about what the loss or compromise of national sovereignty might mean. One form this anxiety has taken is preoccupation with the procedures and processes of domestic politics, as if they existed apart from the external pressures on nation-states. I think the attention being paid by political theorists and politicians to "civil society" as a national problem is a displacement of this kind. Not that the growing interest in institutions mediating between the public and the private, or the political and the familial, isn't in part a consequence of the fall of communism and the desire to implant democracy in the countries of the former Soviet bloc. But references to "civil society" are also part of many discussions about the health of individual Western European democracies, and these references tend to function as an entirely internal gauge of the workings of national political systems. It is as if the national systems (and so the sovereign nation-state) could be fixed if only more attention were paid to civil society; there is little recognition, at least within conversations about civil society, that the problem exceeds this kind of local solution.

The questions of difference and civil society are related for at least two reasons. First, the institutions of civil society are supposed to be the place where differences find a voice that can then be heard in the political realm. Second, conflicts about how or whether to grant political representation for these differences, as well as conflicts about the strength and representability of civil society, can be taken as both symptom and cause of the weakening coherence of democratic nation-states.

In France, a "crisis of representation" was declared by pundits and politicians in 1988–89, at the moment of the bicentennial of the French Revolution. Occasioned by a surprisingly strong showing, in the first round of the presidential election of 1988, of the far right's candidate for the presidency (the National Front's Jean-Marie Le Pen received 14% of the vote), the talk of crisis focused on the failure of "the political class" to fulfill its mandate to represent the nation. Politicians solemnly acknowledged the need to pay closer attention to "civil society," by which they meant the various constituencies that made up the national body, even as they disavowed the notion that elected officials served the particular interests of social groups. The resistance to representing the differences among groups was especially fierce in the face of growing demands by North African populations now settled in metropolitan France for recognition (and correction) of discrimination against them, discrimination based on cultural and religious practices considered antithetical to French standards. Indeed, the bicentennial was marked by a strong reaffirmation of what were said to be the timeless principles of French republicanism: the indivisibility of the national representation and hence the unity of the French nation. The French system rested, in this view, on a unique realization of universalism, the key to which was the abstract individual, who signified an explicit refusal to represent difference. I will examine the terms of this theory in greater detail in chapter one. Here I want to point out that the attention to historic tradition and to the singularity of French universalism came not only as evidence of domestic cultural dissensus grew ever more apparent but also as European unification moved inexorably forward, threatening to deprive France of many of the distinctive marks of its national sovereignty.

The movement for parité emerged at the juncture of these two opposing forces, on the one hand promising to strengthen the nation by realizing a more perfect vision of French universalism (one in which the recognition of difference would not signify a loss of cultural coherence) and, on the other, challenging the autonomy of the nation by bringing the force of European institutions to bear on the direction of French politics. The French *mouvement pour la parité* was the outgrowth of feminist lobbying within the European community for a greater role for women in decision-making, and it was a domestic campaign by French political women for a law that would overturn entrenched male control of access to elective office. The substance of the campaign—its theoretical formulations and tactical interventions—is the focus of this book. But so also is the insight the movement provides into French politics at the end of the twentieth century. When the paritaristes insisted that France live up to the mandates and policies of the European Union, they also appealed to the peculiarities of French republicanism to legitimize their claim. These demands were more often in conflict than complementary, and that was the point. For it was precisely by simultaneously evoking the threat of diminished sovereignty and offering to counteract it by shoring up national unity in a new way that parité made its mark. The strategic successes and vulnerabilities of the movement are best understood in terms of a series of double moves—moves that at once exposed and exploited a moment of contradiction in the history of the French nation-state.

If parité enables us to see that contradiction clearly and to appreciate its force, it is because (as I have argued before) conflicts involving the differences of the sexes are not isolated or marginal phenomena but central issues, or at least key factors, in alignments and realignments of power at the national and international levels. In fact, questions about the place of sexual difference—particularly about the position of women, control of their sexuality, and their access to politics—have become increasingly a focus of international concern. In that sense France, for all its uniqueness, provides insight into a more general phenomenon. The parité movement is a particularly compelling example of the growing importance of sexual difference for politics because it succeeded in passing a law that quite literally makes gender an enduring and undeniable factor in French political consciousness. But the significance of parité also lies beyond the literality of the law, in its demonstration of the inextricability of sexual difference and politics. This is the case in France, where republicanism and certain styles of heterosexual interaction are so intertwined that a critique of one is taken as an assault on the other. But I would also insist that France is a particular example of a more general proposition: histories that focus on sexual difference cannot be written apart from the histories of politics within which they take shape and to which they in turn give form, whereas histories of politics are often illuminated by feminist critiques that, at their best, uncover contradiction and exacerbate it in an effort to transform the status quo.

CHAPTER ONE

The Crisis of Representation

The demand for parité was unlike previous feminist demands for equality. Until 1944, the question of suffrage was paramount; the equal right of citizenship was, above all, conceived of as an equal right to vote. Of course, many feminists assumed that voting also meant that women would run for and hold office; to be a citizen was to have the possibility of serving as a representative. In 1849, Jeanne Deroin campaigned for a seat in the legislature as part of her insistence that the Second Republic allow women to vote. And when, in 1885, Hubertine Auclert drew up an electoral program which demanded that women and men exercise the vote, she also envisioned a legislative assembly "composed of as many women as men."[1] When women did win the vote, however, few were able to gain access to political office. After some debate among members of de Gaulle's provisional government about whether eligibility for office should be extended to women instead of or along with the right to vote (some conservative politicians worried that with men away at the front or in prison camps or dead, the vote of women in the first elections after the Liberation would unbalance the electorate), it was decided that "women are voters and are eligible for office under the same conditions as men."[2] But what was conceded in principle was hardly ever put into practice; women were only occasionally nominated for or elected to office in the second half of the twentieth century. Until 1997 they constituted no more than 6% of deputies in the National Assembly and rarely even 3% in the Senate.[3] Although no law or constitutional provision precluded women from becoming representatives, there seemed to be a tacit agreement to prevent them from doing so. It was that tacit agreement, taken to be symptomatic of male monopoly at the very centers of political power, that parité aimed to expose and overturn. The paritaristes' goal was to gain equal access for women as representatives of the French nation. Like Auclert, they wanted to see as many women as men in all the elective offices of France. Unlike her, they were addressing a situation in which women already had the right to vote; parité was not about being represented but about being a representative.

The call for increasing the number of women representatives was sounded often during the 1980s, particularly within political parties, but it didn't become a "movement" for equality until the early 1990s, when it also acquired a clear theoretical justification. At that point, a full-blown discussion, indeed an argument, about representation was in process. The language was urgent—the situation was deemed a crisis. Although there were few direct references to international pressures and to Europeanization, there was a prevailing sense (in the media and in political circles at least) that national sovereignty was being challenged at its core. The challenge came from two directions. The first was from the growing population of people of North African origin, a postcolonial phenomenon that exposed the inadequacies of cultural assimilation as a route to French citizenship. The second challenge was internal to the political system itself: politicians seemed cut off from contact with the citizens whose mandate they held. They were a professional caste apart, impervious, it seemed, to the needs of "civil society." And they were corrupt. A series of scandals in the late 1980s coincided with impressive electoral showings of the right-wing populist National Front, whose platform centered on ridding France of its immigrant problem. In 1988–89 the questions of immigrants and politicians were joined in a debate about the adequacy of the system of representation for governing the nation in the late twentieth century.

THE SUBJECT OF REPRESENTATION

The debates in 1988–89 grounded their arguments in references to the French Revolution; they mythologized its continuity and immutability. Looking back to the Revolution, they ignored many years of history and identified French republicanism with an unchanging commitment to abstract individualism. It is important here to discuss notions of representation during the Revolution in order to see how they were reified and used in the 1980s and 1990s.

The revolutionaries conceived of the republic in terms of two abstractions: that of the individual and that of the nation. As they dismantled the feudal regime in 1789, they replaced a system of corporate privilege with one based on individual rights. At that time sovereignty was said to reside not in the king but in "the people," the citizens who constituted the nation. This change involved not only the relocation of sovereignty from the king to the people but—according to the historian Paul Friedland—a fundamental shift in the notion of representation itself. No longer did representation denote the "making present" of the nation in the body of the king (as the Eucharist "made present" the body and blood of Christ); now representatives simply spoke on behalf of the abstract entity that was the nation. The National Assembly, the metaphoric body of the nation, had replaced the real body of the king.[4] The nation was now the embodiment of the people, its laws the expression of their will. Since France was too large a country for citizens to gather in one place (as had been the case for the first democracies in the Greek city-states so admired by Rousseau), the revolutionaries agreed that there had to be some delegation of sovereign authority to those who would speak in the people's name. These representatives were not to be, as in the Old Regime, spokesmen for discrete corporate interests; instead, each stood for the general interest of the collectivity as a whole. Unlike the architects of the American system (which was being articulated at the same time, most famously by James Madison in the Federalist Papers), who saw legislatures as arenas of conflicting interests and defined representatives as voices for particular social and economic groups or factions, the French revolutionaries took the abstraction of the nation as the referent for representation. Representatives were the tangible embodiment of the nation as a whole; it was a nation "one and indivisible."

The ability of any citizen to stand for, or to represent, the nation derived from the understanding of political individuals as abstracted from their social attributes—wealth, family, occupation, religion, profession. The abbé Sieyès put it succinctly, "Democracy is the complete sacrifice of the individual to the *res publica,* that is to say of the concrete being to the abstract being."[5] And the Jacobin leader Maximilien Robespierre later agreed: "To be good, it is necessary for the public official [*magistrat*] to immolate himself to the people."[6] Abstract individuals were commensurable and interchangeable units, possessing in common only that independent rationality upon which political life was thought to depend. The nation they constituted was equally abstract, not a reflection of the disparate and divisive realities of society but a fictional entity—a unified totality, the embodiment of "the people." There were no politically relevant differences within "the people," as Sieyès maintained: "There exists only one order in the state, or, rather, there are no longer any orders because representation is common and equal for all. No class of citizens can hope to keep for itself a partial, separate, and unequal representation. That would be a political monstrosity; it has been defeated forever."[7] This view was enshrined in the Constitution of 1791, which rejected even the notion of geographical distinctions among representatives: "The representatives chosen in the departments will represent not a particular department but the whole nation; they have no special mandate from the department."[8] Although, by definition, anyone could be a representative, the choice of especially competent men (often lawyers in this period and through much of the nineteenth century) did not conflict at all with liberal republican theory; if abstract individuals were interchangeable, why not choose those best able to express the will of the nation?

For the revolutionaries the difficult questions revolved not around competence or qualification but around the relationship between individual representatives and the nation. Did the representatives constitute the nation, or did the nation delegate its sovereignty to its representatives? According to the first of these possibilities, individuals were responsible only to themselves; once chosen, their actions were by definition an expression of the general will. According to the second, representatives were understood as reflecting a previously existing will; if their actions did not conform to the expectations of the people, their mandate could be withdrawn. The difference between these two notions of the role of the representative was at the heart of the struggle between the Gironde and the Jacobins during the Revolution.[9] Liberals like the politician and mathematician Condorcet held to the notion that the nation only existed through its representatives. "Representative of the people, I will do what I think is in their interest. They sent me to express my ideas, not theirs: the absolute independence of my opinions is the first of my duties toward them."[10] Robespierre, in contrast, believed that the nation preexisted those chosen to represent it. "It is by an odd reversal of all conceptions that public officeholders have been regarded as essentially destined to direct the public reason; on the contrary, it is the public reason which must be master over them and must judge them. . . . However virtuous a man in office may be, he is never as virtuous as the entire nation."[11] Although the imposition of the Terror by the Jacobins temporarily resolved this difference of opinion, it did not erase it. To this day, aspects of these competing views of the representative (independent agent or people's delegate) can be found in proposals for political reform.

Friedland argues that, despite these different views of the representative, the political edifice of representative democracy "was never intended to be democratic." Instead, it was "predicated on the exclusion from active political power of the very people in whose name their government claimed to rule." As in the theater of the time, the citizenry was divided into actors and audience: "political actors acted, political audiences watched, preferably in silence."[12] Abstract individualism was the legitimating premise of this effective separation of power; it worked to obscure the ways in which political audiences were disempowered, if not disenfranchised. Legislators could stand for citizens and for the nation precisely because they were individuals; the impression of synecdoche served to distract attention from political inequality.

The abstractions of individual and nation were the foundation on which theories of representation were built; they also were the key to a distinctively French concept of universalism—one that rested on an opposition between the political and the social, the abstract and the concrete. The abstractions allowed the revolutionaries to substitute the idea of formal political equality for the corporate hierarchies of the Old Regime and republican unity for the rule of kings. And they held out a promise of universal inclusion in political life. Abstraction, after all, meant disregarding the attributes that distinguished people in their ordinary lives; by this measure any individual could be considered a citizen. Indeed, as Etienne Balibar has pointed out, abstract individualism understands itself to be a *fictitious* universality: "not the idea that the common nature of individuals is given or already there, but rather the fact that it is produced inasmuch as particular identities are relativized and become mediations for the realization of a superior and more abstract goal."[13] In this sense, universality does not rest on the exclusion of the particular but on (socially or politically) agreed-upon indifference to certain particularities. The abstract always must take concrete social characteristics into account, if only to discount them, and so becomes the site of arguments about whether there can be limits to abstraction and of what these limits consist. Jacques Rancière puts it another way. Democracy, he argues, rests on a necessary tension between the abstraction of "the people" and the social reality such abstraction obscures. Democratic politics is the adjudication of the claims by various constituencies to represent or to be represented as the people.[14]

The tensions between the abstract political and the concrete social were present in political debate from the Revolution on, although there is a myth (much in evidence in the 1980s and 1990s) that posits pure abstraction as the enduring essence of French republicanism. Confronted with the logical implications of their rhetoric and worried about the practical consequences of enfranchising all adults (including the illiterate, the propertyless with no stake in society), the revolutionary politicians soon qualified their universalism: they made commonality a prerequisite for, rather than a consequence of, abstraction and excluded those whose difference, they said, was not susceptible to abstraction, those whose difference somehow tainted the purity and transparency of representation. In the 1790s, Jews were admitted to citizenship only when they relinquished allegiance to their "nation" and became individuals for whom religion was a private matter. Clermont-Tonnerre's is the classic formulation of this principle: "Grant nothing to the Jews as a nation and everything to them as individuals."[15] Autonomy was another requirement for individuality; thus people whose circumstances made them dependent—wage-earners and women—were initially ruled ineligible for citizenship. Dependency, however, was not the only ground for the exclusion. When property qualifications for citizenship were eliminated (in 1793, and again in 1848), the difference of their sex prevented women from enjoying the rights of citizenship.

It was not as women, though, but as embodiments of sexual difference that they were excluded. Following the arguments of Rousseau, many of the revolutionaries took sexual difference as a template for division and divisiveness more generally. "There is no parity between the two sexes as a consequence of sex," Rousseau wrote in *Emile.*[16] Where there were women, there was jealousy and rivalry, passion and loss of control among men. Without women, the dangers of such conflict were eliminated. "The two sexes ought to come together sometimes and live apart ordinarily," Rousseau advised. In "a commerce that is too intimate . . . , we [men] lose both our morals and our constitution . . . ; women make us into women."[17] Others considered that women's voice was already represented by the men in their families; it would be redundant to also give women a vote. As one commentator put it, "Husband and wife are one political person and can never be anything else even if they are two civil persons. . . . The vote of the one counts for both; that of the wife is virtually included in that of the husband."[18] The reasons for excluding women from citizenship were offered in sets of binary oppositions that posited women in terms of the concrete, the emotional, and the natural (hence not susceptible to abstraction) and men in terms of reason and politics (hence operating entirely in the realm of abstraction). Pierre Rosanvallon suggests that the difference of sex (which he, like the revolutionaries, assumes to be a self-evident, natural difference—it was not "one social construction among others") could not be accommodated by abstraction. "The individual man and the individual woman cannot be recognized politically in both their equivalence and their difference at the same time."[19] Thus sexual difference, in the person of the woman, was not included in the list of traits that could be abstracted for purposes of citizenship. Women's exclusion was not just about eliminating women's influence. It also served a major symbolic function as a reminder of the existence of irreducible difference—unresolvable antagonism within the national body, which posed a threat to the abstraction and thus the very existence of national unity.[20]

Universality's definition rested on the possibility of reductive commonality. Some, like Condorcet, maintained that women were no less individuals than men for purposes of citizenship since they had reason in common with men.

"Human rights belong to all sentient beings capable of acquiring moral ideas and of reasoning about them. Since women have these qualities, they necessarily have equal rights. Either no individual of the human species has rights or all have them. It would be difficult to prove that women don't have the rights of citizens."[21] The majority of the revolutionaries, however, contended that the irreducible difference exemplified by sexual difference had to be repressed if commonality were to be achieved. "Since when is it permitted to give up one's sex?" thundered the Jacobin Pierre-Gaspard Chaumette to a group of women who dared to enter the Convention. "Is it to men that nature confided domestic cares? Has she given us breasts to feed our children?"[22] Pierre-Joseph Proudhon echoed this view in 1849, when he objected to feminist Jeanne Deroin's attempt to run for office. A female legislator, he quipped, made as much sense as a male wet nurse. Her reply—"Show me which organ is required for the functions of the legislator and I will concede the debate"—exposed the symbolic investments of his argument: well beyond any logical criteria or substantive discussion of the real capabilities and capacities of women, sexual difference stood for difference itself.[23] Not just any difference, but one so primary, so rooted in nature, so visible, that it could not be subsumed by abstraction.

Yet specific exclusions—of the propertyless, of workers, of women—contradicted the stated promise of universal rights and raised the question (always inherent in fictitious universalism anyway) of social influences on the process of abstraction. Was there a flaw in the way abstraction was being implemented, or was the abstract individual the wrong way to represent the nation? Should representation follow an abstract mode or a concrete one—that is, should the nation be conceived as constituted by interchangeable individuals or by members of socially differentiated units? The tension between the abstract and concrete modes of representation has persisted to this day. The defenders of the abstract mode argue that it alone guarantees universal equality; the defenders of the concrete mode do not reject universalism but think equality is achieved by addressing rather than ignoring social distinctions. The debate focuses on the status of difference: the concrete mode, sometimes referred to as *representativity*, calls for differences to be made visible, so that rights can literally be seen to be exercised by all. The abstract mode, sometimes referred to as *representation*, requires the assimilation of those previously excluded on account of their differences; only when the excluded are included (shorn of their attributes, visible only as individuals) will true universalism (the absence of difference, the end of conflict) prevail. In the course of French history, representativity has put constant pressure on representation, exposing its limits and its insufficiencies and forcing compromises in practice that have been deemed impossible in principle. When the pressure has gotten too strong, when representativity seems to be overwhelming representation, the system is seen to be in crisis.

One such moment of crisis came at the end of the nineteenth century when the issue of class challenged the political organization of the Third Republic; another came at the end of the twentieth century when questions about how to represent difference (this time the difference of ethnicity and that of sex) divided the nation. Rosanvallon addresses the first crisis when he recounts the challenges posed by the nineteenth-century working-class movement that resulted in the creation of a political party identified with a specific social interest. (He ignores parallel claims by feminists in the same period, perhaps because theirs was a much smaller movement and not successful in achieving its end. The terms of argument, however, were much the same.)[24] Rosanvallon points out that there was always ambiguity in the nature of the claims being made. Some leaders insisted (in the concrete mode) that workers or women, because of their particular experiences, needed advocates and, by the end of the nineteenth century, political parties of their own.[25] Others (following the abstract mode) suggested that the inclusion of workers, historically destined in a Marxist vision to be the universal class, or of women, whose interest was already identified with the larger community, would signal the final erasure of difference and hence the realization of genuine universalism. It was in this vein that Hubertine Auclert justified the inclusion of women: "French women have a sense of utilitarian democracy. When they are voters and candidates, they will force administrative and legislative assemblies to understand human needs and to satisfy them."[26]

Once universal male suffrage was enacted in 1848, the question of *how* to represent workers—whether as individuals or as members of an interest group—became an issue, while women, still excluded as citizens, pressed for a truly universal suffrage. In 1864, a manifesto by a group of sixty socialist worker-delegates who had been to the Universal Exposition of London (1862) called into question the competence of elected officials to represent "all." There was no way, they insisted, that these "socially myopic" bourgeois could speak to or for workers. "We are not represented, and that is why we dare to pose the question of working-class candidates."[27] (Parallel arguments by feminists such as Auclert criticized the masculine bias of legislators: "It is not possible to be man and woman at the same time. It would be considered strange for a man to play the role of father and mother in a family, and yet men are permitted to play this double role in the legislature.")[28] These comments suggest that only workers or women could represent their respective groups; but there were other possibilities: workers and women could function as individuals representing no particular interest, or their interests could be represented by individuals who were not themselves members of the interest group but who had been given a particular mandate. (Here was the tension between representatives as autonomous individuals or as delegates of some portion of the people; here, too, was the tension between concrete social reality and political abstraction.) The workers' party, an explicitly interest-based political organization formed in the late 1880s, took representation to be the delegation of authority, but in two possible ways. The worker-deputy Christophe Thivrier came to the National Assembly dressed in the smock and trousers of his class, while the bourgeois Jean Jaurès, also elected by the workers' party, nonetheless wore the suit, collar, and tie of his class.[29] This difference of costume illustrated the ongoing tension between the concrete realities of the social (Thivrier stood as a worker) and the abstractions of the political (Jaurès was an individual who held a certain point of view), and between essentialism (identity defined one's politics) and politics (political positions established one's identifications), even as the inclusion of a working-class interest (first in the Section française de l'internationale ouvrière—SFIO— and, after 1920, also in the Communist Party) in the legislature became a matter of course. Inclusion ultimately diminished the tension by absorbing working-class deputies into the ranks of politicians; they were now eligible as individuals to be representatives of the nation.

The formal party system was consolidated during the Third Republic, and it brought a measure of stability to French political life. But that stability was achieved at the price of acknowledging that class conflict divided a nation once figured as "one and indivisible." To be a representative now meant to be a spokesman for some social and economic interest, whatever one's own individual origins. There were periodic attempts to introduce proportional representation into the electoral system in order to make politics more directly reflect political—and therefore social—diversity, but these were resisted in the name of abstract individualism, which, however compromised, was still thought to be the best guarantee of formal equality before the law. If elected officials were now delegates of voter interests, spokesmen for competing ideologies, the subject of representation was still the nation—albeit a nation riven by conflicts of class. Paradoxically there was one concrete trait that made the otherwise warring representatives commensurable and interchangeable units, abstract individuals capable of incarnating "France"—their shared masculinity. As it had since the French Revolution, sexual difference symbolized the irreducible difference that must be excluded if universalism were to prevail.

When women were granted the vote in 1944, General de Gaulle used their inclusion to signal the newly restored unity of a badly divided nation and his commitment (after the shame of the collaborationist Vichy regime) to bring France back into the international democratic fellowship. By 1944, the enfranchisement of women had become associated with the "advanced" democracies of Britain and the United States. But although women now had the right not only to vote but to run for office, they were considered somehow lesser beings when it came to being chosen as representatives. It was one thing to cast a ballot, it seemed, quite another to represent the nation. The pressure to keep women out of the body of the nation (to refuse to allow the body to be divided symbolically) was enormous and effective until the end of the twentieth century—the moment of another crisis of representation, the one that is the subject of this chapter.

In the course of the twentieth century, politics became an increasingly exclusive arena. Political parties were a training ground for officeholders, and they controlled access to candidacy; politicians could hold multiple offices (as mayor and deputy, for example), thus combining and monopolizing local and national power bases; and during the Fifth Republic, technical credentials (including training at the Ecole nationale d'adminstration) further professionalized the job of representative. The fact that the national representation was in the hands of a technocratic, bureaucratic corps strained the notion of representation in at least two ways. For those who believed that the individual was the basic unit of citizenship, politicians had too corporate an identity, and that interfered with their ability to represent abstractly. In the terms of the original revolutionaries, they were disqualified as representatives because they no longer spoke for the general will. For those who believed that social diversity ought to be more directly reflected in politics, these men had become so preoccupied with the business of influence and reelection that they had lost touch with the needs of their constituents. If votes were delegated mandates (sovereignty assigned conditionally to representatives), professional politicians were violating the trust of the voters by substituting their selfish corporate interests for some more universal vision. By the 1980s, the perceived disparity between elected officials and the national representation came to be seen by politicians, journalists, and some scholars as one aspect of a crisis.

The crisis was compounded by the emergence of social movements insisting on the recognition of the difference of their adherents. Whereas class had been taken to be the great divide of the century from about 1848 to the 1970s, differences of other kinds—gender, race, religion, ethnicity—began to claim attention and by the 1980s were at the heart of debates about representation. In many ways, these debates rehearsed concerns that had been expressed about working-class representation in the late nineteenth century, although many commentators did not acknowledge that fact.[30] Instead, they treated the problems posed by former colonial subjects and women as wholly new attempts to refigure the nation in terms not of its unity but of its diversity. Unlike the United States, where affirmative action was the policy offered to end years of discrimination based on gender and race, France resisted "differentialism" in the name of the abstract individualism of republican universalism. Abstraction could overcome all differences, it was argued; that was the distinctive lesson of French political history. Although this was untrue (as the recognition of class had shown), the myth of an unchanging revolutionary heritage strengthened as the pressure to represent differences increased. An antidiscrimination law was passed in the 1970s, which punished expressions of racism (*propos racistes*), but positive remedial action did not follow. Singling out groups for special treatment was taken to be not only counterproductive, because it would exacerbate divisions and make them permanent features of the social and political landscapes, but antirepublican, for it would undermine the universalism (the abstract individual, the abstraction of a unified nation) touted as the defining feature of the French political system.[31] The refusal to grant official recognition to minorities extended to statistical profiles, published in census data, for example.[32] And other government statistics did not take gender into account. In this way the illusion of national unity was maintained by treating everyone only as individuals. But could particular differences of race and gender (marked bodies, ascribed group identities, shared interests created by discrimination) be absorbed into the universalist abstractions of individual and nation? Was this more desirable than representing the nation in all its diversity? And, in the face of the financial scandals of the late 1980s that discredited professional politicians, almost entirely white and male, as representatives, who were the suitable embodiments of national unity? If corruption had replaced integrity and greed reason, was the notion of individual autonomy feasible for thinking about the conduct of representatives? By insisting on universalism as the only solution to the political crisis, politicians and intellectuals exacerbated the tensions between the social and the political. This in turn exposed the limits of universalism when it came to incorporating those "others" defined as inherently or irredeemably divisive outside the unified body of the nation. This was especially true of the two groups that came to the center of attention in the 1980s and 1990s, whose difference was deemed irreducible, not susceptible to assimilation or abstraction: "immigrants" of non-European and, particularly, North African origin (with communal and religious loyalties that clashed with the dominant culture) and women (symbols of internal division and irreparable antagonism). Could those who were identified as belonging to "foreign" cultural communities ever speak in the name of the general will? Was being a woman (embodied, sexed) antithetical to being an abstract individual? If these kinds of differences could not be integrated, did this failure signal the exhaustion of the abstract mode of representation? Was irreducible difference the Achilles heel of French universalism, exposing its dependence on some form of exclusion to define its existence? Implied in the various answers to these questions was an evaluation of the continuing usefulness of the system of abstract individualism, designed as an alternative to the corporatism of the Old Regime, in the much-changed circumstances (postcolonial, multiethnic, postmodern) of the late twentieth century. Was this notion of universalism capacious enough for the political realities of late modern France? These questions were addressed in a series of escalating encounters in which were raised, first, the question of citizenship for North African "immigrants," and then the issue of parity for women in politics.

CONDITIONS OF CITIZENSHIP FOR NORTH AFRICAN "IMMIGRANTS"

Although it had been simmering for a number of years, the "immigrant" question boiled over in the 1980s. The term "immigrants" was a misnomer, since it was those of North African origin—former colonial subjects—who were at the heart of the debate. Moreover, many of those deemed "foreigners" had, in fact, been born in France. It was their perceived allegiance to the alien communal cultural and religious practices associated with Islam that defined their citizenship as problematic. From the early days of colonial settlement, French administrators had distinguished between Algerians who were assimilable and those—Muslims—who were not. "If we have one duty in Algeria, it is to combat Islam, our eternal enemy, in all its manifestations," wrote the viscount Caix de Saint Aymour.[33] France's "civilizing mission" consisted in bringing secular values to North Africa, reclaiming the territory that was once European and had been lost to Islam centuries before. The outlook that defined French colonialism continued in the postcolonial era, but with far less precision than in the past. After independence, whether in the popular press or among politicians, few distinctions were made between secular North Africans and "Arabs," and all, whether religious or not, were taken to be followers of Islam. Islam remains for many French, if not an "eternal enemy," then at least antithetical to French republican values. Islam's very different treatment of sexual difference (codes of modesty in public for women and men, the confinement of sexual relationships to the private sphere) also makes it alien to French sensibilities, which ac-

cept or even welcome public displays of sexuality.[34] Those perceived to be followers of Islam are thus, by definition, irreducibly different, outside the nation,
ineligible for citizenship. The term "immigrant" not only designates all North
Africans as followers of Islam but also defines them as eternally "foreign."[35]

In the 1980s the intensity and divisiveness of the debates about how to deal
with these immigrants pitted members of the same family and/or political party
against one another in uncharacteristic hostility; the situation was likened by
some commentators to the Dreyfus Affair (the false accusation of a French Jewish army captain of treason), which had polarized France at the turn of the century.[36] The resolution of the debates—in the form of a set of government policies
reiterating the principles of republican universalism (against nationalist racism
on the far right and multiculturalism on the left)—set the terms for the treatment of immigrants, and the context for the arguments parité would advance.

Although France has had a long history of incorporating foreigners—historian Gerard Noiriel has pointed out that in the nineteenth and twentieth centuries it was a veritable "melting pot,"[37] assimilating the foreign-born and making them culturally indistinguishable from native-born French—it was North
Africans, among them followers of Islam, who were the focus of controversy in
the 1980s. "In France," Riva Kastoryano writes, "all references to identity or to
some kind of community refer to Islam."[38] Unlike earlier migrants, the North
Africans were former colonial subjects whom the French had set out to "civi-
lize," and they did not seem capable of assimilation; religion, especially, precluded the cultural incorporation that had rendered invisible the long history
of largely European migration that Noiriel recounts. Did the presence of such
a (supposedly) coherent minority community threaten the unity of France?
Did their collective religious and cultural commitments—their identity as a
community—preclude their acting as individuals? How could the integration
of these particular strangers be achieved? In the 1980s, these large philosophical issues tended to dominate the conversation, replacing earlier more pragmatic efforts addressed to the practical needs of foreign workers.

The troubling presence of foreign populations in France, particularly those
of North African origin, was a postcolonial phenomenon. Under the terms
of the Evian Accords, which ended the Algerian War in 1962, Algerians were
granted special rights of access, and children born in France automatically became French citizens at birth. (This was because, unlike most other French
colonies, Algeria had been defined as a "department," an integral unit of the
nation.) In 1970, Algerians were the largest immigrant group in France. Most
were men, working to support families at home or until they had saved enough
to return themselves. Restrictions were put on immigration in the 1970s, and

few new immigrant workers were admitted, but the total numbers grew because family members joined the original migrants, an effect of European Union accords that asserted workers' rights to family. There was no question in the 1980s that Algerians and other North Africans (Tunisians and Moroccans) constituted an increasingly settled population in metropolitan France. Together these groups accounted for 39% of all immigrants. Their numbers were such that commentators who equated all Arabs with Islam predicted that Islam had become the second major religion of France. The families were concentrated in suburban ghettos outside of major cities, where poverty and their distinctive dress, language, and religious/cultural practices made them visibly different and easy to single out as the source of economic instability and crime.

The cultural differences of North Africans were at first encouraged by the French government, which looked upon these foreigners as a cheap and, importantly, temporary source of labor. Following a policy of *insertion* in the 1970s, a range of social welfare services were provided, as well as Arabic and Turkish language courses, often in public schools. Under the guise of tolerance, these measures were aimed at maintaining ties with the workers' home country, which often paid for and provided teachers and religious leaders, and to which, it was expected, the workers would later return.[39] Because it anticipated the eventual repatriation of these workers, the French government respected the laws of the native country that applied to civil status, especially family law. Indeed, during the economic crises of 1977 and 1978, in an effort to alleviate unemployment, the conservative government of President Valéry Giscard d'Estaing paid many thousands of North African workers to return home.[40]

The election of socialist François Mitterrand as president in 1981 brought some changes in the treatment of these resident foreigners living in France. Mitterrand declared his solidarity with the struggles of postcolonial Third World nations and sought to regularize the status of foreigners in France by such measures as distinguishing between the legal and illegal among them. Limits were put on new arrivals, but repatriations ended. And there was even a short-lived proposal to grant foreigners a vote in municipal elections even though they weren't citizens—a way of recognizing the rights of noncitizens in accord with European Union recommendations and of educating them in the practices of democracy. (The proposal was withdrawn because there was such widespread opposition to it.) Mitterrand's government continued to support Arabic language courses in the public schools, now in the name of "the right to be different," a broad policy introduced by the minister of culture, Jack Lang, in 1982. Lang's endorsement of the right to be different applied initially to various cultural minorities within the nation (Basque, Breton, Catalan, Corsican, Occitan, Gypsy), part of Mitterrand's aim to preserve French regional linguistic and other heritages against the homogenizing effects of urban and industrial development. Though its proponents warned against the dangers of "micronationalisms"[41] and insisted that minority cultural identity always be subsumed to national identity, the right to be different could be seen as a threat to national unity, especially when extended to North African Muslims.

The recognition of minorities by the Mitterrand government did not last long. They were sharply challenged in the municipal elections of 1983 by Jean-Marie Le Pen, a far right-wing populist whose anti-immigrant stance attracted a significant following, opening a new era in French politics. When the right, in alliance with Le Pen's party, captured the town of Dreux and drove socialist mayor Françoise Gaspard from office, many feared for the future of the republic. Le Pen and his National Front claimed that immigrants were taking jobs from native French workers, that their welfare costs were eroding national and local budgets, that they were destroying the integrity of cities. He described the immigrants as a new invasion, comparable to the German occupation. These people "breed like rabbits," he said. They will upset "the biological equilibrium," his supporters warned.[42] The solution: "France for the French"; drive the foreigners out. In some cities, the traditional right made alliances with the National Front in a successful effort to defeat the left even while professing repulsion for the extreme racist ideas Le Pen espoused.[43] Le Pen's ability to mobilize voters in cities with large immigrant populations, to win votes away from the Communist Party (which, in an attempt to hold on to its working-class constituency, also took an anti-immigrant stance in this period), and to gain a wide public hearing made the question of immigration the political issue of the moment. But the reassertion of the value of universalism did little to counter Le Pen's appeal.

The discussion of what in the United States was called multiculturalism had a very different aspect, because of a very different political history, in France. There, since the late nineteenth century, the opponents of democracy—its harshest critics and most vigorous antagonists—insisted that racial differences be recognized in order to protect national purity. To deny diversity, they argued, was to engage in a deceptive universalism, one committed to the illusion of equality and its consequences: racial mixing, the weakening of native stock, the feminizing of the nation. From the nineteenth century on, the racism of the right attacked the universalism of the left. In the name of universalism (paradoxically, a peculiarly French universalism), the left made the republic a refuge for victims of discrimination coming from elsewhere.[44] But this welcoming universalism assumed assimilation to French cultural norms.[45] Ernest Renan had written in 1882, "A large aggregation of men, clear of mind and warm of heart, creates a moral conscience that we call a nation. Since this moral conscience proves its strength by sacrifices that demand the abdication of the individual for the good of the community, it is legitimate and deserves to exist."[46] By "community" Renan meant a singular, shared culture with a common past and future. For Renan there was only one community—France.

Although the circumstances of the 1980s made the stark opposition of racism and universalism less tenable—or perhaps because they did so—these positions still organized a good deal of the debate. Thus Louis Pauwels, the editor of the right-wing *Le Figaro Magazine,* wrote that to be a universalist "is to recognize and wish to maintain the existence of different ethnicities and hence of specific cultures and societies; it is to admit, to pay tribute to, and to protect human diversity. To be racist is to deny or refuse this diversity; it is to undertake to restore humanity's singularity."[47] Having reversed the usual associations, making racism the equivalent of the left's universalism and diversity the true universalism, he went on to warn of the consequences of allowing immigrants' children to become French: "When we know that that would result in the greatest biological disruption our country has known since the Frankish invasions, we have a right to raise questions about it." Le Pen made a similar argument about the need to recognize racial differences: "I believe that the white man of Europe is characterized by an alchemy of nuances. . . . We are of the same race and the same spirit. . . . We also respect the foreigner as part of that universality of humanity that makes each man, each group and nation, a distinct being."[48] "Distinct being" meant not susceptible to assimilation or abstraction.

In the 1980s most republicans repudiated Pauwels's and Le Pen's arguments, but no longer in the name of Renan's notion of cultural assimilation. Instead, they put forward the idea of *intégration,* which sought to balance cultural difference and national unity in new ways. There were several definitions of *intégration.* A minority view, offered by the future leaders of parité, Françoise Gaspard and Claude Servan-Schreiber, took the position that social differences must be recognized not obliterated, which was close to an American multiculturalist perspective. Immigrants were here to stay, they said; many of those still called immigrants had lived in France for more than ten years; the children of these people were not immigrants at all (having never lived anywhere else). They had created hybrid cultures, mingling French and North African influences; these cultures needed to be recognized as what they were: part of the reality of French life, not antagonistic to, but rather components of the nation. And they should be given a voice in political life. "Yes, these young people are distinctive: they affirm their existence by asserting their identity. It is their way of making us understand that their integration is less a problem for them than an obligation for us. . . . They want to be recognized rather than assimilated."[49] Gaspard and Servan-Schreiber defined *intégration* as the social and political recognition of difference; there was no question of these immigrants becoming French, they already were. The abstraction of a unified nation, "one and indivisible" didn't correspond to the reality of its diversity, nor to the concrete problems posed by this population.

This was not, however, the view of *intégration* that became the official response to Le Pen. Instead, in the course of the 1980s politicians and philosophers worked out a compromise—based, they said, on the enduring principles of republicanism—that granted cultural difference the right to exist as a set of private commitments (there was no longer a demand for cultural conformity as a prerequisite to citizenship) but required that citizens be thought of only as individuals for the purposes of political representation. *Intégration* was premised, not surprisingly, on abstract individualism.[50]

This theory of *intégration* was articulated in the late 1980s and early 1990s. It was implemented in revisions to the Code of Nationality in 1986, and again in 1993, along with laws tightening controls of foreigners (referred to as the Pasqua laws, named for the minister of interior of the conservative government then in power). Of the many events that consolidated support for the official version of *intégration* (revisions of the nationality code, the continuing militancy of Le Pen and his followers, heated discussion about whether female excision or polygamy, or indeed any non-French family law, should continue to be tolerated), probably the most dramatic was *l'affaire du foulard*, which erupted in 1989 as a kind of perversion of the celebrations of the bicentennial of the French Revolution (and which continues in even more dramatic form to this day).[51] The affair began when three Muslim girls, who insisted on wearing head scarves, were expelled from their public school because, the principal maintained, their scarves were a public expression of religion and thus violated the separation of church and state. "The school is French," he proclaimed. "It is in the town of Creil and it is secular. We will not let ourselves be plagued by religious problems." (That the principal, Ernest Chénière, was worried above all about Islam became clear when he later ran for a seat in the National Assembly, promising to end "the insidious jihad.")[52] A huge controversy ensued. The far right maintained that the affair demonstrated the nonintegratability of these foreigners, the impossibility of their ever becoming French. In opposition to the far right, religious leaders—Catholic, Jewish and Protestant—argued that tolerance of signs of religious affiliation was part of the mission of secular schools. Some republicans insisted that the secular nature of public schools precluded any religious insignia. Particular communal identities were private matters, they said, which must finally have no bearing on public behavior, no public visibility. Only in this way would the equality of individuals before the law be guaranteed. "The figure of French democracy is called the Republic. It is not a mosaic of ghettos where liberty for all cloaks the law of the strongest."[53] Régis Debray, the former radical who had been with Che Guevara in the 1960s, put it this way: "the universal is abstract and the local concrete, and this confers on each its greatness and its constraints. Since reason is its supreme reference, the republican state is unitary and centralized by nature."[54] Taking a more moderate position, historian Jacques Le Goff agonized about many things: whether permitting head scarves contributed to the subordination of women; whether expelling the girls would ultimately defeat the public school's mission of transmitting French values (the values of secular universalism) to "foreign" students, especially Muslims; whether acceding to (what he called) "soft pluralism" would undermine national unity. Some differences, he thought, were irreducible, hence by definition impossible to discount for the French republican system. "We must distinguish between respectable and inadmissible differences, those in particular which compromise the necessary cohesion of a society and a nation. . . . Pluralism is not fragmentation and chaos."[55] In the debate about head scarves (in 1989 as later in 1994 and 2003), women became the synecdoche for Islam, for those "inadmissible differences" which Le Goff worried would "compromise the necessary cohesion of . . . a nation." In this way the long-standing view of sexual difference as divisive was displaced onto Muslims and, at the same time, reinforced in relation to all women. Sexual difference was used to express anxiety about Muslim practices and to shore up a particular vision of national identity in which the difference of sex was antagonistic to universalism.

The *affaire* was settled temporarily when the minister of education, Lionel Jospin, asked for an opinion from the Conseil d'état (or Council of State). The Conseil (the highest administrative court in France, whose task is to deal with the legality of actions taken by public bodies) found that the wearing of the head scarf was not a violation of the separation of church and state since the law applied to buildings and curriculum but not to students unless they engaged in activities that disturbed the peace. Accordingly, school principals had the option of prohibiting the head scarf only if they thought classrooms were being disrupted or students were proselytizing. This ruling did nothing to quell the explosive concern about the place of immigrants in French society. It continues unabated. In 1990, the socialist prime minister Michel Rocard called for an end to Mitterrand's earlier endorsement of the right to difference; government policy should support only "a right to indifference," he proclaimed.[56] And in 1993, when the conservatives returned to power, this notion of *inté-gration* was put into effect.

Under the revised nationality code of 1986 (which remained in effect until it was again revised in 1998), citizenship would no longer be extended as a matter of course to children born in France of foreign-born parents. Instead, as they reached adulthood, each child had to ask to become a citizen, signifying his or her desire as an individual to enter the "social contract." The notion was that one must choose to ignore particularistic communal loyalties in order to es-tablish political identity. In addition, for children of Algerians who were born before independence (when Algeria was still French), the period of residency needed to qualify for citizenship was lengthened, and proof of *enracinement* (rootedness) was required as well. Adrien Favell describes the implications of the change this way: "The symbolic accent on the *volonté* of immigrants to em-brace French nationality is . . . the first step toward establishing a new, indi-vidualist conception of the *contrat social* in France: the social contract that guarantees the political and social order of France as a political entity. In stat-ing their voluntary adhesion to the nation, new members engage in a new moral relation to their adopted nation, which puts the accent on their individual rights and responsibilities."[57] To become a citizen, a report from the Haut con-seil à l'intégration argued in 1993, meant enjoying full freedom of private com-munal association but rejecting "the logic of there being distinct ethnic or cultural minorities and, instead, looking for a logic based on the equality of in-dividual persons."[58] France might be culturally diverse—liberty of association guaranteed this—but politically it was homogeneous; individuals were equal before the law, their rights conferred and protected by the laws of the state. Favell argues that the requirement that French-born children of immigrants declare their desire to become citizens was seen to constitute their autonomy and their moral agency as individuals, and it implied that the only collective identity conceivable in the political realm was that of being French.[59] *Intégra-tion* did not hold up the old standard of cultural assimilation, but it did de-mand a singular national identification: for the purposes of political participa-tion there were only individuals, and they were the embodiments not only of the law but of the nation.[60] National identity was antithetical to any represen-tation of difference.

Harlem Désir, a founder of the antidiscrimination organization SOS Racisme (which had protested the expulsion of the girls who wore head scarves to school) and himself biracial (the son of Antiguan and metropolitan French parents), argued eloquently for pluralism, but insisted, too, on the priority of a single national political identity. *Intégration,* he said, necessarily reaffirmed a conception of the nation as founded "not on identity but on citizenship, not on blood, race or religion but on principles, on the social contract, on universal values."[61] The recognition of differences, he maintained, must not interfere with collective—that is political—life.[62] To that end, he urged that immigrants be treated as individuals, not differently from anyone else, not assigned a distinctive place because of their difference. The point for Désir was "not to deny diversity, but to refuse to restrict the individual to the supposed determinations of his origins."[63] This was, in effect, an argument for ultimate assimilation, if not to all aspects of French bourgeois culture, then to the political—secular, republican—values held to be universal. What many perceived to be the threatening powers of Islam (as exemplified by fundamentalists seeking to undermine the Algerian government or issuing fatwas against Salman Rushdie and, less violently, by different understandings of gender and sexuality) would be slowly undermined by republican schooling in France and by the eventual triumph—individual by individual—of French national identity over communal identity. As Favell states it, the new site of cultural integration was now the *political* sphere.[64]

The new scheme of *intégration,* by putting all emphasis on individual rights and universal values, did little to solve the problem of "immigrants" in French society. In fact, it drew attention away from the social and economic realities faced by North Africans living in France and perpetuated discrimination based on negative assessments of their different cultural practices and their threat to the "French" way of life. Though supposedly tolerated as private commitments, these were taken to be at odds with the universal principles that define what it means to be "French." So even when they formally became citizens, Muslims (and the many secular non-Muslim North Africans to whom the "Islamic" attribute attached anyway) remained strangers by virtue of their ethnicity, "immigrants" whose interests were perceived to be tangential, irrelevant, or dangerous to the collective interest of "France." Needless to say, such people were hardly considered eligible to represent the nation. Though fully French under the law, these "immigrants" continued to be associated with a difference that could not be abstracted.

The reaffirmation of republican universalism in the context of the immigration question in the 1980s and early 1990s was articulated in mythologized terms (the history of accommodation to working-class representation conveniently forgotten). Reaffirming the enduring principles of the Revolution, universalism was offered as the only solution possible for the problems posed by the increasing cultural diversity of the French population. National unity was to be maintained in the face of this diversity, by the all-inclusive, nondifferentiating, abstracting principles of universalism. There was to be no representativity, only representation. And if there was universalism (equality of individuals before the law), how could there be discrimination? But if there was discrimination based on ascriptions of group identity, how could it be rectified within the terms required by the newly minted myth of "traditional" French republicanism? Was there some way of changing the notion of the individual, expanding its capacity for abstraction to include differences once thought irreducible? This was the challenge addressed by the feminists who founded the parité movement.

"MALAISE DANS LA REPRÉSENTATION"

The continuing and bitter debates about immigrants came to a head in the presidential election of 1988.[65] Although Mitterrand was elected for another term, Jean-Marie Le Pen, the candidate of the National Front, won some 4.5 million votes (14% of the total) in the first round. On the eve of the bicentennial of the French Revolution, some intellectuals and journalists wondered if the future of the republic was in danger; there was serious dissatisfaction, and ordinary politics didn't seem to address it. Their anxiety was fueled by other indicators: a rising rate of voter abstention, a decline in the kinds of party and trade union activism that usually mobilized voters, internal quarrels within the parties, and a series of financial scandals that "degraded the image of the political world."[66] Things only got worse in 1989, when the parliament declared amnesty for all those politicians who had been implicated in the scandals.

Diagnoses of the causes of the problem varied, but they tended to emphasize internal structural issues, all of which suggested a weakened democracy and a weakened nation-state: "presidentialization," begun under de Gaulle and carried on by Mitterrand, had undermined parliamentary democracy by transferring power and attention to the head of state; the legislature was further weakened by the Gaullist administrative apparatus, including the use of the Constitutional Council to overturn laws passed by the parliament; real power now lay with the government, whose members were not necessarily elected officials; and the media paid little attention to debates in the Assembly, focusing instead on the opinions of "leaders" outside the parliamentary arena.[67] Newspaper editorials and public opinion polls seemed better indicators of the "general will" than anything that happened in the legislative forum. Elected assemblies at all levels had lost prestige and power as a result.

To make matters worse, the defining institutions of French republicanism weren't working as they should. The world of elected politics was out of touch with the voters; the gap between politicians and "civil society" was enormous. "Civil society" was a term that substituted for "the social" of nineteenth- and twentieth-century discourse. It referred to relations of citizens in ordinary life; it signified the realm of concrete ties and interactions as opposed to the political—where abstraction reigned, stripping individuals of their social identities so that they could represent the nation. The idea that politicians should be more in touch with civil society did not necessarily deny the value of the abstract individual; it did, however, suggest that there must be greater responsibility, greater attention to the needs of the nation. Whether exercising their own reason or holding a mandate from the people, politicians were supposed to be embodiments of the general will. But this no longer seemed to be the case. They did not speak for the nation; they were not abstract individuals but were themselves examples of difference and division. The weakened legislature was at once a symptom of "presidentialization" and the cause of its own demise.

In addition, the institutions that had evolved during the Third Republic to represent "the social" and that could put pressure on the legislature had declined. Political parties could no longer count on stable constituencies, and trade union membership had dropped sharply. In their place, according to some commentators, were fractured and individualized forms of affiliation. Instead of analyses about "social forces," the personal characteristics of politicians were blamed for the nation's problems.

The world of politics had been so compromised that it could not challenge the president's power even if it wanted to. The "political class" was a closed system that no longer fulfilled a representative function, preoccupied as it was with the business of holding on to sometimes multiple offices (politicians could serve as, say, deputies and mayors concurrently) and the technicalities of administration. Bureaucrats and technocrats had taken the place of the old ideological warriors. And their differences of values and interests set them apart from the nation as a whole. Rather than embodying the integrity of France (integrity taken both as wholeness and upright behavior), they stood only for themselves—and not as individuals, but as members of an interest group. They had lost the ability to represent abstractly. As a result, the illusion that a vote was a delegation of the nation's sovereign will was dispelled by a deepening cynicism; politicians were deemed irrelevant and corrupt, unfit either to reflect or to constitute the nation. Growing abstention rates (along with votes for Le Pen) called into question the process of the delegation of authority from voter to elected official, which legitimated the essential function of the representatives. On this legitimacy, the entire parliamentary system—indeed, the whole notion of national sovereignty—had rested.[68]

The votes for Le Pen were taken as a sign of a growing populism, the consequence of the insensitivity of politicians to those populations grappling with economic insecurity, unemployment, and uncertain futures. There was, Rosanvallon opined, "a gap between real life and the concern of the political system."[69] Socialist party leader Michel Rocard concluded that the state apparatus had "become too distant from civil society." And President Mitterrand vowed that in his second term his government would be more open to "civil society."[70] But exactly what "civil society" meant was never clear. Some, like Rosanvallon, argued that society itself had become so fragmented and individual identities so fluid that there were no clear group interests for politicians to represent. "It is collections of individuals, and no longer classes or professions, that express their discontent today."[71] If there was division, it no longer took recognizable social or political form: "Increasingly, divisions between the mass and the elite are given greater credence than those between right and left."[72] Marcel Gauchet added a note of ironic nostalgia: "In retrospect, what fun the class struggle was, how beautiful the civil war."[73] Clear divisions of class had been addressed legislatively within the terms of a "general will," no such clarity was possible in a world of highly individualized wills. So even if politicians weren't corrupt, there was little chance they could speak for or to "civil society."

Others, of course, did see groupings within "civil society," and they talked of the problem posed for political representation by "minorities." But they rarely addressed directly the questions of discrimination or cultural differences that feminists and those speaking for North Africans had raised during the 1980s. Instead, the term "civil society" made a gesture to "minorities," signifying the heterogeneity (the fractionalization, the individualization) of the population, but it didn't address the question of how politicians might be more responsive to minority needs, more representative of them. This may have been in part because "difference" was not perceived as equivalent to the lost category of class, which had attained legitimation and representation within the political system. It also followed, of course, from the equation of individuals with political representatives, from an insistence that French republicanism was about representation, not representativity. But these assumptions were only implicit, since the question of difference and of the access of differently marked groups to political influence was surprisingly absent from these analyses of crisis. Bernard Lacroix has suggested that this was because the "crisis" conversation was really internal to the political class, drawing new boundaries of power between old-line politicians on the one side and newcomer journalists and social scientists on the other.[74] In his view, the real questions of democracy—whether elections could ever offer legitimate representation for the diversity of the population—were absent from the discussion.[75] I would add that the focus on both the estrangement of the political class from the nation and the weakening of parliamentary power was, at least in part, a way of displacing the questions about the representation of irreducible difference that the "immigrant problem" had raised. "Civil society" was, to be sure, an indirect way of acknowledging them, but it also fudged the question of representation versus representativity. Was civil society something akin to the general will, in whose name politicians legislated? Or was it a realm of fractious diversity, which must be represented as such? Conceiving of "civil society" as an entity distracted attention from the more radical notion of representativity. And it left in place the myth of a timeless republicanism. But it also raised troubling new questions: If this closed caste of politicians was unrepresentative of the nation because it could not represent abstractly, what would it take to achieve genuine representation? Was there any longer a legitimate divide between civil society and politics? And was breaching it the only way to repair it? However vague the definitions were of civil society, once it was cited as a protagonist, it acquired voices to speak in its name. Those of women, long active in demanding a greater role in political parties and increased access to elective office, were prominent among them.

CHAPTER TWO

The Rejection of Quotas

As journalists and politicians analyzed the crisis of representation, feminists seized the moment to demand a greater role in political life. These were women who for years had been agitating within political parties and in the legislature for an end to the discrimination they faced. Their goal was greater access to decision-making. From one perspective, their claims had nothing to do with the issue that had precipitated the crisis—the relationship of civil society to politicians and the question of citizenship for those of North African origin. Women were already citizens; the problem was whether North Africans could be. In addition, the problem for North Africans, whether naturalized or not, was perceived to be their communal loyalty, which seemed to spill over from the private realm, where it was tolerable, into the public realm, where it was not. The problem for women was not whether they could be French but their sex, a "natural" attribute, which they could not choose to shed and which had long been considered an obstacle to their participation in politics, first as citizens and then as representatives. There was, however, something that both groups had in common: their differences seemed resistant to abstraction and so raised the specter of division in the body politic. Seizing on the fact that the laws on nationality had admitted the possibility of abstracting foreigners, notably Algerians and other North Africans, from their communal difference, feminists sought to abstract women from their sexual difference. But they arrived at this strategy only after some twenty years of unsuccessful efforts to change the rules of the political game.

WOMEN ACTIVISTS IN POLITICAL PARTIES

During the 1970s and 1980s, as part of the general feminist ferment of the period, continuous pressure was exerted by women activists to gain more leadership roles within the parties and to widen access to elective office. The organized feminist movement tended to avoid the institutions of formal party politics and to condemn participation in them, but women in political parties, especially on the left, were equally feminist in their demands for an end to discrimination based on sex. The issue for party activists was defined as a matter of fairness, and the goals were numerical: increasing the numbers of women in elective office and in party leadership positions. Among politicians there was at least a rhetorical commitment to the idea of more women holding office; women activists pressed to turn campaign promises into deeds. But the project of increasing the numbers of women representatives raised troubling issues: By what standard could progress toward equality be measured? How many women would it take? And what should these numbers refer to? Would quotas do the job of increasing the numbers of women in office and permanently reversing discrimination? And did the existence of quotas introduce unacceptable terms of differentiation into the national representation? Were concrete social differences corrupting the necessarily abstract rule of political representation? Was representativity replacing representation? The "woman question" in this period illustrates a classic problem that discrimination poses for liberal democracies: how to remedy exclusion based on ascribed group identity without making that identity the grounds for inclusion. Put in terms of the mode of abstract representation, the question was whether women could ever be detached enough from their association with sexual difference to become "individuals." The history of efforts to remedy discrimination against women in the 1970s and 1980s suggests that sexual difference posed an obstacle that the traditional notion of abstract individualism could not overcome.

Initially, attention to the condition of women and, especially, attempts to increase women's participation in politics came under the banner of "modernity."[1] François Mitterrand began his long campaign (in 1965) to capture political leadership from the Gaullists for the left by associating himself and his party with the "modernization" of France.[2] De Gaulle had already spoken of modernization, by which he meant economic and industrial development under the aegis of the state and its president. In his view, modernization required or would result in an end to social and political divisions; the establishment instead of a national consensus. While Mitterrand, too, equated economic growth with modernization, he emphasized "democracy" as well. If there was to be economic growth, it must be accompanied by "equality," by the inclusion in policy making of workers and their unions, by greater party influence in politics, by extended civil liberties, and by recognition of the rights of individuals—the right of women to control their own bodies, for example, which Mitterrand took to require legalizing contraception and abortion.

In his quest for votes, Mitterrand sought to mobilize new constituencies for the coalition of left-wing parties he was building. One obvious target—because they constituted some 52% of voters and because of the discrepancy between their improved educational and occupational attainments, on the one hand, and their lower wages and civil status, on the other—was women. By the 1960s, highly educated women pursued careers as teachers, nurses, social workers, and white-collar workers in the public and private sectors. Although the law mandated equal treatment, women's wages were consistently lower (by about 34% in 1968) than men's.[3] Moreover, even after the reform of the marriage law in 1965, paternal authority ruled the household (granting the father sole rights over his children and the husband the sole right to decide where the couple would live), and women's adultery was (as it had been since 1804) more severely punished than men's. Even though sexual practices had begun to change, the law of 1920 that prohibited both contraception and abortion was still in force. If "equality" was a sign of "modernity," the situation of women was an indicator of backwardness. In 1965, Mitterrand declared his commitment to improving the condition of women in an interview in *La Femme du 20e siècle* (the journal of a "cell of women," the Mouvement démocratique féminin):[4] "Without their even knowing it, women are at the center of modern politics," he said. "They have to learn that politics influences their future."[5] This statement assumes that women can be absorbed into the system as individuals, but it also reveals the gendered nature of politics in two ways. First, there is the recognition of the growing importance for politics of issues typically associated with women (life, death, sex, fertility, health—what Marcel Gauchet refers to as "l'ordre vital").[6] Second, it is Mitterrand—and not women—who sees what needs to be done. Women are a group; Mitterrand "the tutelary father"[7]—an individual leader. "Without their even knowing it," he writes, they are the center of modern politics, even as he publishes his article in a journal whose goal is to open space for women at the center of the noncommunist left.

Mitterrand's insistence that women were at "the center of modern politics" found its echo among politicians on the right, particularly Valéry Giscard d'Estaing, who won the presidency in 1974. In tight electoral contests, where every vote counted, where politicians were aware of a "gender gap" before it was so named,[8] and where, at the height of the women's liberation movement in the

1970s, there was significant pressure for women both to abstain from politics entirely (it being defined as hopelessly patriarchal) or to found their own political party, women were courted with promises of more adequate representation, and some concessions were made to them. In the Communist Party, which could garner more than 20% of votes in elections in this period, the practice of "feminization" had begun after World War II, and this greater apparent concern for allowing women to play leadership roles and run for office undoubtedly spurred the other parties to action. So while Mitterrand promoted women to national leadership positions within his party and encouraged the formation of a committee to identify and act on women's problems, Giscard (and his prime minister, Jacques Chirac) created the first women's cabinet position, secretary of state for the condition of women,[9] to which he appointed journalist Françoise Giroud (a founder with Jean-Jacques Servan-Schreiber of the news magazine *L'Express*) and named Simone Veil (who would successfully lead the fight to legalize abortion) minister of health.[10] The presidential prerogative for appointing ministers was an effective way of bypassing entrenched resistance to women within the political parties. (When he was elected in 1981, Mitterrand would use this strategy as well.) Presidential appointments did not do much to promote women's access to elective office, but they did demonstrate that women were individuals capable of playing the game of politics, and they set a standard for future governments. Nevertheless, Giscard was fully aware of the resistance of established politicians to this practice (and, more generally, of the limits of setting aside a certain number of places for women): "Places are rare and promises numerous," he wrote, "The political milieu sees no reason to complicate this problem further by reserving places for women ministers."[11] The "political milieu" was by definition a long-standing corps of men, whose status as representatives was automatically masculine.

If the politicians expressed a variety of motives in their appeals to women, they nonetheless uniformly invoked justice and equality. Equality was loosely defined as an end to discrimination; associated with modernity or modernization, equality for the most part meant fairness, more attention to definably women's issues, better treatment (as wage earners, wives, mothers, political party members), and a larger share for women of the political pie. But if equality might mean that women could be considered abstract individuals, the difference of sex was never far from politicians' calculations. Giscard, for example, by way of justifying the pathbreaking appointments he had made, talked of the distinctive contribution women made to politics in terms that emphasized their collective difference from men: political women, he said, "could bring to our public life elements now lacking: greater realism, more prudence in arriving at judgments, a more accurate feel for the realities of daily life."[12] This statement suggests that there might be some use in political life for the differences women embodied, but it doesn't touch on the capacity of women to represent others, on their status as universal prototypes—individuals. Rather, women provide a supplement, in the form of a particular set of qualities, to the (universal) business conducted mostly by men. Mitterrand, less essentialist, stressed the need to end women's economic exploitation, and in 1982 he endorsed a goal for political inclusion that had been offered more than a decade earlier during the Estates General of Woman sponsored by the fashion magazine *Elle.* The delegates to that assembly, arguing that attention to women's issues would come only when women had a significant presence in legislative bodies, had aimed for "representation [for women] that corresponds to their actual proportion in the electorate."[13] Echoing them (and a militant feminist current within his own party), Mitterrand noted that "women should have access to civic responsibility fully and in closer relation to their social role and to their numbers in the population."[14] Here the idea of social differences included in the national representation didn't necessarily conflict with the republican notion of the interchangeability of abstract individuals because proportionality was a way of evaluating fairness to individuals, not a means of group representation. In any event, Mitterrand's comment was more a pious hope than a practical suggestion. It was women activists who proposed to attack discrimination by using quotas as a means of correcting distortions in political representation.

QUOTAS

The idea that establishing either voluntary or mandatory quotas would correct discrimination against women was first adopted by the Socialist Party (PS) in 1974. Quotas were also among the recommendations for affirmative action that came from the United Nations Decade for Women conference in 1975. Special temporary measures, which could include quotas but were not mentioned as such, were also specified in the UN international convention on the elimination of discrimination against women (CEDAW) that France ratified in 1983.[15] The UN position on quotas took difference to be unacceptable as a ground for exclusion but necessary as a temporary way of achieving inclusion. The use of quotas thus paradoxically identified a group in order to allow its members eventually to be abstracted from group membership and treated as individuals. It was, its proponents argued, a technique to end discrimination, a form of positive discrimination.

Among French politicians in the 1980s, the discussion of quotas foundered not on the question of difference itself but on quantity. What constituted a reasonable percentage for representing women? Should quotas reflect some reality about gender, the numbers of women party members, party activists, voters? Since none of the major parties kept statistics on the gender of their members (an aversion to recognizing difference tied to their universalist philosophy), it was not clear what the quotas referred to.[16] Different groups seem to have used different referents; some seem to have arbitrarily chosen a figure. In the PS there was greater willingness to accept quotas for the leadership structure than for candidates for office. But whatever the reference, all discussion of quotas involved tactical maneuvers that expressed vastly different tolerable limits: the percentages offered by feminists represented a barely acceptable minimum—a starting point on the road to full equality (when difference of sex would no longer be a reason for exclusion and the numbers of men and women elected to office would be roughly the same); those coming from party leaders were the maximum concession imaginable (a grudging acknowledgment of the need to remedy discrimination in some token way, but no concession to the idea that women were as capable as men were of representing the nation as elected officials). The struggle over quotas revealed to women activists the limits of male politicians' commitment to ending discrimination and the futility of voluntary and incremental measures. Repudiated as "humiliating" and "even pernicious," quotas became unacceptable to feminist activists. "Once a quota is achieved, it becomes almost impossible to exceed it because it was not conceived to reach toward equality," wrote the Belgian jurist Eliane Vogel-Polsky, reflecting on her country's experience and that of France. "Its aim is to find an 'acceptable' compromise and nothing more."[17] Politicians' attitudes to quotas exposed the persistence of the association of women with an unacceptable division of the body politic. Despite all the positive talk of equality, the sexual difference of women still symbolized an antagonism at odds with images of republican unity. The struggle over quotas led some feminists to the conviction that if genuine equality were to be achieved, something more radical was needed—something that would address this symbolism by unsexing political representation.

In her "One Hundred Measures for Women" (1976), Françoise Giroud suggested that in municipal elections there be no more than 85% of candidates of the same sex. Municipal elections were seen as a first step, a way of educating women and bringing them into greater party activity, thus creating a larger pool of women politicians who would contest other elective offices in the future. Such elections were also deemed a more appropriately feminine arena—local, concerning issues that touched on family, education, welfare, geographically close to home, in one way or another an extension of the domestic hearth.[18] The wording of the proposal—placing a limit on candidates of one sex—was intended to avoid the appearance of protecting or favoring one sex over the other. The wording also spoke to the question of the adequacy of political representation. If it was overwhelmingly male, it was particularistic and so could not represent abstractly.

One of Giroud's successors, Monique Pelletier, proposed in 1979 that there be a limit of 80% of candidates of the same sex—which meant a quota of 20% women—on electoral lists in municipal elections. The following year, the government of conservative prime minister Raymond Barre sent a law to the National Assembly that would have implemented Pelletier's plan. It resoundingly passed a first reading but never came to another vote, leading one commentator in *Le Monde* to conclude that the effort had been merely a symbolic gesture to consolidate women's support for the upcoming presidential elections.[19]

Within the Socialist Party, ever in search of a winning strategy against the right, the issue of quotas became an important bargaining chip between party leaders and feminists. In 1975, women activists—taking literally Mitterrand's commitment to equality and the party's endorsement of a 10% quota the year before—insisted on increased representation in party offices and on electoral lists. Nothing was gained, however, until 1977. Then veteran party activist Yvette Roudy became a national party secretary, and the feminists returned to the party congress with a new set of demands, among them this time a quota of 20% (thought to reflect the number of women members of the party). When a resolution for 15% passed with no debate permitted, the feminists threatened to disrupt the proceedings with a sit-in and a press conference.[20] Eager to avoid public scrutiny of women's dissatisfaction in their ranks, the party leadership delegated Roudy to settle the matter. She engaged in intense negotiations with feminists; a compromise resulted, which maintained the 15% quota but elevated Roudy's office to the highest level of party administration and called for a convention (to be held the following year) to draft a major policy statement on women for the party's consideration. "The deal finally haggled out was: you may have only 15% now, but you will have a convention."[21] While the PS acknowledged the need to remedy its treatment of women, it refused (by insisting on the 15%) to concede their capacity generally to represent the citizenry.

In 1978, in the wake of socialist victories in the municipal elections of March 1977 but no increase in women elected to office (only 1.9% of elected socialist mayors were women), the feminists were back, this time working to form a third "current" (or faction), *le courant 3*, within an already divided party. (To receive official recognition, "currents" had to have support of at least 5% of the delegates at a party congress; then they were in a position to offer motions and lists of candidates.) There were at the time two "currents," the majority led by Mitterrand and the minority led by Jean-Pierre Chevènement. The plan for a third led to an intense debate about how women's voices could best be heard in the PS—as outspoken members of existing currents, inserting women's issues at every point, or as a separate interest group. There was even an attempt to form a pressure group, with women on the right and in the Communist Party, so as to increase women's influence within the parties generally. Françoise Gaspard recalled that, upon hearing of this effort, Mitterrand, who had gotten wind of it, called her in and asked, "But in whose name are you negotiating?" To her, "the question showed that the first secretary of the PS was afraid that women would do politics without a mandate from their leaders."[22] In the end, the feminists were divided over whether to remain integrated or separate. And, once again, Roudy offered a compromise: a quota of 30% women on the Socialist Party lists for the upcoming election for deputies to the European Parliament. Gaspard, the spokeswoman for *courant 3,* replied that 50% was the only acceptable figure because "in Europe, one of every two citizens is a woman," but after a tense conversation with Roudy in the corridor during a meeting of the party leadership she accepted the compromise. (The standard of 50% took voters, not party members or party activists, as its referent, and it echoed the feminist movement's egalitarian slogan, "one of every two men is a woman.")[23] For the European elections of 1979, the PS did present a list with 30% women on it, but the practice was short-lived. In the elections of 1984, 1986, and 1989, if women were candidates at all, they were at the very bottom of party lists.[24] The party leadership could justify their inaction by pointing to a decision of the Constitutional Council in 1982 that quotas were unconstitutional.

THE RULING OF THE CONSTITUTIONAL COUNCIL

In 1982, Mitterrand was president and the socialists had a majority in the National Assembly. During the campaigns for the presidency and then for the assembly, many promises had been made about increasing women's representation, but of the 491 deputies elected in June 1981, only 26 were women.[25] When a law revising procedures for municipal elections was introduced into the assembly in July with no mention of quotas, feminist lawyer Gisèle Halimi, a socialist deputy (who had formed her own group, Choisir, in 1978 to put forward women candidates but who ran as a socialist in 1981) rose to protest. She offered an amendment stating that no more than 70% of municipal council seats could be held by members of one sex (30% was considered the minimum necessary for creating a critical mass of women who would tip the balance of power).[26] The PS quickly amended Halimi's figure to 75%. After some debate in which deputies worried about whether voters' liberty of choice was being constrained, whether women would be insulted by being treated as a "category," and—most significantly—whether the amendment was constitutional, the law overwhelmingly passed its requisite two readings.[27] At that point, several deputies asked for a ruling on the constitutionality of a provision of the law that had nothing to do with quotas. The Constitutional Council, which had no women members, met and (contrary to its usual procedure) reviewed the entire law, not just the questioned provision. On November 18, 1982, it overturned the reference to quotas and let the rest of the law stand.[28]

In retrospect, feminists found this decision a particularly galling aspect of the affair, a measure of the hypocrisy of political men on the right and left. There were signs, to be sure, during the debates on the law that the deputies would look to the Constitutional Council to overrule a measure they felt they had to pass. Jurist Danièle Lochak noted the number of times deputies (even those who voted in favor) had referred to the dubious constitutionality of quotas: they undermined universal suffrage, divided citizens according to inadmissible "categories," and introduced new forms of discrimination. The minister of the interior had even asked that Halimi's amendment be made a separate article so that its eventual invalidation wouldn't prevent passage of the rest of the law.[29] And Françoise Gaspard, a newly elected deputy, remembers that the head of the socialist caucus in the National Assembly, Pierre Joxe, walked over to the opposition as deputies were being polled, securing their votes by assuring them that the quotas would eventually be ruled unconstitutional.[30] By deferring the issue to the Constitutional Council, the assembly could seem to be supporting the feminist agenda without ever having to implement it. One deputy of the Union for French Democracy (the UDF, a center-right party founded in 1978 by Giscard d'Estaing), declared he would vote for the law but bemoaned the fact that the socialists would get credit for opening municipal council seats to women when it was really the former government of Raymond Barre that had acted first—though not competently—on the issue.[31]

The grounds on which the council ruled referred to both the 1958 Constitution of the Fifth Republic and the 1789 Declaration of the Rights of Man and Citizen (which has a status similar to the U.S. Bill of Rights). Article 3 of the constitution is about the sovereignty of the people and stipulates that suffrage is "universal, equal, and secret," is open ("under conditions determined by law") to adult citizens of both sexes and cannot be denied to them. Article 6 of the declaration declares: "The law is the expression of the general will. All citizens have the right to participate personally or by their representatives in its formation. It must be the same for all, whether it protects, or whether it punishes. All citizens, being equal in its eyes, are equally eligible to all public dignities, places, and employments, according to their capacities, and without other distinction than that of their virtues and their talents."[32] Taking these two articles together, the council ruled that the constitution already considered women part of the sovereign people and that quotas, because they established an inadmissible distinction of sex, not only threatened the unity required for sovereignty but also contravened the notion of careers open to talent in article 6 of the declaration. By joining the two documents, the council endorsed a vision of the nation that rested on the immutability and continuity of the revolutionary tradition based in abstraction: the sovereignty of the people was embodied by abstract individuals. The constitutional principles, the council members found, were "opposed to all divisions of voters or candidates by category" even if the purported goal of quotas was precisely to realize equality of access to office.[33]

Critics of the council's ruling insisted that quotas were a political, not a constitutional, issue, designed to level the playing field for those women whose "virtues and talents" as individuals had remained invisible for over a century. The Declaration of Rights, after all, was written to eliminate feudal privilege; its authors did not even accept the idea of a female citizen and so could not address inequality based on sex. The critics also pointed to the weaknesses of the council's rationale as evidence that the judicial body had overstepped its function. The quota was a practical measure, a last resort aimed at realizing women's rights: "it is the ultimate means of opening a situation when all other measures have failed."[34] And quotas in themselves didn't deny voting rights to anyone. There were already limits on eligibility for office: relatives couldn't serve on the same municipal council, and candidates had to satisfy residency requirements. Moreover, the very existence of a list limited voters' options in the free exercise of their vote. The wording of the law didn't favor one sex over another; it said simply that there could be no more than 80% of either sex on a list. This did not pose an impossible numerical demand (as it might for other genuinely minority groups) since women were half the population. And since the law already recognized sex as a characteristic of citizens (it did not, in contrast, recognize race or religion, although it outlawed discrimination based on those qualities), no new divisions were being introduced.[35] Indeed, more than one critic of the council's ruling argued that since sexual difference cut across every other category, social distinctions of the kind feared by the authors of the Declaration of Rights were an irrelevant concern. "Strictly speaking, [women] don't constitute a social 'category' like youth or the aged or the handicapped.">[36] In other words, they were individuals, though of a different sex from men.

This claim had already been made in the debate on the law in the assembly, but it seemed to have gone unheard. Instead, the council agreed with deputy Serge Charles of the Rally for the Republic (RPR—the heir to Gaullism), who abstained from the final vote but had warned ominously of the risk of multiplying categories of the citizen, "who is one and ought to remain that way. The road you want to take is very slippery and can lead you one day to use other classifications whose foundation and nature I dare not imagine.">[37] If the "slippery slope" argument was misogynist (women will open an unimaginable abyss fatal to the integrity of France) and elitist (the polluting effects on the assembly of the presence of social "others"), it nonetheless rested on references to the hallowed principles of abstract individualism as contained in the revolutionary tradition. The citizen was an individual—one—and must remain so; all attempts to divide or multiply him must be resisted. In effect, the council suggested that since sexual difference was an irreducible difference—not susceptible to abstraction—it could not be recognized even as a source of discrimination.

After 1982 there were no further attempts to legalize quotas, although they would be used as a campaign ploy in the 1990s and as a way of seeming to accommodate feminists without granting parité. At these moments, the parties ignored the reasoning of the Constitutional Council, implying by their actions that quotas were indeed a practical political matter, a way of letting a few women in while getting many women's votes. But the issue of constitutionality remained a challenge to those who thought that the (quixotic) self-interest of parties was inadequate as a guarantee of equal access to elective office for women; only a law, they concluded, could end discrimination. When the movement for parité took shape to demand that law in the early 1990s, it not only explicitly rejected quotas (as arbitrary limits on what should be equal opportunities for women) but also addressed the relationship between sexual difference and abstract individualism.

The ruling of the Constitutional Council had an important effect on the ways equality could be implemented, since in the name of abstract philosophical principles it made concrete arguments for affirmative action difficult to maintain. In the name of French republican universalism, social differences were deemed an impermissible ground for action to correct discrimination. The nation's integrity depended on unity: it could not recognize difference. So to get a law passed, the parité strategists had to find a way to remain within the boundaries of republicanism and yet change its terms. This they eventually did by endorsing the principles of abstract individualism while radically insisting on the duality of the individual—the individual was not one, they insisted, but two, man and woman.

In preparing the ground for parité, the fourteen years of the Mitterrand presidency may have made its greatest contribution by granting the validity of feminist claims without satisfying them, at least in the realm of party politics. Mitterrand's election in 1981 raised great expectations among feminists, particularly those who had long campaigned for changes within the PS. Among his first actions as president was the designation of Yvette Roudy as ministerial delegate for the rights of woman. (Mitterrand's preference for the singular, though the plural had been recommended, gave some feminists pause even at this early stage.)[38] The fact that her office reported directly to the prime minister signaled that she had more influence than her predecessor, as did a vastly increased budget (which, among other things, supported feminist scholars and activists dedicated to making women's issues more visible). Roudy pushed hard and successfully for reforms of civil and family codes, for state reimbursement to women who had abortions, and for laws outlawing sexual harassment and job discrimination.[39] Her office financed studies of pay and employment differentials, documenting inequalities between women and men that must be remedied by legislators. Advances in these areas made the delays on the political front more striking; when it came to running women candidates—and electing them—the socialists did little better than their opponents.

For the legislative elections of 1981 (when the PS combined with other left-wing parties), women constituted 8.5% of candidates on the left; with all parties taken into account the figure was 11.9%. (Of those actually elected, women made up 5.3%.) The number of candidates rose significantly in 1986 because the electoral law had been changed the year before to have all elections decided by proportional representation.[40] Women constituted 24.7% of candidates in all parties in that election, but the numbers elected (5.9%) did not correspond at all to that proportion because women were placed so low on the party lists that they rarely had a chance of winning a seat even if their party prevailed.[41] Two political scientists commented on that election: "The double peculiarity of March 1986 appears to be a record number of women candidates and a record number of women not elected."[42] In discussions about the effects of proportional representation, Mitterrand had suggested that women would be the great beneficiaries of the new procedures. (In fact, the concerns of the socialists at this moment were practical: to secure more seats for their majority

and to weaken the center right, but they had little to do with gender representation.)[43] The outcome of the election proved Mitterrand wrong and Roudy,
who had disagreed with him, right: "Proportional elections are a good thing
for women on condition that they are not left up to local party leaders."[44] As
long as local bosses drew up the lists, women had little chance of being elected
because they were placed too low to benefit from a party victory. In any case,
proportional representation did not help the left in 1986; the right returned to
power. Right-wing parties restored majority elections for deputies in 1988, and
the numbers of women candidates fell to earlier levels; those elected from all
parties were 5.7%. (The PS presented 9.4% women and elected 6.1%.)

Overall, the Mitterrand years disappointed those seeking to break into the
male culture of party organization; from the point of view of feminists, the 1980s
were (in the words of political scientists Jane Jenson and Mariette Sineau) "un
rendez-vous manqué." There were, to be sure, some impressive presidential
appointments, the most visible of which were Edith Cresson, who in 1991 became the first female prime minister in French history, and Noëlle Lenoir, a first
for the Constitutional Council.[45] Mitterrand used his presidential prerogative
to bring young women into government positions. (Departing from typical
practice, which placed elected politicians in cabinet positions, he chose graduates of the elite professional schools as his protégées—adding new faces to the
ranks of PS activists—but also, given their credentials, adding women who were
seen to be exceptions, not typical of their sex.)[46] Not much was done, however,
at the institutional level to provide more women with the credentials they needed
to fill ministerial posts, if not to run for elective office. The Ecole nationale
d'administration, for example, the training ground created by de Gaulle for
high-level functionaries, admitted only a small number of women each year
(10% in the 1970s, no more than 25% in the 1980s and 90s), and no attempt was
made to remedy the situation. Even more to the point, the parties operated as
they always had, seemingly oblivious to the president's pronouncements about
the need to bring women into the system. Surveys of women who were elected
in these years reported on the extreme hostility they experienced. One such
woman commented, "You have to know that to be a woman elected in the PS
is truly . . . like a declaration of war." Another deputy confided that she never
felt like a "real" deputy because she was a woman. Others told of receiving obscene threats and insults (often from members of their own party) as they campaigned for office.[47] Still, there was a growing awareness that the situation
needed remedying. The funding of feminist research, the passage of laws designed to counter some forms of gender discrimination, the appointment of
new women to high government office, and the calculated (if sometimes en-

tirely instrumental) appeals to women voters made the recalcitrance of the political parties all the more apparent and all the more frustrating.

The attention to gender discrimination in France echoed and drew on concerns developing in European institutions in this period. As the Council of Europe (an intergovernment organization dating to 1949) and the European Commission (part of the executive arm of the European Union charged with preparing propositions for the parliament to consider) took up requests for membership from former communist countries after 1989, discussion turned to standards for evaluating democracy. Advocates for women argued that those countries setting the standards must themselves demonstrate a commitment to equality by ending evident discrimination against women. "Democracy without women is not democracy," became their watchword. In 1989, the Council of Europe organized a seminar on *démocratie paritaire*. And that year, the European Commission began an inquiry into the persistent wage differentials between women and men. One outcome of this inquiry was recognition of the very few women in negotiating and decision-making positions. In response to feminist pressure, working groups were set up to examine women's situation and to make policy proposals. In 1992, the European Experts' Network on Women in Decision-Making was established to collect information on member nations' treatment of women and particularly on their access to political office; without political clout, it was felt, there would be little change in the economic and social positions of women in member countries. At the first meeting of the network, in Athens in November 1992, a declaration of principles was issued whose intention was summed up by a ringing statement: "Democracy requires parité in the representation and administration of nations."[48] The Athens meeting spurred action within member countries providing both incentives and information for delegates in their home countries and visibility for women in the European political context. Comparative figures on women's political participation in member nations showed France to be persistently near the bottom of the list—the "red light" of Europe—and this low ranking became a rallying cry for political women in France, who now had a European-wide forum within which to point out the limits of Mitterrand's goal of "modernization."[49] Drawing on European resources and demanding implementation of European policies, the activists addressed themselves to improving the political scene within France.[50]

Parité took shape in this context as an expression of exasperation and determination. Clearly, quotas would not do the trick, and the hope that politicians would voluntarily open their ranks to women was vain. Discussions in the European networks pointed to the need for domestic as well as international legislation. Discrimination, some feminists concluded, could only be ended by a law that in France would forcibly overthrow the belief that the difference of sex could not be reconciled with the abstractions of individual and nation. When in 1988 the republican system of representation was declared to be in crisis, a way was opened for a new feminist offensive.

RESPONDING TO THE "CRISIS OF REPRESENTATION"

In 1988–89, feminists seized on the discussion of the gap between politicians and civil society and offered women as the solution. Rebuking the PS for its recalcitrance, Edith Cresson (who in 1989, when she offered this opinion, was the minister of European affairs) warned that if the party did not advance more women to leadership positions, it would, like the rest of the political world, be "a deformed caricature of society . . . which had nothing to do with civil society."[51] The absence of women was taken to be symptomatic of the oligarchic structure of party politics, which gave priority to those who already held political office, usually at more than one level, and was "very detrimental to the renewal of French political personnel, to openings to new and more dynamic elements: the young, women, or activists from the business world."[52] In a similar vein, Françoise Gaspard, explaining the basis of the parité strategy, picked up the theme of democracy in danger. Speaking to a feminist seminar in 1992, she offered a reinterpretation of the crisis. The key to the "rupture between representatives and those represented," she argued, lay in the absence of women in politics. "It is not only the absence of workers and young men, it's the absence of women workers and young women. Women cut across the entire crisis of representation. Their absence is a symptom of the rupture between politics and civil society."[53]

To exclude women (or, more accurately, sexual difference) was to ignore the necessarily contentious diversity of society and the challenges it posed to the nation. Like Cresson, Gaspard did not argue that women needed a separate representation of some presumed common interest; nor did she claim that women would bring a different perspective to the operations of politics. She did not liken women's plight to that of immigrants; rather, their situation was symptomatic of all other exclusions. She argued that democracy would prevail, the gap between representatives and the represented would be closed, if genuine universalism were realized—that is, if the distorted nature of the political representation (its nearly exclusive masculinity, its gender dis-parity) were corrected and differences deemed irreducible were admitted to elected assemblies. The point was not demographic accuracy but power, the ways in which political and social power were mutually reinforcing.[54] The citizenry was conceived not as belonging to fixed interest groups but as a diverse collection of individuals with different experiences (some of them based on ascribed group identities). The abstraction of the nation remained, but it would no longer be figured as homogeneous. Universalism would be expanded to include its excluded others and so would become truly universal. To attain this refiguration required not only new policies but an assault on the symbolic structure that legitimated the existing system. The moment of perceived crisis provided exactly the opening that feminists needed, and theirs was a kind of homeopathic solution: to resolve the crisis by intensifying it. This was the strategic creativity of the movement for parité.

CHAPTER THREE

The Dilemma of Difference

As debate about the crisis of democratic representation unfolded in 1988–89, feminists pointed out that the absence of women in elective office was both symptom and cause of the problem. There were at least two aspects to their critique. One was an elaboration of the point—made by politicians after 1988—that the political class was out of touch with "civil society."[1] To the extent that women were part of civil society, their absence from the ranks of those elected to office (like the absence of members of other social groups) was a telling reminder of the gap between representatives and those they were presumed to represent. The idea was not that women (or, for that matter, any other group) needed representatives of their own to speak in their name, but rather that elected assemblies should in their composition reflect the diversity of the French population. The extreme homogeneity of incumbent politicians—the fact that they were overwhelmingly male—distorted the national representation by vesting power in a particular group and making it impossible for its members to represent abstractly. There was no contradiction, these feminists maintained, between the idea of France as one and indivisible and a representative body composed of people of varying social backgrounds, races, ethnicities, and genders. In a democracy, they argued, participation in decision-making ought to be open to all types. Representatives would, of course, act as individuals (as republican theory presumed they would) in the interests of "France," not of some subgroup or faction, but their different experiences might be brought to bear in the conversations that resulted in new laws.

Feminists also attacked the false universalism of the abstractions of "individual" and "citizen." The lack of diversity among decision-makers, they said, resulted from a monopoly enjoyed and defended by the political class. That this class consisted almost exclusively of men was not an accident of history but the result of the fact that universalism and masculinity were taken to be synonymous. Or, as historian Michelle Perrot put it, the universal is "in fact . . . a fig leaf that merely covers over the masculinity that has served to exclude women from the government of the polity."[2] The gender disparity in the national representation meant that elected officials were not neutral individuals; they had become a special-interest group, a homogeneous political class that protected its monopoly by excluding those who were different. The republican theory of representation (which these feminists granted) was based on the idea that individuals were interchangeable units, made identical by their capacity for reason; no other traits mattered. Women's ability to reason had long been established (in laws granting equal education at the end of the nineteenth century and in enfranchisement in 1944), but women had yet to be deemed worthy of representing the electorate and, by extension, the nation. They were not, in other words, considered identical to all other individuals, not universal enough to transcend the difference of their sex. Their exclusion suggested there might be other exclusions too, since the representative individual turned out to be a member of a particular interest group ("the political class"), not at all the general abstraction imagined as a republican individual. Instead of following the precepts of abstract individualism and ignoring difference, male politicians used their own difference as a criterion for holding office and so corrupted the universalist principles which were supposed to secure the abstraction of the nation. A group of women politicians who announced their support for a parity law in 1996 diagnosed the problem this way: "The functions and fulfillment of representation have been captured by a ruling group, few in number, and extremely homogeneous, as a result of training in the *grandes écoles* and by early inclusion in the senior branches of the civil service and ministerial cabinets. Stable in its composition and difficult to penetrate, the ruling group constitutes a 'democratic aristocracy' under cover of being a republican elite. It is high time we finished with these stereotypes and blockages."[3]

The paritaristes proposed to end the "stereotypes and blockages" in an unusual way, by guaranteeing that women would hold as many elective positions as men. In an echoing of the traditional arguments used to exclude women—that their sex distorts their ability to be abstract individuals—the paritaristes insisted that the male monopoly of political office also distorted; but this time it was the political body of the nation, not the individual, that was at issue. Just as individual women had been typically portrayed as incapable of abstract representation (they could not be detached from the particularities of their sex), so feminists insisted that a political body made up overwhelmingly of men was incapable of representing abstractly. If a small group of men had declared themselves to be the nation, the nation was no longer representative of the people and the republican system was in danger. As evidence that this was the case, supporters of parité pointed to the growth of the right-wing populist party, the National Front, as well as to corruption scandals in the mainstream political parties.

To end discrimination in the selection of national and local representatives, some feminists called for a law that would implement women's right to equality by requiring elective positions to be evenly divided between women and men.[4] In 1992 they began to campaign for parité. They rejected the suggestion that they seek passage of an antidiscrimination law instead because, they said, such laws did not promote total equality; moreover antidiscrimination laws took for granted the existence of minority groups defined by biology or culture.[5] Following arguments developed among feminists in the European Community, the proponents of parité insisted that antidiscrimination laws were always partial and simply reinstituted differences that must be abolished. Rather, the principle of a fundamental right to equality must be enunciated and then implemented by law. This equality was not to be conceived as *between* women and men, because that notion assumed that men were the standard against which women were measured, but as the equality *of* women and men, for that assumed human equivalence as the foundation of social organization.[6] Parité was meant to overturn the misogynist premises on which the French liberal state rested. What the literary scholar Eliane Viennot referred to as the phantasmatic male dream of asexuality had been realized by the exclusion of women from politics.[7] Women in public, theorists from Bodin to Rousseau had argued, introduced sexual difference and so the play of desire into a realm that should be ruled by reason. The point of parité was to create a place for women in the political sphere, to democratize politics with no reference to the kind of extrapolitical considerations (such as cultural ideas about gender) that had long justified inequality.[8] By insisting on the equality of women and men, by recognizing that any abstract individual was sexed, the paritaristes hoped to *unsex* the agglomeration of abstract individuals that constituted the political body of the nation. The apparent contradiction—recognizing that abstract individuals were sexed in order to remove sex as a consideration for representation—was at the heart of the theoretical impulse of the parité movement. Françoise Gaspard put it this way: "Our fight for parité is situated in a different perspective, that of equality of the sexes based neither on difference glorified nor on difference denied but on difference exceeded—recognized in order better to be disposed of wherever it produces inequality."[9]

For women to achieve the status of individuals, escaping the limits of group identity, the paritaristes believed that nothing less than full equality was required. Dismissing quotas as inadequate because they settled for less than equality, they called initially for a 50/50 division of seats; 50% was not a quota, they argued, but a reflection of the fact that whatever other qualities they might have, individuals always came in two sexes. Anatomical difference was universal, but the meanings attributed to it were social and cultural. Philosopher Elisabeth Sledziewski thus distinguished between a living being and its sexual attributes, between the ontological identity of the subject (man and woman) and the characteristics ascribed to it by social relationships. "This recognition of sexual identity, like that of physical individuality, is independent of the status and importance attached by particular cultures to the difference between the sexes or to the individual dimension of the human subject. . . . The idea that there can be no human substance without sexual identity implies that we cannot legitimately define human rights, which are attributes of this substance, otherwise than as the rights of man and woman."[10] Ascribed meanings were the source of inequality. Until now, the paritaristes reasoned, the universal abstract individual had been figured in terms of symbols that associated reason and abstraction with masculinity, passion and the concrete with femininity. In order to extend the possibility of abstraction to women, anatomical difference had to be separated from its symbolizations; it had to be desymbolized. The way to do this was to insist on the *duality* of the human species (not the difference between the sexes): the universal individual was man and woman.

This was not the same as the nature/culture, sex/gender argument that American feminists first used and then deconstructed, because no inherent meaning, upon which gender was constructed or to which it could be referred, was attributed to anatomical duality. Indeed, biology itself was understood to be "cultural"—concrete, not abstract, a discourse attempting to account for the brute "fact" of the anatomical difference of sex.[11]

The aim of the reconceptualization was to break the link between maleness and individuality by extending the status of individual to women. This involved sexing abstract individuals in order to unsex political representation, rejecting the very notions of difference that led to the exclusion of women—not by denying difference but by refusing the opposition between sameness and difference. As Eliane Vogel-Polsky put it, "a male-dominated society is a society in disequilibrium. The idea of parité—which encompasses similarity and difference—permits a displacement of prevailing paradigms."[12] A paradigm shift, as Thomas Kuhn had described it, was what the paritaristes had in mind.

Equality of the sexes was the principle. The means of its implementation had to be a law, since only the law had the power to overcome the resistance of politicians and political parties and to redefine the terms of operation—symbolic and practical—of the political field. Before the law could do its work, it had to be passed, and that required an appeal to politicians and public opinion. The appeal on behalf of women consolidated them as a social group even as it sought to strip sex of its social characteristics. With parité, women were to become simply female individuals and, by virtue of their individualness, representatives capable of embodying the nation. The proponents of parité did not claim that women would represent only women; nor did they suggest that all women elected to office would act in the same way. They argued just the reverse: that women were as capable as men of representing the nation and that they were as varied in their opinions and assessments as men. "It is a question not of women representing women but of giving to women as many possibilities as men to influence the common destiny; of permitting women to think about the global future of society and not only the problem of day care; of having society recognize itself in them as it does in their male counterparts."[13]

This conception of parité is an example of what Etienne Balibar refers to as "ideal universality." "Ideal universality" he defines as the existence of "absolute or infinite claims which are symbolically raised against the limits of any institution."[14] Balibar points out that the argument against discrimination requires naming an excluded group, which, however, defines its exclusion as a violation not of particular rights but of the ideal of human universality itself.

> Inasmuch as women struggling for parity transform resistance into politics, they are not trying to win particular rights for a "community," which would be the "community of women." From the emancipatory standpoint, *gender is not a community.* Or perhaps, it should be said that the only gender which is a community is the masculine, inasmuch as males establish institutions and develop practices to protect old privileges (and, it should be added: by doing so males virtually transform the "Political Society" into an affective community, where processes of identification can take place). . . . There is nothing like a "women's culture" in the sense in which it can be spoken of as the culture of a community (be it ethnic or social/professional). But on the other hand, *every* community is structured by the relationship of genders with specific forms of sexual, affective, and economic subjection. Hence it must be recognized that the position of women (both the "real" position in the division of activities and the distribution of powers, and the "symbolic" position which is represented in discourse) is a structural element which determines the character of every

culture, be it the culture of a particular group, a social movement, or a whole society with its inherited civilization. . . . The struggle of women for parity, therefore, being a complex struggle for non-indifferentiation within non-discrimination, creates a solidarity (or achieves a conquest of citizenship) without creating a community. In Jean-Claude Milner's terms, women are typically a "paradoxical class," neither united by the imaginary of resemblance of "natural" kinship, nor called by some symbolic voice, which would allow them to view themselves as an "elect" group. Rather, this struggle virtually transforms the community. It is therefore immediately universalistic, which allows us to imagine that it could transform the very notion of politics, including forms of authority and representation, which suddenly appear particularistic.[15]

This was exactly the claim of the parité movement: to realize true universalism in the French political system, not by agreeing to ignore social differences (as in fictitious universality), but by making anatomical duality a first principle of abstract individualism.

In articulating the justification for a law on parité, feminists encountered what I have called (borrowing the phrase from the American legal scholar Martha Minow) "the dilemma of difference."[16] By this I mean the difficulty of desymbolizing the differences between the sexes, thinking about this difference outside its usual social meanings. The paritaristes distinguished between two registers of thinking: the abstract and the concrete. Abstraction, they rightly believed, was what republican politics claimed to depend upon; the concrete pertained to the realities of society. They thus posited a distinction between anatomical dualism and sexual difference: the one was an abstraction—the assertion of the neutrality, the essential meaninglessness, of sexed bodies; the other was substantive, it designated the social, cultural, and psychical attempt to establish meaning. The problem was that it was hard to detach bodies from the meanings attributed to them, especially since the meanings usually offered nature as their justification. So the invocation of "men" and "women" could call up the very symbolization the paritaristes wanted to change—anatomical duality became sexual difference. However precise their formulations, the proponents of parité were often misheard, their arguments distorted. Some feminists charged that the paritaristes were betraying decades of attempts to break the connection between nature and gender, and some republicans accused them of trying to substitute American multiculturalism for French universalism. Conceptualized as a form of humanistic egalitarianism, parité was understood by its critics (and by some of its supporters) as nothing other than identity politics.

This chapter examines the debates parité provoked as a dilemma of difference. I'm not suggesting that parité was a movement about women's identity or that there was a good alternative to the justifications offered for the law. Even if, as Françoise Gaspard suggested in conversation, there had been a time limit put on the 50/50 measure—defining it as a temporary strategic correction for discrimination rather than as a fundamental principle of political representation—the call for a parité law would have occasioned much the same debate. That is because the mention of women, however carefully abstracted, evoked the very social meanings the paritaristes wanted to avoid. The arguments slid easily from the register of abstraction to the register of embodiment. Yet there was no way to avoid mentioning women in a campaign aimed at ending their exclusion from the position of political representative, as Eliane Viennot well recognized:

> In the last analysis, parité is more of a battle for the extinction than for the intensification of sexual difference as a major criterion for the identification of individuals. But at first, in order to be inscribed in the law, there must be a phase in which difference is recognized and even exacerbated. . . . We must explain that, at the end of what will probably be a very long process, when "man" and "woman" cease to mark political, social, and symbolic difference, the law will no longer be necessary and can be forgotten. In order for women to become men's equals, we must first admit that they are not.[17]

Combating discrimination required the assertion of a *political* identity, "we women," whose aim was not to claim representation of a particularistic community interest but instead to expose and alter the power relations that used gender to justify inclusion and exclusion.[18] But maintaining the distinction between sexual difference as a cause of unacceptable discrimination and anatomical duality as a ground for inclusion proved difficult. Even among supporters of parité the lines between the abstractions of political theory and concrete notions of gender often blurred. This was because the parité movement was above all a political movement, not a philosophical one, so the exigencies of particular polemical contexts often made consistently nuanced arguments difficult to sustain. Indeed, the difficulty in political discourse of treating anatomical duality as an abstraction, removed from cultural attributions (from sexual difference), led some of the original supporters of the law to insist, usually from hindsight, that their emphasis on two sexes had been instrumental, with no theoretical or philosophical basis, from the start. "Parité," philosopher Geneviève Fraisse famously commented in 1998, "is true in practice and false in theory."[19] She was wrong! There was good theoretical justification for parité as a universalist concept and for the strategy of law as a way of achieving it.[20] Indeed, it was the practical implementation of the theory that caused most of the problems.

SEXING THE ABSTRACT INDIVIDUAL

The prehistory of the parité movement included the feminist activism described in chapter 2 and the increasing attention paid to women in politics in the European community in the late 1980s and early 1990s. But its founding moment was 1992 and its founding text *Au pouvoir citoyennes: Liberté, égalité, parité.*[21] The authors of this text—Françoise Gaspard, Claude Servan-Schreiber, and Anne Le Gall—came to the project from different vantages. None was a trained philosopher or theorist; all three were political activists. Yet their thinking was undeniably theoretical; an example perhaps of philosophy in practice or practical philosophy and also of the ultimate inseparability of theory and politics. Gaspard had long experience in the PS; she had served as mayor of the town of Dreux (until 1983 when, in an election that became the ultimate signifier of immigration politics, she was unseated by an alliance of the traditional right and the National Front) and as a twice-elected deputy from the Eure-et-Loire department, and she had been active as a feminist within the PS in the 1970s and 1980s. In 1992 she was a member of the European Commission's network of experts on "women and decision-making." Servan-Schreiber was a journalist who had published *F-Magazine,* a counterpart to the American feminist magazine *Ms.* in the 1980s; in 1990, she was preparing a study of the feminist *courant 3* in the PS.[22] Gaspard and Servan-Schreiber were partners, and they knew Le Gall from socialist and feminist circles where she was an outspoken rank-and-file militant. As part of her research, Servan-Schreiber had invited Le Gall to her country home outside of Dreux for an interview. Le Gall remembers many details of the visit (the weather, the food, the comings and goings of Gaspard in the course of the day, and her disappointment at the initial caution that greeted her idea) with the clarity one has about such pathbreaking events. According to Gaspard and Servan-Schreiber, it was Le Gall who argued for a *law* on parité. Her background was in law, and so she insisted that male domination was a function not so much of the social as of the juridical structure; as such, it could only be overturned by a law that implemented women's right to participate in political representation. Over the course of several days the women continued to talk; from their conversations the book evolved. Le Gall says she didn't do any of the writing ("I talk, but I don't write"), but she did play a crucial role in formulating the argument.[23]

Au pouvoir citoyennes made a strong case for the determining role of law. Rejecting functionalist, culturalist, and psychoanalytic theories of male domination that referred inequalities of power to the facts of sexual difference, the authors insisted that law, not nature, established and hence could abolish those inequalities. Law was constitutive of subjects, they maintained, and it established the actual and symbolic relationships among them. Wrote Gaspard, "The social and political prejudices resulting from differentiations constructed on the basis of biological sex remain with us, as does an unequal balance of power (favoring men), which finds expression in particular in the domain of political representation and sites of decision-making. This imbalance clearly shows that there exists an unspoken 'order' of men. The achievement of strict equality between men and women in representative assemblies, whether national or local, therefore has great symbolic weight."[24] Distinctions of sex were introduced into politics; they did not follow necessarily from biology. The realms of biology and politics were separate, brought into relation only by man-made law. Law had formative power, but it was also mutable. The abbé Sièyes had recognized as much during the French Revolution, when he had stated that women, "at least for the moment," could not be considered active citizens (their exclusion was thus "not natural, only temporal").[25] The revolutionaries' concept of the individual was, according to the authors, inimical to women's political rights. Women's citizenship was recognized in 1944 when, with the stroke of a pen, de Gaulle granted women the vote, paying no heed to previous assertions about their incapacities. This demonstrated for the authors that arguments used to legitimize women's exclusion were mutable since they were "political in nature. Entirely political."[26]

The underrepresentation of women in politics was not a reflection of nature (of women's innately driven preferences for the private, the domestic, the relational, or the sexual) but the effect of discrimination stemming from male domination. Law had the power to rectify discrimination in two ways: by making sex an invalid ground for exclusion and by symbolically extending the status of individual to women. In order to guarantee genuinely equal status, the invidious distinction that takes women to be men's inferiors for purposes of representing the nation must be replaced by a law that rules the sexes equal and so makes it possible to imagine women in the role of representatives. Women might be able to govern, Geneviève Fraisse argued, but they aren't yet considered truly representative. "The symbolic representation of the people is not open to women."[27] The need for a law on parité, added philosopher Françoise Collin, was to change this symbolism: "to make apparent and to recognize that women are representative of the universal in the same way as men are."[28]

There was no achieving this aim without deciding (according to the terms of fictional universality defined by Balibar)[29] which differences were to be discounted for purposes of abstraction. "In democracies," Gaspard pointed out, "the legal system constantly takes differences into consideration in order to institute the conditions for equality. Its function is to impose what does not happen 'naturally.' Law is 'differentialist' whenever its goal is to eradicate inequalities produced by society."[30] Law has traditionally addressed power relations directly, aiming not at behavior but at the field of force that enables discrimination. Under the parité law, other supporters wrote, women would be recognized as individuals, not as "men." "The struggle to establish parité is for the recognition of the political legitimacy of women."[31] Anatomical difference, instead of being a ground for exclusion, would become "a normal condition of political life."[32] The law on parité, from this perspective, is not just an ordinary law but "a law that will change the very conditions under which laws are drawn up."[33] "Change in the quantitative division of women and men in the direction of parité in the power to represent will lead to qualitative change in this representation, that is to say to a change in the very conception of the general will."[34]

To recognize the political legitimacy of women serving as representatives required addressing two universals: the legal fiction of the abstract individual and the so-called natural fact of sexual difference. Sexual difference had long been used to discount charges of discrimination. Women's particularity (their difference from the normative male standard) was said to mark them in ways incompatible with abstract individuality. One way of arguing against this logic was to insist that sex was an irrelevant criterion, a physical and social characteristic that didn't count in the definition of the political individual. Another was to redefine representation in more democratic terms, as the function not of abstract individuals but of socially located human actors. (These two positions were those of more conventional feminisms, the one asserting that gender was entirely cultural, associated with so-called equality feminists; the other insisting on the special qualities women would bring to the table, dubbed "differentialist.") The authors of *Au pouvoir citoyennes* took a third course: they argued that sex was relevant for the definition of the abstract individual, not as sexual difference, not as a set of culturally defined attributes, but rather as anatomical duality—the bare fact of genitally distinct bodies. Since humans all came in one of two sexes, and since sex had been used to disqualify women and to favor men, the way to equality was through the redefinition of the human individual as plural, as a type of two. The parité strategy was designed to expose the hypocrisy of a universalism that historically had privileged the male sex (the French words for "individual," "citizen," and "representative" are masculine in gender) by equating men with the general and the abstract (signified by reason), and women with the particular and the concrete (signified by sex). The strategy was also designed to avoid the more radical democratic (multicultural) alternative that had been ruled out by the republican consensus established around immigration. Only by insisting on the necessary duality of the human species could a truly inclusive individualism exist, one in which sex no longer mattered. "It is paradoxical, but interesting to argue," commented Françoise Collin, "that it was universalism that best maintained the sexualization of power, and that parité, by contrast, attempts to desexualize power by extending it to both sexes. Parité would thus be the real universalism."[35]

The authors of *Au pouvoir citoyennes* were aware of the traps posed by "nature" in discussions of sexed bodies, but they expected that the law, once in effect, would bypass those traps. In justifying the need for a law, however, they had to address a commonsense understanding that took for granted the biological determination of gender. There were no comparably simple, seemingly self-evident formulations about the influence of culture or law that could be readily deployed; instead, the paritaristes were constantly reaching for new conceptualizations that could be distinguished from the essentialist views upon which discrimination against women had been based. So, for example, at a seminar on *Au pouvoir citoyennes* in October 1992, Servan-Schreiber refuted the idea that parité was a way to recognize "the true nature" of women, their essential "difference." The point wasn't to defend some special "women's interest," or to bring a uniquely feminine capacity to lawmaking ("that way we'd fall into a differentialist discourse, which I don't accept at all"),[36] but rather to make women plausible representatives of the nation. Insisting on the anatomical duality of the human was a way of claiming the equal right of women to represent humanity. "The human species is a unit that stands upright on two legs—two legs that are part of a single body and are not interchangeable. We seek *political* recognition of this duality—not of difference, but of duality. That's what parité is."[37] While "difference" came laden with all sorts of cultural assumptions about the inescapably biological capacities and characteristics of women and men, Servan-Schreiber thought "duality" avoided those associations. Women and men were not, in one sense, interchangeable; if they were, women would be subsumed and thus effaced by dominating males. The argument against such obliteration (against discrimination) required that women be distinctly visible. Equality implied recognition of duality, in this case that the human was man and woman, in order to qualify women as individuals, elim-inating their sex as an obstacle.

　　Duality was not, however, an argument about complementarity, nor about the necessary heterosexual foundation of society—these were cultural defini-tions, not abstractions. Rather, men and women simply existed as the two hu-man types; discrimination had prevented women from becoming representa-tives in elected assemblies. This was a violation not of nature—nature had nothing to do with it—but of the principles of democracy:

> Democracy is a universal aspiration; universality encompasses women and men. There is, therefore, no representative democracy if represen-tation isn't equal [*paritaire*]. Today, the underrepresentation of women in elected assemblies is so constant in its disproportion that it reveals a deficit of thought and consequently of law. Because of this dispropor-tion a new democratic contract is needed. The word "contract" pre-sumes equality between the contracting parties. Only the adoption of a parité law will insure that this equality is not a sham.[38]

Anticipating objections from those who saw parité as the tip of a differentialist or communitarian iceberg *à l'américaine*,[39] the authors denied that they were treating women as a "class" or a "social group." They were opposed, they said, to "a social corporatism that fractures the unity of universal suffrage." There was no "women's interest" at stake here, since women cut across all interest groups. Electing women would not mean introducing a separate, unified ele-ment into the legislatures; they would likely be found in every party, on all sides of contested issues. It was "pernicious," they said, to put women on the same plane as classes, social categories, or ethnic communities: "Women are every-where. They are in all classes, in all social categories. They are Catholic, Protes-tant, Jewish, Muslim, agnostic. . . . And they can't be compared to any pres-sure group . . . that demands to be better represented. . . . Women are neither a group nor a lobby. They constitute half of the sovereign people, half of the human species."[40] Blandine Kriegel also rejected the equation of women with a minority group. "Femininity is a universal," she wrote, "and just as one is hu-man when one is masculine, so when one is feminine, one is human."[41] The law on parité was meant to implement not a differentialist vision of women (as a group with definable attributes) but the universalist principles of democracy. "Parité," asserted Gaspard, "obviously concerns not only women but the very construction of democracy."[42]

THE SLIPPERY SLOPE OF ESSENTIALISM

Despite the rigor of their arguments, the paritaristes could not avoid the dilemma of difference. It appeared most prominently in the objections offered by critics—both feminist and republicanist.[43] (Interestingly, the division between supporters and opponents of the law did not follow traditional party or ideological lines.) There were, of course, also some supporters of the movement who could not hear the claims for women's right to become representatives in other than essentialist terms. "Women," for these critics (and some supporters), was a permanent category of identity overflowing with social attributes taken to be "natural," one whose existence was confirmed by common sense and could not therefore be abstracted or altered by changes in the law. Desymbolization was not possible for them with regard to differences of sex.

Supporters of Parité

As the paritaristes grappled with abstract arguments about the power of law to transform women's access to the position of representative, they were often asked to justify their claims in practical terms. Equality was a fine principle, but what difference would it really make if there were more women in elective office? The question implied some notion of women's difference, indeed that women were a group with shared traits, who would fill a perceived lack in the political realm. But it revealed a fundamental misunderstanding of the goal of parité—to insist, against prevailing assumptions, that women were, or could be, individuals, just as men were. To remain consistent to their argument, the paritaristes probably should have refused even to entertain this question, insisting that the principle of equality, implemented by law, was their only goal. This was the advice of the Belgian philosopher Jean Vogel, who cautioned against any "extrapolitical" arguments. "Parité is about equality and democracy; it is therefore in relation to the internal workings of democracy, as a self-criticism of democracy, that it must be justified, and not in relation to extrapolitical considerations."[44] Irresistibly, however, the paritaristes did try to respond, sometimes because a particular debate seemed to require it. And of course there were some among them who believed that, whether because of experience or nature, women were essentially different from men—that sexual difference was an irreducible antagonism that law might reflect but could never change.

The authors of *Au pouvoir citoyennes* carefully avoided any claim about the complementarity of the sexes or about the ways in which a feminine presence might increase legislative sensitivity or bring greater harmony to lawmaking, but they did argue (quite reasonably, it seems to me) that discrimination had given women a different perspective on the political process. "It is permissible to think," Gaspard insisted (with a combination of sarcasm and defensiveness), "that women will bring a particular expertise as a result of their specific experience."[45] That experience, according to PS militant Jean-Pierre Chevènement, derived from women's relationship to power, different from that of men, and so would bring new concerns to the table. He was careful to add, "This doesn't mean that women by nature hold the keys to an alternative political practice, but that their contribution will help to shake things up."[46] On the basis of this same notion of experience, Servan-Schreiber told a feminist gathering that she was willing to "bet" that when women were in positions of power they would "not always vote against the interests of other women," that there would be some solidarity on women's issues. Her use of the negative—"[they would] not always vote against"—was a way of avoiding the essentialist argument that women would necessarily represent a women's interest. This kind of circumlocution is evidence of the difficulty of reconciling practical considerations and abstract conceptualizations.[47]

Others took for granted the historical or cultural constructions of women's different experience and generalized more broadly about women's potential contribution. Thus Yvette Roudy (who hardly fit her own description) suggested that "beyond stereotypes, women saw things in life differently, settled problems otherwise . . . and approached politics from a different perspective."[48] Like Roudy, Janine Mossuz-Lavau, a political scientist who became one of the important voices in the parité campaign, summarized the results of her research on voter preferences by invoking the public/private distinction: women were more attuned to the private, men to the public. "Men define politics by institutions and parties, while women talk of people and what can be done for them." As a result, "women express themselves less about unemployment than about the unemployed." The particular, not the abstract, was their concern.[49] When ten leading female politicians published their manifesto for parité in 1996 (the Manifesto of Ten), they took some of these notions further, at least in part in a calculated attempt to appeal to commonsense notions of difference and perhaps also to reassure their public that they didn't intend to overturn the social order symbolized by the difference of sex. The manifesto stated that the exclusion of women "by the Jacobins" at the founding of the republic had introduced an unfortunate but persistent opposition between virility (hierarchical, centralizing, arrogant, rationalist, abstract) and femininity (understanding others "as they are," sensitive, concrete, and attentive to the cares of daily life).

Instead of rejecting this opposition, they accepted it and lamented the lack of women's input on contemporary matters ("the circulation of information, the diffusion of knowledge, interindividual and collective relations"), contending that "women, because of their identity and their history, are well placed—if not better placed than men—to take up challenges that arise."[50] Still, they did not argue that women would represent only women, just that their input would bring a different perspective to common political deliberations. The next step was to take these historically constructed oppositions and make them even more enduring. So it was that Green Party leader Dominique Voynet pointed to the necessary complementarity of women and men "in all aspects of life."[51]

As parité gained momentum and became a prominent and controversial movement (see chapter 4), it drew followers who were less wary of the traps of essentialism and who, even while rejecting identity politics, naturalized the male/female opposition that others attributed to law or history. They conflated anatomical duality and sexual difference while the founders of the movement sought to distinguish them. There were feminists, for example, who had long believed that the difference of sex—whether biological, psychological, or symbolic—was "primary and irreducible." For Julia Kristeva, one had only to consider the "elementary structures of kinship" to grasp the connection between the recognition of sexual difference and human culture. "Parité finally reflects humanity rendered in its constitutive duality . . . , a humanity that has not lost its sense of the sacred—neither that of sacrifice nor of procreation."[52] It was not far from this argument (and from Kristeva's other writing, emphasizing maternity as a key to femininity) to one that maintained that complementarity in politics would reflect the natural order of the heterosexual couple. This was what philosopher Sylviane Agacinski began to argue in her *Politique des sexes* in 1998.[53] Written while a law to recognize the rights of homosexual couples was being debated (and with that debate in mind), Agacinski grounded her support for parité in a nature that had always been cultural; not only were there two sexes, but theirs was a necessary relationship of heterosexuality, based in procreation. While the paritaristes originally sought to depoliticize the difference between the sexes (distinguishing between the reality of anatomical duality and the attribution of meaning to it), Agacinski made those attributed meanings foundational to biology, social organization, and politics.

I will discuss Agacinski's arguments in relation to the family law reform and their impact on the parité debates in chapter 5. They were the turning point, the essentializing moment, in the parité campaign. Here I want only to point out the way in which her intervention illustrates the dilemma of difference. Having set forth "women" as the object of their campaign, the paritaristes could have a hard time controlling its meanings; the difference of women (replete with cultural attributes) came to be seen not as the effect of political power but as a natural essence to which power must refer. Even some of those most ardent in their support of the law tended to invert the causality Gaspard, Servan-Schreiber, and Le Gall had proposed. For Gaspard and her coauthors, law could change the social relations between the sexes; there was nothing inherent in anatomical duality that determined what those relations should be. For Agacinski, law must respond to a previously existing natural order, which was not an abstract dualism but a set of differences full of meaning. In her thinking, men and women were not individuals who happened to be sexed, but necessarily opposites: husband and wife. The universal individual was not simply pluralized but replaced by the universal couple. Perversely, Agacinski's argument ended up outside the frame of the republican consensus, denying women the very equality *as individuals* that Gaspard and her colleagues sought.

Critics of Parité

Critics of parité fell into at least three groups, according to sociologist Yves Sintomer. One consisted of classic antifeminists, like Philippe de Gaulle (the general's son), who claimed that from the beginning of time ("depuis le monde est monde") women existed to bear children, men to fashion the world.[54] This traditional public/private distinction well articulated the hierarchy that supporters of parité, from Gaspard to Agacinski, sought to combat. A second group, consisting mostly of intellectuals identified with the left, acknowledged that equality was desirable but objected both to what they took to be parité's implied essentialism and to its endorsement of the liberal principles of representative democracy that privileged formal (legal) over substantive (social and economic) rights.[55] A third group of critics, while agreeing that the exclusion of women from politics was lamentable, thought parité threatened to replace republican individualism with an American-style communitarianism. I refer to this group as "republicanists."

Leaving aside the antifeminists, whose reactions were entirely predictable (and who, ironically, recognized parité for what it was—an attempt to alter the gendered bases of power), the second and third critical positions illuminate the dilemma of difference. Each heard the demand for parité not as a correction of long-standing bias but as a call to elect women simply because they were women—as a form of "communitarianism" or identity politics. Republicanists objected to the idea that a new requirement was being added to the standard criteria for office holding (talent, aptitude, skill), namely, "being of the female sex."[56] And those on the left admonished the paritaristes for treating women as a group. "Women do not constitute a homogeneous social category in themselves any more than men do."[57] This comment must have struck the authors of *Au pouvoir citoyennes* as absurd, since they had argued so hard against the idea that women were a homogeneous social category, but it also demonstrated the difficulty of conducting a political struggle with complex concepts (anatomical duality rather than sexual difference, the power of the law to transform social and symbolic relations between the sexes or even to render gender irrelevant) aimed at altering the grounds on which discriminatory practices rested. If republicanist critics found parité's attention to anatomical duality dangerous because they took it to mean sexual difference, critics on the left (who also conflated anatomical duality and sexual difference) thought that attention to sexual difference was too restrictive because recognizing this difference occluded other more salient differences such as class. But in offering their own alternatives, the critics were unsuccessful at resolving the dilemma of difference. They had no solution to the problem of discrimination—a discrimination based on a belief that women's difference of sex was not susceptible to abstraction.

The left-wing critique. Critics on the left offered many objections to the parité campaign. Above all, they maintained that parité, contrary to its own intentions, could only reify rather than dissolve the naturalized opposition between women and men. Among other things, this reification denied women the possibility of acting as individuals or as members of other groups. There might be discrimination against women, but the argument for ending it should not be made for women as women. "That would leave the impression that women can only accede to politics as members of a homogeneous group. . . . From this perspective, the potential for singular contributions to public life from individuals, a fundamental condition of citizenship, still remains blocked."[58] These feminists could hear "women" only as signifying a social group, so they believed that women's legitimacy as representatives would be undermined by their having been elected because of their group identity, not for their individual capabilities.[59] Parité would thus confirm rather than disrupt the prejudice that made it almost impossible for women to be representatives of France. In this view, parité was a trompe-l'oeil for feminism; the recognition of a difference based on biology would lead inexorably to its reproduction and not to the promised equality.[60]

If women did have an identity, these critics argued, it was not because of their physical makeup but because of the social and economic oppression they suffered. This gave them common cause with a larger group of the oppressed. "The only possible alliances are political projects that develop an alternative to the world as it exists, based on the interests and needs of men and women, on multiple and often contradictory views of domination."[61] For these critics, it was more important to point out that women were vastly overrepresented among the unemployed and as heads of impoverished households than to complain that they were excluded from holding office. In the one case, feminism was dedicated to social justice, in the other to securing a few otherwise privileged women access to better jobs. Failing to distinguish among different kinds of exclusion ran the danger of reducing all forms of social antagonism to sexual difference and ignoring the plight of others—immigrants, the unemployed. The parité campaign was accused of political elitism, interested only in advancing the careers of a few *patriciennes* who aspired to enter the halls of power on male terms.[62] Pierre Bourdieu, an early supporter, worried later that parité's critique of universalism "risks intensifying the effects of another form of fictive universalism by giving priority to women from the same social space as the men who now hold dominant positions." And he urged, instead, action against "all the effects of domination" in all the institutions of society (without, however, specifying what concrete forms such action might take).[63]

Even if its proponents did not actually endorse the notion that only women can represent women, historian Eleni Varikas argued, parité logically implied "that women should exercise their citizenship as women."[64] She then extended the logic to require that any woman candidate must be preferable to a man. But this was a betrayal, she said, that would lead feminists to encourage voting for such candidates as the National Front's Marie-France Stirbois just because she was a woman. Such an approach denied the need to support substantive policies that would benefit those women (and men) who were victims of real inequality.

Parité's emphasis on political matters—representation and the passage of a law—seemed so much liberal distraction from more fundamental economic inequalities in French society. Was parité a call for social justice or simply for legal reform, these left-wing critics asked? If social justice were the issue, then there must be pressure across the board for more democratic—that is, more representative—representation. The crisis of representation had opened the way to claims for genuine democracy; parité was closing the door on this chance for democracy by accepting the terms of the old universalism (that of the abstract individual) instead of redefining it. Parité sought to integrate women into the existing republican system; critics on the left wanted an alteration of the system itself so that all underrepresented groups could find a voice. This could not happen, they insisted, by legal means. "In the present state of the world, this idea maintains the illusion that a change in power relations between men and women is possible, that antagonisms such as these can be transformed by simply passing a law."[65] Even if women won 50% of the seats in elected assemblies, men would still have more power because law itself could not change existing "relations of power." To the argument that an assembly with 50% women would have a powerful symbolic effect, reversing stereotypes about women, Varikas replied that the relation between symbols and reality "is much more complex and mediated than is readily recognized."[66] The economic and social powerlessness of women would influence perceptions of women in all domains, including politics. Here disagreement with the founders of parité was fundamental. For left-wing feminist critics, law merely followed social change; it didn't precede or cause it. Politics was to the social and economic as the symbolic was to the real; the political and the symbolic always reflected (and never constructed) the realities of social and economic life. Moreover, while the paritaristes understood change as incremental, as a series of cumulative advances in the direction of greater equality, their left-wing critics had a more dramatic and totalizing—a more revolutionary—notion of how change would occur and what it would entail.

The left-wing critics of parité did not deny the need to recognize that social differences divided French society; indeed, they assumed that such recognition was the only way movements could be organized to transform existing structures of power. They objected, however, to parité's focus on anatomical duality (which they equated with sexual difference) both because it neglected other, more salient differences such as class and because it seemed to assign biological rather than economic causality. They further rejected the paritaristes' idea that law was the source of this assignment of biological causality and so could alter it. Their call for political alliances among those who were oppressed (*les dominés*) avoided the charge of essentialism but did not guarantee that sexual discrimination as such would be addressed. Indeed, as Varikas herself admitted, in left-wing movements notorious for ignoring hierarchies based on gender, the absence of specific attention to women might perpetuate rather than end discrimination.[67] Her solution was to create a better movement, more attentive to the needs of its diverse constituencies—a new form of democratic politics in the long run.

According to their own logic, the left-wing critics of parité were caught in the dilemma of difference: they could not think about women except as an already symbolized social category. And they struggled with two unsatisfactory alternatives. Singling out women inevitably reproduced the terms of discrimination against them, while subsuming them in the category of *dominés* did not. But defining women as *dominés* drew attention away from the specifics of discrimination against women based on their sex (Varikas's use of the masculine "dominés" is symptomatic of this problem)—specifics the left-wing feminists acknowledged but were finally unable to address.

The republicanist critique. Like the left-wing critics of parité, those critics who were self-styled defenders of the Republic (many of these were, of course, also on the political left) could not hear or refused to accept the distinction between abstraction (anatomical duality) and attributed meanings (sexual difference) and therefore strongly objected to the implicit essentialism of the movement. They thought it would set back generations of feminist accomplishment. Thus Elisabeth Badinter insisted that parité sought to "concretize" the universal, which must be necessarily abstract.[68] By changing the demand from "equality of the sexes" to "equality between the sexes," claimed law professor Evelyne Pisier, parité introduced difference into what must remain an abstract universal principle.[69] (Here she was mistaken: the paritaristes were calling for "equality *of* the sexes," not "equality *between* the sexes.") Historically, Pisier argued, the point of feminism was to deny the significance of sex for purposes of political participation. Since anatomical dualism was inevitably rooted in biology, it would be used to justify all sorts of discriminatory treatment of women. In her view, the concrete could never be separated from the abstract.

The republicanists objected to what they considered the inevitable essentialism of parité. "To rely on biological determination . . . creates no community of existence, no chance of liberty, but it does recreate the conditions of discrimination that always threaten to reappear."[70] The notion (offered in the Manifesto of Ten) that there was something inherently feminine that transcended class, education, and political affiliation infuriated Elisabeth Badinter, perhaps the most vocal and frequently cited of republicanist critics. "I feel much closer to a man who shares my values than to a woman who does not share them."[71] And she found nothing to confirm ideas about their difference in the deportment of those few women who had managed to enter the assembly or the government. "Excuse me for being skeptical, but when I rub shoulders with women who have power, graduates of the ENA or the polytechnics, I find them very similar to their male colleagues; same attributes, same faults."[72]

Another objection was to the danger of "communitarianism." Unlike the left-wing critics who attacked it as conservative, republicanist commentators decried parité as an attempt to radically alter the French political system and replace it with "the communitarian democracy of quotas, imported from the

United States."[73] America was the foil for these criticisms, its multiculturalism a stark warning to anyone who would tamper with the principles of French republicanism. Parité was likened to American affirmative action—by definition a failed attempt to reverse discrimination. "Discrimination is never positive and always ends by turning against the person who is the object of discrimination," Badinter asserted, and she gestured (without further elaboration) to "American Blacks" as proof of this statement.[74] Danièle Sallenave too cited the American case, pointing out that its most severe critics were those who were presumed to benefit from the practice.[75] The complex facts of the American experience were beside the point in these arguments; it was the image of America, riven by conflicting ethnic, religious, and racial communities, that served as the antithesis of the desired unity of France.

America was differentialist, France universalist. Above all, the republicanists thought parité dangerous because it tampered with a hard-won universalism. In the history of French politics, they recalled, discourses of difference were invariably associated with the right; by implication, parité opened the door to enemies of the republic. For this reason Badinter thought that parité carried "mortal implications for our secular and universalist republic."[76] "To put parité into law is to renounce the equality of citizens and to accept the end of the French Republic."[77] And though she granted that women's situation in the political realm was deplorable, she pledged to "fight with all my strength to protect the foundation of the Republic as one and indivisible."[78] The foundation was necessarily the traditional notion of abstract individualism. For Dominique Schnapper, "the nation defines itself by its ambition to transcend particular memberships—biological, historical, economic, social, religious, or cultural; to define the citizen as an abstract individual without particular identities or aptitudes, above and beyond all concrete determinations."[79] The nation's indivisibility, indeed its very existence, here rested on the absence of perceptions of difference (an absence signified since 1789 by the exclusion of sexual difference in the form of the exclusion of women). For senator Robert Badinter, "sovereignty, like the Republic, is an indivisible whole." It was incomprehensible, he maintained, to conceive of sovereignty incarnated in two halves of humanity any more than it was plausible to refer to a "concrete universalism." "Universalism is universalism, nothing more, nothing less!"[80] For Elisabeth Badinter, "humanity" was the abstraction that dissolved difference: "The greatness of the concept of humanity is that it is common to all of us despite all of our differences."[81] There might be all sorts of differences in reality, added Pisier, but these must never be allowed to affect "the legal principle of indifferentiation."[82] After all, it was an appeal to their rights as humans, not as women, that had won women the vote and that should now be invoked to gain them access to politics. Abstract individualism because it "transcended" difference was the guarantee of inclusiveness; any recognition of difference in the realm of politics was inevitably destructive. For Pisier, there could be no abstraction of the kind the paritaristes offered because there was no inherently meaningless anatomical duality.

The fierce reassertion of the principles of the republic was meant to stave off not only parité but demands for fairer representation from other groups. Granting this system of "quotas" (for parité was nothing but a quota in the eyes of these critics) would introduce "corporatist" principles and thus open the door to all manner of demands for proportional representation. "Who is it more difficult in a society such as French society to be: a *beur* or a woman?"[83] Instead of campaigns for rights, Sallenave warned, there would be campaigns for the recognition of all sorts of different collectivities. Then where to draw the line: "Blacks or *Beurs,* homosexuals or Muslims, Seventh Day Adventists?"[84] The listings varied (the handicapped were often mentioned, as if to suggest that lesser or deformed humans might also have to be included), but the overwhelming preoccupation seemed to be with "immigrants"—the North Africans whose status had been at the center of disputes about nationality during the 1980s and early 1990s. Parité threatened to reopen what the 1986 and 1993 reforms of the nationality acts had refused: the granting of special recognition to the needs and interests of immigrants. Thus the anxiety of Elisabeth Badinter: "You have to be deaf and blind not to see that the rise of communitarian pressure in France is enormous. And what can the paritaristes say to the North African 'community,' which includes millions of people who can look at the National Assembly and say indignantly: 'And what about us? Aren't we excluded from the universalist Republic?'"[85]

Most of these critics acknowledged the problem of discrimination against women that parité sought to correct, but proposed other means for improving women's access to elective office. The issue, they maintained, was not rights for women but the facts of discrimination against them. It was not principles but practices that were at fault. In an opposition based on the myth of a timeless republicanism, republicanists posited principles as immutable, as against practices, which changed. They rejected entirely the idea proposed by the paritaristes that an as yet unstated principle of equality (*of* rather than *between* men and women) was at stake. Thus, Elisabeth Badinter thought the male monopoly of political power, defended by the misogyny of political parties, could be corrected by specific measures. If the practice of multiple officeholding were eliminated, more positions would be available for women. If the behavior of political parties were influenced by financial incentives, more women might be listed as candidates. Badinter supported a constitutional revision that would require political parties to implement existing commitments to equality. The "real causes" of the underrepresentation of women would thus be addressed.[86]

On the question of causality, the republicanist critics' disagreement with the paritaristes was fundamental. For the republicanists, the universalism of abstract individualism was antithetical to discrimination; for the paritaristes, they had been mutually constitutive since the Revolution. For the former group, discrimination could be overcome only by ignoring difference; for the latter, only the restatement of difference as duality could allow discrimination to be addressed. The two positions exemplify the dilemma of difference. While republicanists predicted that parité would only reproduce discrimination, they had no answer to the question of how—or whether—women could be considered individuals in the face of discrimination based on their sex. Could existing notions of universalism remove the marks of sexual difference, a difference historically taken to be irreducible, not susceptible to abstraction? Parité advocate and Green Party activist Alain Lipietz suggested they could not: "There is an enormous difference between women and workers" as elected representatives, he said. "A woman elected remains a woman because she is immersed in social relations that immerse her in that identity; whereas a worker once elected is no longer a worker."[87] What the paritaristes considered the "real cause" of exclusion—conceptions of women's unsuitability as representatives of the nation based on the difference of their sex—could never be made part of the republicanists' remedy. Instead, for the republicanists, the fiction that individuals have no sex (and that sex is the equivalent of any other social characteristic) had to be maintained in politics, even if sex (conceived as more fundamental than any other social characteristic) was the basis for discrimination against women.

෴

From the publication of *Au pouvoir citoyennes* to the passage of the parité law in June 2000, these debates raged. From an American viewpoint they are remarkable for their high level of philosophical engagement (even as they were venomous and passionate) and for the involvement of some of France's leading intellectuals. Some commentators tried to dismiss the debates as a family quarrel on Paris's Left Bank, suggesting that for all its rhetorical brilliance philosophy ultimately had no bearing on politics. Although the law did pass despite the force of the critics' objections, these debates do seem to me to have had important political relevance. Not because they did or did not directly influence legislators and public opinion, but because their very unresolvability demonstrated the need for a law. Only a law, the authors of *Au pouvoir citoyennes* had argued, could cut through arguments in which philosophy and ideology, epistemology and political allegiance, were entangled. Only a law that implemented a new principle of equality could begin the process of structural and ideological change required for the reconceptualization of women as individuals. Whether such a law would ultimately render sexual difference irrelevant in the sphere of political representation could only be known long after it was put into effect. The aim of the movement now was to get the law passed.

CHAPTER FOUR

The Campaign for Parité

The divisions among intellectuals, evident in intense philosophical debates about sexual difference and republicanism, were not replicated in the general public. Instead, the debates seem to have made parité an increasingly familiar and popular term. Within fewer than five years of the launching of the campaign, opinion polls showed overwhelming support (with hardly any distinction between men and women) for gender equality among elected representatives. Although there is a strong notion among observers outside of the country about French conservatism on matters of gender, public opinion was not opposed to increasing the numbers of women in politics. This may have been the result of many factors, including the long experience with women as voters, the more immediate public disgust with politicians, and the way in which the parité campaign made its appeal. Whatever the reasons, the pressure of public opinion was such that deputies and senators, as well as party leaders, swallowed their hostility and included parité in their vocabularies (even as they tried to limit the definition and the realization of its goals). Between the defeat of the Socialist Party in the legislative elections of 1993 and its recapture of the majority in the National Assembly in 1997, parité gained enormous currency as a statement of principle and a commitment to action. Politicians understood that a stand on parité might make or break their party's electoral success, and, indeed, that seems to have been an accurate perception. Widespread public support made passage of some kind of law inevitable by the end of the decade.

The popularity of parité was the result of a sustained feminist campaign against injustice and for equality. This was not a movement aimed at establishing a coherent female identity; what commonality there was came from the experience of discrimination. This was evident both in the form the movement took—a loosely coordinated network of established women's associations, with little in common beyond a critique of the existing system of representation—and in the minimal nature of its demand: parité meant nothing more than "perfect equality." Perfect equality was about fairness in access to decision-making; it was not an endorsement of an essentialist vision of sexual difference. There were, to be sure, essentialist traps inherent in the dilemma of difference, but the actual movement managed to minimize them in its heyday.

PARITÉ: THE SLOGAN

The leaders of the parité movement took a term that was already "in the air," coined by the German Green Party and feminists to refer to equal political representation of women, subsequently employed in discussions in the Council of Europe and the European Union, and brought to the center of public discourse in the course of the 1990s. Parité was a goal, the alternative to, and thus a critique of, discriminatory treatment of women in politics. As far as its chroniclers can determine (and there is inevitable disagreement about this), parité was first used in French feminist circles around 1986. Those associated with Arc en ciel, a group consisting of ecologists and members of the far left, implemented parité in the leadership and the conduct of their organization (even the time allotted to speakers at meetings was the same for both sexes). In another feminist group, Ruptures, Monique Dental and Odette Brun also began to speak of parité. In 1988, the French Green Party included parité in its statutes and applied it to its lists of candidates. In the Council of Europe, from at least 1989, with pressure from jurist Claudette Apprill, *démocratie paritaire* was theorized in seminars, with important contributions from French philosopher Elisabeth Sledziewski and Belgian jurist Eliane Vogel-Polsky. In 1992 a network of national experts devoted to women's equality of opportunity was established, this time by the European Commission. Later that year, the first European summit on "women in power," meeting in Athens, proclaimed that "democracy requires parité in the representation and administration of nations." The text of the Athens conference became the byword for European feminists and a standard they could use as they worked to expand women's role in politics in their own countries. (The term "parité" became so popular that Antoinette Fouque, who had—much to the annoyance of fellow feminists in the 1970s—copyrighted the designation "Mouvement pour la libération des femmes," sought once again to establish an exclusive claim. But since parité was considered by the patent office to be a term in common usage [like liberty or equality] and therefore not patentable, she had to be content with a copyright for "Parité 2000" as the name of her group.)

The women in the European network began to lobby for parité as something more than a rhetorical endorsement of women's equal rights. They also sought to develop an awareness of the inadequacy of formal notions of equality, tied as they were to theories of liberal individualism that were implicitly bound to masculine norms. "Formal democracy, egalitarian democracy, is an illusion because it allows a small group of men who have made a profession of 'representing the people' to seize power, excluding, in addition to women, the vast majority of the French population. It's a caricature of democracy."[1] Parité was the articulation of a new notion in which women's rights were assumed to be the same as men's from the beginning. This wasn't a matter of simply ending discrimination by eventually extending men's rights to women (a compensatory move at best), but of making equality of the sexes foundational, a constitutive principle upon which social and political structures were to be built. "No real democracy is possible . . . if the question of equality between men and women is not posed as a political precondition, pertaining to the constitutive principles of the regime, in exactly the same way as universal suffrage and the separation of powers."[2]

In their 1992 book title, *Au pouvoir citoyennes: Liberté, égalité, parité*, Gaspard, Servan-Schreiber, and Le Gall took a cue from the European network and boldly rewrote the French national motto, significantly replacing *fraternité* (the brotherhood of men) with *parité* (power shared by women and men) and explicitly calling for a law to implement it. The abstraction of equal rights was no guarantee of real equality, they argued; parité was an attempt to breach the divide between principle and practice, abstract and concrete. "Parité is the application of the principle of equality," Gaspard wrote.[3] As principle and practice, it was more than formal equality. A pamphlet published in 1995 elaborated the point: "The word 'parité' signifies 'perfect equality.' Parité of the sexes thus means equality of women and men not only before the law but in reality."[4] The notion that parité was a remedy for a defective equality, but also something more than equality, was built into the campaign that took form with the foundation, in January 1993, of the Réseau femmes pour la parité (referred to by its members simply as "the réseau").[5] If sexual difference as a criterion for participation were eliminated by, paradoxically, insisting on sexing the abstract individual, then "a society codirected by women and men" would follow.[6]

The vision of codirection (a sharing of responsibilities and power) had a long history among feminists, but the notion of parité as a constitutive principle or prior condition (*un préalable*) of politics was new. Inevitably, there were disputes about the exact status of the concept: Was it a principle or a slogan? Did it rest on sound philosophy or practical utility? Could it be reconciled with liberal theory? In fact, the answers to these questions mattered little in the course of the political campaign (except among intellectuals). Parité took hold because it couldn't be figured into familiar rhetorical schemes. Indeed, it was precisely this reaching for something new that infused the movement with much of its excitement and creativity. There was no detailed map of the future, just a set of directional signals and one clear goal: a major realignment of gendered power relations in French society beginning with elected representatives. The description of parité as "an opening" occurs repeatedly in the comments of its advocates. "For me," Eliane Viennot wrote, "parité represents an opening. It is a goal that will allow us to completely reconsider the various haphazard attempts we have made until now."[7]

Beyond installing gender equity, parité promised to fix a political system that had lost the confidence of voters. Polls regularly showed massive disaffection with parties and politicians, a disaffection that deepened in the course of the 1990s.[8] The inclusion of women was appealing to many ordinary citizens because it seemed a first step toward making the national representation more representative, both demographically and socially. The question of women's citizenship had long been settled, so the idea of female candidacies was welcomed as an alternative to stagnant party rule. "In this chorus of prevailing mediocrity," a (male) journalist wrote, "the question of representation for women in politics looks like an exception. It's been a really long time since we've witnessed such a lively battle of principles." At stake, he added, was the very conception of the nation.[9]

Endorsement of parité was not limited to women voters. Indeed, the essentialism that critics attributed to parité was in these years not a serious factor in its popular appeal. Campaigning in rural market towns in 1997 (when, looking to capture a pro-parité vote, the PS had committed to run 30% women candidates), one candidate reported to interviewers that she initially defined herself as a women's candidate and got a decent response. When she told the women she encountered that she was one of them, "a woman for women," they replied, "Okay, that's good, why not?" It was not as a woman though, but as a symbol of a fresh approach to politics that she drew interest from both sexes. "Besides, men also say that this might change things."[10] Another female candidate was approached by a man in his forties who said, "I'm voting for you because we're the same." By this he meant, as he explained, "You women, no one listens to you. But no one listens to me either. Thanks to you, I'll have more of a chance of being taken into account."[11]

PARITÉ: THE NETWORK

The appeal of parité was enhanced by the form of the campaign organized in its name. Indeed, it is clear from dictionary entries written since the parité law was passed in 2000 that the movement and its object are inseparable.[12] But "organized" is a misnomer for this movement, since it was precisely a lack of formal organization that won its many adherents. The mouvement pour la parité consisted of a few dedicated activists who mobilized the leadership of preexisting women's associations (with combined memberships of some 2 million) to address themselves to a simple goal: the need to improve women's access to political office. Actions were coordinated to achieve maximum impact; events that would draw publicity mattered. The point was to generate widespread support and to open national debate on the issue.

In the early days of the parité movement, action was initiated under two different auspices: the Réseau femmes pour la parité and the Commission parité of the Conseil national des femmes françaises (CNFF). Both groups took their inspiration from the declaration of the 1992 Athens conference, "Women in Power," calling for *démocratie paritaire* in the nations of the European community. The declaration (which had symbolic but not legal force) was signed for France by Edith Cresson and Simone Veil; the point now was to turn a recommendation into reality.[13]

The réseau came into being at a meeting at the Maison des Femmes in Paris in January 1993, called by Odette Brun and Monique Dental. It consisted mostly of members of feminist groups dating to the 1970s and of representatives of the Greens and some left-wing parties, including the Socialist Party. Françoise Gaspard and Claude Servan-Schreiber belonged to the réseau. The CNFF had been founded in 1901 and was an umbrella for a number of traditional women's associations.[14] Its commission on parité seems to have been the brainchild of Colette Kreder, principal of the highly regarded Ecole polytechnique féminine (an engineering school for women). The commission's only other member was Françoise Gaspard, France's "expert" on the European Union's Network on Women in Decision-Making. The title of expert played a critical role in establishing the legitimacy of the commission and of the actions undertaken in its name, as did the prestige of the CNFF. Kreder appealed to both when, at the National Assembly in December 1992, she organized an informational meeting on the Athens conference for representatives of feminist and women's associations as well as for political women. (The meeting at the National Assembly was a hugely successful attempt: it brought together more than two hundred women who since the liberation had not met this way.) Continuity and publicity for the work of both groups was provided by a newsletter, *Parité-Infos*, founded and edited by Claude Servan-Schreiber, the first number of which appeared in March 1993.[15] A key means of communication, the newsletter provided philosophical, strategic, and informational articles on developments in France and Europe.

After a year of organizing the publication of a manifesto and major demonstrations at the National Assembly, the réseau dissolved, riven by internal squabbles and long-standing personal and sectarian rivalries.[16] It was replaced in 1994 by Demain la parité, with new leadership and a different notion of the movement's constituency. Françoise Gaspard used her position as European "expert" to appeal to traditional women's associations, among them Elles aussi, itself a network of six associations: Action catholique générale féminine; Alliance des femmes pour la démocratie; Fédération des associations des conseillères municipales et femmes élues; Femmes d'Alsace; Union féminine civique et sociale; and Grain de sel-rencontres.[17] Working in conjunction with Kreder, Gaspard, through Demain la parité, succeeded in creating a broad grassroots constituency. This was not the kind of constituency that provided large numbers of bodies for mass meetings or demonstrations. Instead, it operated through the leaders of existing organizations who could claim to represent their followers and who could elicit support in the form of petitions and opinion polls. Parité built on an already mobilized constituency—an innovative tactic in the history of social movements. The associations affiliated with Demain la parité formed the network along which information passed and action was undertaken in Paris and the provinces. The response to parité often came from outside the network in actions it neither initiated nor organized.

The network seems to have operated by consensus. It had no official spokeswoman; policy (if it could be called that) was decided action by action. As parité became an increasingly popular idea, calls to sympathetic journalist friends could bring needed press coverage. And the simplicity of the movement's goal seems to have consolidated its constituency. The term "parité" was the inspiration for action, the node of affiliation, the shared purpose of the members; common projects were undertaken in its name. The endorsement of parité was a principled stand in favor of gender equality in politics. On the eve of the presidential elections of 1995, a petition that circulated across the network (in the name of "several large women's associations") was, in effect, a pledge of allegiance to parité: "Yes, I'm in favor of parité. I agree that there should be as many women as men elected as representatives in public life. I demand that political parties that propose candidates for elections, and the candidates themselves, publicly endorse parité and commit themselves to implementing it."[18] Parité had concrete, if limited, meaning here; it was not, as some have suggested, so open as to invite any kind of attribution.[19] It clearly endorsed a goal of equal numbers of women and men in elected office and called upon politicians to implement it; nothing more (not the greater capacity or the special interests of women) nor less (not some vision of gender complementarity) was at issue. One sentence in the preface to the petition did note that women's "different points of view and different experiences" were often neglected by men, but there was no claim that this amounted to a special women's interest. If some who supported the movement did hold this view, they were constrained by the concreteness both of the definition established for parité and of the goal of the movement. The point was to end discrimination and to institute equality long denied.

The descriptions of parité offered by its advocates expressed the hope that the usual lines of social, class, and ideological division would not prevail in their movement. Women must come together to protest shared discrimination: that was the only commonality they would acknowledge. Even women politicians might overcome the boundaries of party loyalty on this question—so imagined the organizers of a meeting on International Women's Day (March 8, 1993) at the National Assembly.[20] (It would be three years before this wish came true.) By bringing together women across party lines, the movement aimed at restructuring the "rules of the game" in politics. "The parité movement aims to build not a women's party . . . but a coalition of effective women, within the parties and outside them, in order to compel—in partisan arenas as in all of society—the recognition of the political and symbolic place that is their due."[21] There was all the difference in the world between "a women's party," with its essentialist or identitarian implications, and "a coalition of effective women" aimed at gaining women the recognition prevented by a discrimination based illegitimately on the difference of their sex.

The gloss on demonstrations offered by spokeswomen for parité also reflected this aim of the movement, to attract "women of the right and left, women heads of small businesses and militant feminists side by side, together demanding *'liberté, egalité, parité.'*"[22] This was to be a different kind of politics, "not typical of French practices," as one activist put it.[23] Instead of warring factions, there would be commonality. And, in fact, as the intellectuals debated in Paris, a groundswell of support came from the grassroots, not in the characteristic form of French movements, through massed bodies in the streets, but through carefully constructed associational networks.

PARITÉ: THE MOVEMENT

1992–93: Beginnings

The mobilization of public support was a result of the ingenuity of the network leadership, its talent for acts that captured the public imagination and exploited the political moment. There were also other new groups formed around the theme of parité; these included Parité 2000, led by Antoinette Fouque, and Régine Saint Cricq's Parité. In addition, existing associations began to support the demand for parité; Gisèle Halimi's Choisir: La cause des femmes was a prominent example. These, and others, often lent support to actions organized by the réseau and then by Demain la parité. Many different projects were undertaken—demonstrations, colloquia, petitions, advertisements, media contacts, lobbying—but they were basically of two kinds. The first had to do with exposing in detail the gap between principle and practice in the French republic; the second with demanding public response from politicians—men in power or aspiring to it—to the question of why women had been excluded from political life for so long. Neither involved the assertion of a positive women's identity; what was sought above all was an end to discrimination, an opening to a new politics. Actions of both kinds were at once symbolic and political, and they were necessarily intertwined. For that reason it seems best to treat them chronologically.

At its initial meeting, the réseau decided to ask all candidates for the upcoming legislative elections to endorse the Athens declaration and its call for parité. This was the first of many actions designed to pressure politicians and draw media attention to the movement, and it met with modest success: some candidates responded, and their response was reported in the press. But what could not have been anticipated was the outcome of the national elections. In March 1993, the Socialist Party went down to ignominious defeat, losing 205 of the 258 seats it had held since 1988 (and leaving President Mitterrand to "cohabit" with a conservative prime minister). The paritaristes had not expected this development, but perhaps more than any other single event it opened the political space within which calls for parité had to be taken seriously by party leaders. As parité became an increasingly audible demand, the socialists saw in it an opportunity for redemption. Parité's success cannot be understood apart from the political climate created by the drive of the PS to recoup its losses—a drive that succeeded in 1997 thanks, in some measure at least, to the leadership's willingness to let more women run for office. Since parité appeared to be the only concrete solution to the crisis of representation, to be in favor of it signaled a commitment not only to modernizing the political system but to taking effective measures to do so.

Soon after the election, the commission on parité issued the results of a study it had sponsored. (Although the CNFF, its parent body, agreed to sign off on the report, it refused to pay for it; so much of the work was done pro bono.) In the quest for information to support the movement's criticism of the unbalanced political system, a team of researchers had been assembled to study the fate of women candidates in the 1993 legislative elections. The team was headed by Françoise Gaspard, not only France's designated "expert" in the European network but a trained sociologist/historian as well. Since neither the state nor the political parties made public (or, in some cases, even kept) records that distinguished the sex of voters and candidates, the team undertook to expose the mechanisms by which women were excluded from officeholding.[24] Gaspard's study was released in April to extensive publicity. One television station featured it as the first item on the evening news. The study showed that the larger and more successful a party was, the fewer women it presented for elections; when large parties did run women, they most often assigned them to seats considered lost in advance. The phenomenon of significant numbers of women running for office but failing to gain it could be explained neither by voter preference nor by the weakness of female candidates. Women disappeared with the defeat of the marginal parties on whose slates they typically ran.[25] Gaspard's conclusion was cited by *Le Monde:* "The political system functions as a machine that systematically excludes women."[26] This comment implied a critique of the premises and operations of the political system and a call for its reform—parité was the standard according to which these practices were assessed. Gaspard's comment was also an invitation to the political parties—especially to the PS, with whose members she had long been affiliated—to seize the initiative and reclaim the power they had just lost.

On April 2, when the new assembly returned to work, three hundred women assembled by the réseau and representing at least a dozen organizations greeted the deputies with banners proclaiming no to the "Assemblée natiomâle," yes to parité between men and women. Other placards offered information about the gender asymmetry in the assembly: "Women are 53% of voters, 6% of those elected; find the error." Others commented ironically on traditional divisions of labor: "Women give birth to political men, they can also raise the levels of political debate." Still others played on homophony to make their point: "You

love us when we are mothers (*mères*) or whores (*putains*), why not when we are
mayors (*maires*) or deputies (*deputées*)?"[27] None made the case that women
had something unique to contribute to the political process. Press coverage
was extensive; this was an issue that was not going to disappear.

At the end of April, the réseau began to organize what they hoped would be
a major media event: the circulation and publication of a manifesto to be signed
by 577 people (the number of seats in the National Assembly), 289 women and
288 men. The text was brief and free of identity politics. It rehearsed the inequities in the system of representation (women had had the vote since 1945,
were 53% of the population and just 6% of the National Assembly) and insisted that the minuscule number of women in political life was a mark against
democracy and, internationally, a disgrace for France. This theme—the defense of national pride—resonated widely. When it came time to pass the law,
many legislators invoked it. The manifesto called for a law that would require
all elected assemblies to be composed of as many women as men. Representatives of groups within the réseau volunteered to collect signatures from across
the political and social spectrum, and Servan-Schreiber set out to raise the
money needed to finance the effort. She managed to secure grants from public
and private sources (among them the fashion designer Sonia Rykiel) and,
through her journalist contacts, a reduced rate for the publication of the manifesto in *Le Monde*.[28]

At the end of May, the paritaristes' attention turned to the Socialist Party,
which had organized an Estates General for July to consider its future. "We had
received a huge blow to the head . . . and it was a question of analyzing the reasons for the defeat."[29] Unlike party congresses, where formal decisions were
taken, the Estates General was a deliberative body for the exchange of ideas, a
chance for constituents to voice their opinions. The question of women and
parité was prominent on the agenda. In preparation, Yvette Roudy had called
women politicians of all parties to a meeting at the National Assembly in June
to consider the relations between shared power and democracy. In July, feminists turned out in large numbers at the PS meeting, hung parité banners at
their information tables, and gave eloquent speeches, which were reported on
the nightly news. At the word "parité," which was uttered often, the audience
clapped and stamped its feet. In an impassioned speech former deputy Denise
Cacheux detailed the ways in which women were marginalized in the party and
were ridiculed for complaining about it. (Had she shown her speech to the
leadership beforehand, she commented later, she probably would not have
been given the podium.)[30] Things were changing, she warned, and women were
organizing. The party could not afford to lose their support. Her call to "dare"

to endorse parité was both an invitation and a threat.[31] While local party bosses were heard in the corridors to profess their grudging accommodation to parité "someday," Michel Rocard, the provisional head of the party, anxious to surprise the party establishment and demonstrate his greater sensitivity to contemporary issues, seized the moment to promise a future in which "women will not only be equal voters, they will also be equally elected to office."[32] Rocard was moved, he said, by a sense of justice, but also by the results of a poll the PS had commissioned that showed a significant portion of respondents favorable to parité lists.[33] He took action in a qualified way at the end of October, when he startled the party congress (women were jubilant, men stunned) by announcing that the PS lists for the next European elections would consist of half women, half men. Rocard did not use the word "parité" (perhaps not wanting to endorse either the principle or its radical vision), nor did he promise 50/50 lists for all future elections; he just hoped, he said, that this decision for the European elections would, in the circumstances, "move things forward."

Meanwhile, the réseau continued its campaign, organizing a "summer university" in Normandy at the end of August to hone women's political skills and acquaint them with the nitty-gritty of political processes. *Au pouvoir citoyennes,* which emphasized law and politics, never women's identity, was required reading "so that we don't waste time dealing with questions that have already been resolved."[34] The sessions were devoted to such practical questions as What is the political system? What is the difference between a project of law and a proposition of law? What are the different types of ballot? How is a list for the European elections constituted? This method of training future political candidates had been initiated in the early 1990s by Elles aussi, which continued over the course of the next years to hold day-long forums in provincial cities and towns to recruit and support women candidates.[35] During 1994–45, for example, Elles aussi held thirty-five forums, attended by anywhere from 50 to 150 women, on the question "Why not a female municipal councillor?" These meetings not only began to prepare women to run for local office but also received wide coverage in the local and regional press (more than two hundred articles were inventoried by *Parité-Infos*), as well as on radio and television.[36]

Small but visible demonstrations in the streets kept occurring. The opening session of the National Assembly on October 2 was greeted by a chanting crowd of feminists organized by the réseau, calling for parité. In November, a group of some two hundred women, led by a delegation from Marseilles, arrived at the Pantheon carrying flowers on the two-hundredth anniversary of the guillotining of Olympe de Gouges. "To great women no longer with us [*aux grandes absentes*], from a grateful nation," their banners proclaimed, feminizing the dedication on the Pantheon (which reads: "To great men" [*Aux grands hommes*]). Even the nation's memory, this protest revealed, was contrived to minimize or exclude the contribution of individual women, whose remarkable achievements were lost because of their sex.[37]

Thus far there had been at least one event a month for the press to cover. Then, on November 10, the Manifesto of 577 appeared in *Le Monde*.[38] The number and reputation of the names (from the arts, sciences, academia, politics) drew extraordinary coverage from reporters for the print media, television, and radio. (In France, where the public sphere is a more visible and coherent presence than in the United States, a declaration of this kind becomes an important political event.) There was no longer any question of depicting parité as marginal, the preoccupation of *femmes agissantes,* noisy feminists. It had come to the center of political discourse; one was either for or against it. The topic was on many agendas: there were television and radio programs; the Grand Lodge of Women Masons held a forum on women's role in politics; the left/liberal weekly *Nouvel Observateur* published a special issue on "women and power"; academics organized a conference on the history of women's exclusion from French politics and then published the proceedings in book form; there were local meetings to discuss parité in Paris, Toulouse, and Lyon led by signers of the manifesto.[39]

The effect of the Manifesto of 577—which called for a law requiring equal numbers of women and men in all elective offices—was to generate discussions that were, for the most part, practical. How would the law be implemented? What effects would it have? Would half of all male officials have to cede their posts to women? Should the number of elected positions be doubled to guarantee equal gender representation? Was such a law feasible, constitutional? Should differences of sex be represented at all? Whatever the particular answers offered, and whatever the tone associated with them, there was no doubt that a probing examination of the premises and institutions of French politics had been launched. Here was the "opening" to a reform of the system of political representation that parité promised.

1994: Pressure on the Parties

The campaign continued in 1994 with its multipronged strategy. There were demonstrations: on April 2 the returning assembly was greeted by women who released 577 balloons bearing the message "Parité: as many women as men in the National Assembly." There were meetings to educate and enlarge the constituency: on April 20, a gathering to commemorate the fiftieth anniversary of women's suffrage heard Simone Veil propose a constitutional amendment for parité; on April 23–24, an Estates General of women in politics was called by the Socialist Party's Assemblée des femmes. Articles were written commenting on a range of issues; the authors of one article, in response to President Mitterrand's announcement (on International Women's Day) that Marie Curie's ashes would be transferred to the Pantheon, wondered if she would be lonely there, as the only woman in residence.[40] A seminar convened by feminists (including Gaspard and jurist Marie-Louis Victoire) at the Maison des sciences de l'homme during the academic year 1994–95 brought together scholars and activists for extraordinary sessions. In the seminar, history sharpened strategy; social research fed political analysis. Here was a pooling of collective wisdom in the service of feminist politics.[41] In a personal gesture designed to draw public attention, Françoise Gaspard refused to accept the Légion d'honneur until the group she was nominated with consisted of as many women as men.[42]

The pressure on the parties continued, especially around the European elections in June, when the PS indeed presented lists of candidates on which every other name was a woman's. The combined right lists (RPR and UDF)[43] ran a far smaller number of women (about 21%) but made much of the placement of one prominent academic woman (Hélène Carrère d'Encausse) in second position. Since not all the parties ran parité slates, there was only a small increase— about 7%—in the number of women in the French delegation.[44] But those parties that did adhere to parité and that won seats (the PS and the Communist party—two of the six successful parties) significantly improved women's representation in their groups. On the PS list, women constituted 49.4% of the candidates and 46.6% of those elected; on the Communist Party list, 51.4% and 57.1% respectively. In addition, polling data indicated higher percentages of women than men voting for the PS—proof, to the leaders of the parité movement, that their strategy could widen the gender gap in the socialists' favor. The media attention to the entire effort delighted the parité leaders: "The mobilization of the last two years around the demand for parité has produced astonishing results," wrote Gaspard. But the fact that most parties had refused to open the process of nomination to more women and that no party, even those with parité lists, had endorsed the European women's network call to "vote for a balance of women and men" meant there was still work to be done.[45] "The struggle for parité," *Parité-Infos* reminded its readers, "is also a struggle for more democracy and for more transparency in the internal mechanisms of all of French political life, which remain especially opaque."[46]

Party intransigence was one side of the issue, public opinion another. Polls indicated a steady increase in public support for adding parité to the constitution and also a remarkable willingness (84% in May 1994) to contemplate a woman as president of the republic.[47] A Louis Harris poll showed that the majority of French voters preferred that the next prime minister be a woman (conservatives designated Simone Veil; socialists Martine Aubry).[48] A questionnaire sent to mayors about increasing the numbers of women on municipal councils showed more than half favorable. And the women's nongovernmental organizations (NGOs) preparing their reports for the UN's decadal meeting on women for Beijing in 1995 pointed to the embarrassing fact that France was on the low end of the international scale for women's political inclusion and called for the expansion of women's presence at all levels of decision-making. As attention turned to the presidential election set for April 1995, parité was made a central topic for discussion.

1995: Presidential Politics

When the PS convened to nominate its presidential candidate, the Paris delegation, though split, was all male. There was an outcry and some derision ("Not even one token woman! Parité!"), which was captured for television audiences, much to the distress of the party leadership.[49] On the eve of the election, Colette Kreder, in the name of the commission on parité, invited the major presidential candidates to comment on parité—a first in the annals of feminist history.[50] Seated in the auditorium of the Palais des Congrès in Paris were 1600 women representing most of the major women's associations of the country, and Kreder asked members of these groups to pose questions. It was a grand media event: Edouard Balladur, Jacques Chirac, and Lionel Jospin appeared in turn. All of the candidates agreed, in principle, on the need to grant women more access to politics. And though much of what they said can be dismissed as electioneering opportunism, it is nonetheless interesting to see how much of the feminist language they felt constrained to employ. "Everyone uttered the word . . . 'parité.' Edouard Balladur, Lionel Jospin, and Jacques Chirac have discovered, in the course of their campaigns across France, that they can't avoid the word if they want to attract the female electorate."[51] Balladur deemed parité desirable in the long run, "on the horizon of the evolution of national habits."[52] Chirac lamented the underrepresentation of women and its effects on the Republic. ("As long as that's the case, we will have a crippled Republic, a democracy that limps.")[53] Correcting the situation was a matter of justice, he opined, but one that required neither laws nor quotas, only a slow evolution of mentalities. Perhaps the state could contribute to this evolution by offering financial incentives to those parties that increased the numbers of their women candidates. Jospin too endorsed the idea of financial incentives, and he pledged, more loftily, in the name of women and democracy, to promote "this great idea of parité."[54] The candidates all promised, if elected, to take up a recommendation to set up an official body (the Observatoire de la parité) that would monitor the status of women and the progress of gender equality and prepare regular reports to the prime minister and the parliament.

Chirac won the election and appointed Alain Juppé his prime minister. Juppé named twelve women to his cabinet, most of them as secondary ministers (secretaries of state) but still with great media effect. Referred to mockingly in the press as "les jupettes" (a play on the word *jupe,* "skirt"), the gesture was nonetheless taken at first as promising. Among the appointments were several—the secretary of state for transport, Anne-Marie Idrac was one—who set out to increase the numbers of women administrators in the areas they represented.[55] In October, Juppé created the Observatoire de la parité and appointed RPR deputy Roselyne Bachelot as its head. The eighteen members of the Observatoire had only two feminists among them, but Bachelot assured readers of *Parité-infos* of her intention to scrupulously sponsor research on gender inequities in politics and other areas as well.[56] (This did not deter feminists, led by Janine Mossuz-Lavau, from creating their own watchdog, the vigilance committee for parité, to monitor the work of the Observatoire.)[57] On November 7, only a few months after assuming his post, Juppé reorganized his cabinet in the face of a growing economic crisis, and, much to the surprise of the country, he fired eight of the twelve women, replacing them with men. The prime minister, who months earlier had insisted that his female appointments were not mere decorations ("I chose women not just to add color to the photos taken on the steps of national buildings but because I needed them to help me reform our country to make it fairer and more unified"),[58] now explained his action as impelled by the seriousness of national circumstances. He needed experts, with long experience—competent ministers, professionals who would speak with one voice.[59] The equation of homogeneity and masculinity was a clear reminder that women's difference did not disappear when they became politicians. The brutality of the action and its justification brought home the paritaristes' message about the marginalization and underrepresentation of women in politics and won new adherents to the cause. In an interview with political scientist Frédéric Besnier, one of those dismissed talked of how the experience had forced her to think of herself only as a *woman* politician. "Our eviction from the government created a deep wound, which humiliated women. Our firing gave the impression that women as a group were judged to be incompetent."[60] *L'Express* commented on the shocking effect of the action.[61] Newspaper headlines blared, "Women locked out," "Women sacrificed." And Françoise Gaspard noted wryly that Juppé "has rendered a great service to the parité movement."[62]

In the tumultuous period that followed, there were meetings, demonstrations, television programs and newspaper articles. A wave of strikes in December 1995 protesting Chirac's attempt to roll back the French welfare state pointed up not only economic difficulties but the continuing political crisis of representation. In this moment of disgust and discontent, parité seemed to offer a glimmer of hope, a chance to recast a political system that, by all evidence, wasn't working at all well.

1996: The Manifesto of Ten

The theme of political renewal continued in 1996. The first report of the Observatoire de la parité diagnosed major obstacles to women's participation as the reason for the low numbers in elected office and recommended that the National Assembly discuss proposals for constitutional revision and quotas. Meanwhile, in concert with their European counterparts, the paritaristes mapped strategies keyed to elections. In the face of continuing political unrest, parité was offered as the best hope of recasting the political system by taking it out of the hands of a closed caste and opening it to new faces, new influences. There was large attendance at colloquia: two were held at the UNESCO headquarters, one organized by Gisèle Halimi, the other by Demain la parité.[63] Increasing numbers of books on the parité theme appeared, among them autobiographical accounts of the humiliations and mistreatment women politicians had encountered; street demonstrations continued as did local meetings in the provinces; in Rennes and Marseilles, feminists began campaigning to rename streets in honor of women who had had an impact on public life—another way of making women an integral part of the national memory; the pro-parité petition circulated by Demain la parité was garnering thousands of signatures; and more women politicians publicly declared their support. In May, women politicians of the member states of the European Union gathered in Rome (as they had at Athens in 1992) and issued a declaration under the title "Women for the Renewal of Politics and Society." (Corinne Lepage, minister for the environment, was the representative for France.)[64] In the declaration they recommended voluntary and legislative action to make shared power between women and men a reality. Then in June, in an action parité leaders had long worked for but had had no direct hand in organizing, ten of the most prominent female politicians in France (representing all the major parties) published a manifesto in the newsweekly *L'Express.* Far less radical than the Manifesto of

577 (and in the name of "women" as a group with supposedly shared traits), the Manifesto of Ten called upon the political parties to commit voluntarily to parité, to take measures to increase the number of women elected to at least 30%, and to pass antisexist laws. They also suggested a referendum to revise the constitution to permit affirmative action.

While nominally committed to the slogan of parité, the Manifesto of Ten altered its meaning in ways that seemed to justify a charge of essentialism. After detailing the extent of discrimination against women, they attributed it to the influences of Jacobinism in republican culture, which had been first and foremost "a men's affair." Jacobinism "is a kind of concentration of virile qualities." This meant the exclusion of women and the unique sensitivity they brought to politics: "relating to others as they are, sensitivity, the concrete, concern for daily life."[65] While the original paritaristes had scrupulously avoided the attribution of specific qualities to the sexes (the Manifesto of 577 denounced discrimination and simply called for equality), the Manifesto of Ten seemed to endorse the very oppositions upon which discrimination had been built. "It is high time to finish with these stereotypes and blockages by feminizing the Republic," they wrote. Rejecting the stereotype of apolitical womanhood, they went beyond the paritaristes, who had insisted only on anatomical duality, and emphasized sexual difference: "Women's point of view, their experience, and their culture are cruelly lacking when laws are developed."[66] Such statements can be explained both as a kind of knee-jerk essentialism and as products of a certain political opportunism, grasping on obvious notions that might appeal to commonsense ideas about gender. By joining the parité campaign, these women helped advance the campaign while beginning to transform the message, leaving the register of abstraction (and universalism) for the realm of the practical and the concrete. The philosophical effect of this shift was minimal in 1996, but its practical effect was extensive.

The result of months of planning by a hard core of women who had held ministerial positions (and who therefore had instant name recognition), the Manifesto of Ten became a major news event and, as a result, swayed previously skeptical political leaders. Displaying a picture of the ten on its front cover, *L'Express* reported: "From the left and the right they demand as many women as men in political parties, in the assembly and in the government." Bold letters next to the photograph announced the results of the magazine's exclusive poll: "71% of the French approve."[67] Inside was a breathless account of the origins of the manifesto and a definitive judgment of its import: "this revolutionary text, this political act par excellence." The magazine made much of the fact that the signers had set aside their usual disagreements in order to open "a great national debate." And it presented the outcome of that debate as already decided: in favor. Not only did the poll suggest that French men and women (with little difference between them) saw parité as a remedy for other social and economic inequalities; even children seemed naturally inclined to share power. *L'Express* cited PS deputy Ségolène Royal's recent report to the National Assembly of a comprehensive survey conducted among schoolchildren (aged nine to eleven, and living in a representative sample of towns and cities), who "elected" 305 girls for seats in an imagined parliament (of 577).[68] The critical comments of Elisabeth Badinter and Evelyne Pisier—who rejected the essentialist arguments in the manifesto because they contradicted universalism—were reported in the course of one article, but they were either minimized or dismissed. Pisier's argument that no new rights were needed to achieve equality was countered by Elisabeth Schemla, who wrote the story for *L'Express*. Since the existing political system permitted no solution to the problem of inequality, Schemla noted, something more—"a deepening of the law"—was needed. Parité, in other words, was neither the simple implementation nor a restatement of equality; it somehow exceeded equality. This point, far more than the manifesto's critique of Jacobinism as a form of male domination and its praise of women's special qualities, was emphasized in *L'Express*'s coverage. At this stage of the campaign, parité was associated with an aspiration for equality and for political reform, with an end to the shameful record of France compared to the rest of Europe (as illustrated in *L'Express* by charts). It was not yet equated with prevailing norms of sexual difference.

L'Express asked Lionel Jospin and Alain Juppé for their views on the Manifesto of Ten, and both rushed to endorse parité. (The interviews were accompanied by American-style photographs of each man in warm and close conversation with his wife.) Jospin regretted his failure to name women as university rectors during his term as minister of education and promised to work for parité in his party and in the nation. He thought a revision of the constitution would be necessary to overcome the objections that the Constitutional Council had raised about quotas in 1982; when this was done, the parties would eventually comply. A referendum was risky and unnecessary. Proportional representation (something the PS had long favored) for all elections would improve women's chances, he believed. To an interviewer's question whether proportional representation might also benefit the National Front, Jospin replied that the women's vote would counterbalance the force of the extreme right (a claim the paritaristes had not made). He was opposed, he said, to the manifesto's recommendations on antisexist laws and on affirmative action. "I don't want to import American 'political correctness' into France."[69] For him, parité was not about a community or a minority but was a reflection of the "complementarity of the human species." He was very optimistic about what could be accomplished, necessarily in stages. Realistically, Jospin thought, it would take about ten years to arrive at parité among elected representatives.

Juppé, for his part, preferred a referendum if there was to be a constitutional revision. He was in favor, he said, of parité, and thought it could begin to be implemented in the next round of legislative elections (then scheduled for 1998). He explained that he had fired the women in his cabinet not because he doubted their abilities but because they had been recruited outside of the usual party circles and so lacked the necessary influence to win votes for his program in the assembly. The scarcity of women within the party was a problem, he admitted, one that needed to be addressed, perhaps by offering financial incentives to parties to find and run women candidates. Juppé firmly rejected the idea of proportional elections for the legislature, pointing out that the socialists' experiment with it in 1986 had done nothing to increase the presence of women among the deputies. As head of the RPR, he avowed his intention to increase the number of women candidates, even aiming for parité on the lists for the upcoming regional elections.

Jospin, the contender, seemed more in tune with paritariste demands than Juppé, the incumbent prime minister. But their differences were less significant than their common commitment to bringing more women into politics in the foreseeable future. Both associated removing obstacles to women in the party system with "modernization" (a theme sounded by Mitterrand as early as 1965). Of course, each wanted to capture and tame parité, and they did this in various ways, most visibly by opting for quotas rather than the "perfect equality" sought by the paritaristes. Quotas, of course, might be a practical remedy, but they missed the point parité was aiming at: a presumption, to become fact, concerning the complete equality of men and women as individuals and hence as representatives of France.

Jospin, in September, announced that the PS had reserved some 160 districts (out of 577) for women for the legislative elections. Local party organizations would be free to name their female candidate, but they must work closely with the national committee charged with finally choosing the candidates. *L'-Express* speculated that of the 160 seats, 40 were probably winnable, which would increase the number of female socialist deputies by 36 (dramatic, but far short of the 30% goal suggested in the Manifesto of Ten).[70] The newsweekly also reported on behind-the-scenes maneuvers that granted flexibility to party leaders such as Laurent Fabius, who complained that his first priority was not to enforce the mandate but to help male deputies who had been defeated in

1993 to regain their seats. Here was a conflict, not easily resolved, between male career politicians and women who were also experienced politicians, more than a third of them having held office either as deputies, substitute deputies (those elected to replace deputies who moved into cabinet positions), or municipal councillors. Many of the "newcomers" came from trade unions or other associations. Though hardly novices in politics, they were often depicted that way by local party bosses seeking to protect men's positions. As the PS struggled with its leader's decision, public pressure continued to build.

1997: Debate in the National Assembly

Early in 1997, Demain la parité announced that its petition had over ten thousand signatures. In the assembly and in the senate, members of minority parties (greens, communists) began to offer proposals for a law on parité. On March 8, there were demonstrations all over the country on the occasion of International Women's Day. Although massive resistance to the idea continued among politicians, public pressure could not be denied.

On March 11, debate began in the National Assembly on the question of "the role of women in political life."[71] Juppé had called for this deliberation in accordance with the recommendations of the Observatoire de la parité, but the debate was more gestural than practical, since no vote was to follow. It was a way of seeming to take the issue seriously without having to do anything about it. In his introductory remarks, Juppé proposed a ten-year plan for overcoming discrimination against women. It involved constitutional revision and a temporary quota law to be applied only to those elections in which proportional representation prevailed—this in the face of a survey of the 577 deputies in the assembly, published in *Le Monde* on March 8, that showed overwhelming hostility: of the 54% who bothered to reply, 75% were opposed to parité, 60% did not support quotas, and 77% refused a referendum. Nothing, in their view, needed to be changed. A majority of the assembly's 32 women were against any action to increase their numbers (an attitude not reflected in their speeches on March 11.)[72] The leadership was going to have a hard job winning the measures they were proposing to appease public opinion. It would take another year, and the electoral success of the PS, to convince the legislators that some kind of action was unavoidable. On March 11, 1997, however, the very fact of a debate in the National Assembly on women's access to representation had enormous symbolic significance; parité was on the national agenda, and feminists "in the street" had put it there. The substance of the debate revealed that although a process of recuperation had begun, parité was still understood to concern not women's identity but women's access to the position of representative.

The grand sense of an opening to a new kind of politics began to be narrowed, however, when the political professionals brought parité into the realm of established politics. In the debate it was clear that the parties and the individual speakers had very different ideas about how to rectify a situation they all agreed was embarrassing to France. (Laurent Fabius, a former socialist prime minister and president of the socialist caucus in the assembly, noted with alarm that France had a poorer record than Uganda when it came to the percentages of women in elected office.)[73] Not only was there disagreement about the need to revise the constitution (socialists and communists thought it wasn't necessary; speakers for the RPR and the UDF thought it was), about the advisability of quotas, about the feasibility of offering financial incentives for voluntary compliance by the parties, and about the chances for proportional representation to better serve women's interests (the communists and socialists thought yes, the Gaullists were vehemently opposed to proportional representation itself); there was not even consensus on the meaning of the word "parité."

"Parité" was often used synonymously with quotas by participants in these discussions, contrary to the way the founders of the movement defined the term. For the paritaristes, 50/50 meant the acknowledgment of the anatomical duality of the human as a principle of political representation; it did not refer to social and psychological differences between the sexes. "Parité" was also used interchangeably with *mixité,* a word most often associated with coeducation and the complementarity of the sexes, and which denoted neither full equality nor the strict 50/50 the paritaristes had demanded.[74] The idea of a law requiring a 50/50 result was put aside, and various forms of affirmative action (temporary quotas especially) took its place. The focus moved from mandating electoral outcomes to the more uncertain terrain of candidates for office. The constitution would have to be revised, it was argued, if "quotas" for candidates were to meet the objections of the Constitutional Council's ruling of 1982. (The fact that France had ratified a UN convention against sex discrimination in 1983 was not considered a strong enough counter to the ruling.) As the pressure to revise the constitution built, parité was increasingly equated with quotas for candidates. Press coverage tended to treat the issue as a matter of party negotiation too, emphasizing the drawbacks of quotas and the unwillingness of men to yield their places to women. *La République des Pyrénées,* for example, remarked that "our deputies adore women. But elsewhere, in the next district, in the neighbor's party, they are for equality, though decidedly not at home."[75]

The reluctance, if not hostility, of male deputies (regardless of party affiliation) was underscored by the conduct of the debate in the National Assembly. For the most part, individuals spoke their party lines. More striking was the low turnout of male politicians and their dwindling numbers as the day progressed. The speakers were overwhelmingly women, signaling that for all the rhetorical gestures to the future of French democracy, most deputies considered this debate a women's affair. After an eloquent denunciation of the machismo of the Jacobins and the disgrace for French civilization of the current composition of the assembly, Prime Minister Juppé left well before the session concluded, having advised women to start at the bottom—in the municipalities—before aspiring to higher office.

If parité became confused with quotas in these debates, more attention would nonetheless be paid to correcting discrimination and less to essentializing arguments when the revision of the constitution was enacted in 1998–99.[76] Those who supported some kind of affirmative action—though not, of course, the American kind—held to the paritaristes' argument that a women's interest was not the issue. Thus Juppé rejected the idea that women were a minority group. Rather, "they are one of the two parts of humanity." Here he cited Genesis 1:27—"God created man in his image. . . . He created him as man and woman"—to underscore the sameness of women and men.[77] One UDF deputy (Nicole Ameline) emphasized that temporary quotas did not lead to the categorizing of society (to the creation of permanent lobbies as in the United States). Véronique Neiretz, a long-time supporter of parité, insisted that "the individual is dual, man and woman, and . . . the rights of man are also the rights of woman."[78] Using the paritaristes' language about the duality of the individual, none of these statements insisted on complementarity or essentially different traits of women and men. In this sense, the debate remained true to the movement's goal: thinking of women as a variant of the individual, gaining access to representation on the same terms as men. The conflation of quotas with parité did not yet detract from the fact that this campaign was about sharing power and not about the politics of identity.

June 1997: The Legislative Elections

On April 21, 1997, President Jacques Chirac dissolved the National Assembly, calling for elections a year early. This was a gamble (since the right held the majority) aimed at winning a mandate for his attempts to bring the French economy into line with the demands of the Maastricht Treaty. Chirac wanted immediate approval for austerity measures that would only worsen by the time of the scheduled legislative elections (March 1998). If the right held the National Assembly, there would be no elections for five years, ample time to begin to roll back the welfare state; if the right lost, Chirac would remain president until 2002, forcing the socialists to compromise whatever plans they had. Although the election campaign focused on economic issues (especially those related to requirements of European Union membership and to the question of whether a unified European currency could ever be implemented), the parties of the left, especially the PS, drew attention to themselves for the numbers of women who ran on their slates—this while the combined rightist parties tried to woo voters from the far-right National Front. The gesture to parité was important for the PS, not only because it endorsed a widely supported goal, but also because it was a concrete action, a real reform, at a time when criticism abounded but practical solutions to the economic situation were in short supply. By implementing its promise to open more elective offices to women, the PS could be seen as demonstrating a broader commitment to change.[79]

In the event, the PS triumphed, and that triumph too was attributed to its emphasis on renewal, signaled, at least in part, by its "feminized" roster of candidates. The PS captured 250 seats and close to 40% of the vote in the second round; with other left-wing parties, it now held a majority. The number of women elected to the National Assembly nearly doubled, from 35 or 6% in 1993, to 59 or 10.2% in 1997; among the socialist delegation, 41 of 251, or some 16%, were women. Those numbers were not enough, the paritaristes pointed out, to improve France's standing internationally, but were enough to convince politicians to take seriously the question of women in politics.[80] There was much celebrating among proponents of parité when, as promised, Jospin, the new prime minister, chose 8 women for his cabinet of 26 (30.7%), several for ministries never held before by women.[81] In the line up of prestige, Martine Aubry was second only to the prime minister as minister of employment and solidarity; Elisabeth Guigou was the first woman to be named minister of justice; and the government's spokesperson was Catherine Trautmann, also named minister of culture. Green Party leader Dominique Voynet was named minister of the environment. All of these women had had a great deal of party experience (Aubry was the daughter of the renowned politician Jacques Delors and, as *Le Figaro* pointed out, had long since learned to be an *homme politique*); many had been trained at the Ecole nationale d'administration and had won office as mayors, deputies, or representatives to the European Parliament; and several had fought for years to improve the political position of women.[82] Media coverage commented on these historic "firsts," also mentioning the absence of "elephants" (we would call them dinosaurs) in the new government.

The old guard had been displaced by new faces, many of them female, and this seemed to accord with parité's promise for renewal. *Le Monde* noted that Jospin had broken with a long tradition on the left and right, which consisted of only token representation for women. "This time there are lots of women— 8 out of 26—and they have important responsibilities."[83] *Le Figaro* insisted that Jospin was only following the lead of Alain Juppé, without mentioning either that Juppé's appointments of women were to decidedly minor posts or that he had fired most of them in short order.[84] Still, the papers were filled with biographies of the women and with discussions of "feminization" more generally. *Le Monde* columnist Pierre Georges reported that the theme was "the same in all the commentaries, common to all the eulogies, the same in everyone's thoughts: Women at last. Women everywhere. Lots of women. Women not to beautify things or to make them feminine. Not to provide a secretary of state for macramé or for flowers in villages or for children at risk, or to provide 'juppettes' or 'jospinettes.' Real women in real positions [of power]!"[85]

Jospin, taking the PS victory as a mandate on feminization from the electorate, announced that he would introduce a constitutional revision the following year to prepare the way for a law on parité.[86]

> The modernization of democracy requires not only institutional reforms but also profound cultural changes. First we must permit French women to engage unhindered in public life. In this domain, progress comes first with the evolution of mentalities and changes in behavior. The socialists and the majority have set an example and proposed the route, especially since the last elections. We must go further. We will propose a revision of the constitution in order to inscribe in it the goal of parité between women and men.[87]

In November, Jospin, who had no minister for women's rights in his cabinet, appointed feminist philosopher Geneviève Fraisse as his special delegate (*déléguée interministérielle*) to oversee the promotion of the rights of women and the implementation of parité. At this time, a long-standing feminist demand to "feminize" titles and functions received new attention as a result of debates about what the gender of the word "minister" should be. Did one address Elisabeth Guigou as Mme *le* ministre or Mme *la* ministre? The Académie française, ferociously opposed to the feminization of titles, insisted on "le" because, it said, customarily the gender of words had nothing to do with the gender of persons; but feminists convinced Jospin to opt for "la," arguing that the presence of women was obscured when the masculine was used to describe their jobs. The question of language was symptomatic of the broad range of issues opened by Jospin's commitment to parité.[88]

But if there were purist positions to take on linguistic usage, the moment had come for the compromises of practical politics. Negotiations for a revision of the constitution had eliminated the word "parité" from the document (a condition of President Chirac's support). Although this was a huge loss for the movement and appeared to deny its radical vision of gender equality, gaining a law seemed to make the concession worthwhile. (In fact, when the law did pass in 2000, it was referred to, even in official government publications, as the parité law.) Just as significant was the conflation of quotas with parité, and this the authors of *Au pouvoir citoyennes* resisted stubbornly, pushing hard for their alternative—a law that would require 50/50 representation in all elective offices. Still, for the time being they supported Jospin's tamer efforts because the initial aim of the movement—to have women defined as equally capable of representing France—looked achievable. At the end of 1997, when *Parité-Infos* bid its readers farewell, the need for coordinated networks and sustained popular pressure seemed to have subsided. There would, of course, still be intense negotiations, but some form of parité law was now in sight.

No one anticipated, as the politics of revising the constitution began to take shape, that another project of legal reform would intersect and profoundly shape the final stages of the parité campaign. But in the course of 1998, a huge controversy about the rights of homosexual couples did exactly that. As legislators, sociologists, anthropologists, moralists, and psychologists argued about what counted as a family, the question of sexual difference was widely discussed in terms that could not but influence understandings of parité. If essentialist possibilities had, from the beginning, hovered around parité's notion of the duality of the individual, they were not the primary impetus of the movement. In 1998, however, these essentialist possibilities came to the fore, but not in ways some early critics had expected. Instead of women, with their special traits and interests, becoming the focus of attention, it was the heterosexual couple that came to be seen as the foundation of the family and the state, and thus of the egalitarian politics promised by parité.

CHAPTER FIVE

The Discourse of the Couple

"Is it obvious . . . that sexual preference ought to be the object of institutional recognition?"[1] This rhetorical question, from an opponent of a proposed law on domestic partnerships, the Pacte civil de solidarité (or PaCS), during debate in the Senate on March 17, 1999, was at the heart of a public controversy that had been raging for several years. How, if at all, should homosexual partnerships be legally recognized: As private contracts? As forms of cohabitation? As marriages? And what did legal recognition imply: The need to address a host of practical matters made visible by the AIDS crisis? An end to discrimination based on the choice of one's sexual partners? Acceptance of the fact of homosexuality as a sexual and social relationship? As a relationship like any other, or definably different from the heterosexual norm? If legal recognition rested on some principle of universality (as it must in this French republican context), was this principle an individual (private) right to choose one's partner, or a collective (social) right—that of any cohabiting couple—to the same benefits enjoyed by those formally married? Did this collective right mean that unmarried couples (homosexuals included) were families? That homosexuals too could bear, adopt, and raise children? Here was a Pandora's box from one perspective far more dangerous than the one opened by parité. For while parité worked within the familiar framework of individual rights— the right of women to be representatives, individuals elected to incarnate the nation (not to represent the female sex)—the PaCS dealt with couples and with the terms of recognition granted to them by the state. What was a couple? A practical domestic arrangement or a universal form of loving union? A mutable legal category or the embodiment of the eternal fact of sexual difference?

In the course of 1998–99, parité and the PaCS—until then two parallel movements—intersected, and the discourse of the couple replaced the discourse of the individual in discussions of sexual difference. It was now the relationship between women and men, their necessary complementarity, that was at stake, no longer the interchangeability of women and men as representatives of the nation. The meaning of parité's demand for 50/50 representation took on new significance, becoming the endorsement of an essentialist/differentialist notion of sexual difference instead of an antidiscriminatory/individualist claim for equality. In the intertwining of the PaCS and parité debates around the question of the couple, notions of equality, sexual difference, and universalism got tangled in contradictory ways, demonstrating not only the malleability but the historical contingency of these supposedly immutable abstractions. At this point in the story, it seems necessary to take some time to consider the debates over the PaCS in order to understand more fully their impact on the campaign for parité.

THE CAMPAIGN FOR A DOMESTIC PARTNERSHIP LAW

During the 1990s, as feminists demanded an end to discrimination against women in politics, proponents of gay rights sought legal protection for homosexual couples. The movements were parallel but distinct, though both linked their fortunes to the success of the left. Both movements also wrestled with the dilemma of difference, albeit in different forms. While parité was concerned with the status of women as abstract individuals, homosexual activists focused on the social question of the couple; parité was framed as an elaboration of the universalist principles of the republic, while the gay rights movement sought to reconcile the rights of a specified group (the concrete social) with the requirements of universalism (the abstract political).

As individuals, homosexuals already enjoyed some legal protection. The criminalization of homosexual acts ended in 1982, and an antidiscrimination law went into effect in 1985. As the AIDS epidemic became increasingly visible, there was of course concern that new antidiscrimination measures were needed to protect those individuals who were HIV-positive, but AIDS more pressingly raised the question of the status of gay couples in France, as it did elsewhere.[2] There were no legal protections for inheritance, joint property ownership, shared health benefits, the transfer of leases, power of attorney, or rights of hospital visitation. A few attempts to recognize gay partnerships as instances of cohabitation failed to win approval. When, in 1989, a court rejected one such request, ruling that cohabitation (*concubinage*) "can only refer to a couple consisting of a man and a woman," advocates concluded that a new law was needed to change that definition of the couple.[3]

But how would such a law be framed? There were several possibilities. The first would be simply to specify that gay couples were entitled to certain financial and other protections; they were, in effect, a special case or class. Arguments along these lines were offered by those interested in ending discrimination without normalizing the status of gay partnerships by including them in some larger category. (This approach was closest to U.S. domestic partnership legislation: antidiscrimination law for the special needs of a particular group.) The second possibility was to include homosexuals in a general category of cohabiting "duos" (which extended from elderly ladies sharing a home, to a priest and his resident housekeeper, to a brother and sister or a parent and child), in that way playing down the specificity of gay sexuality. This was the approach of a proposition for a civil partnership offered to the Senate in 1990, for a contract of civil union (CUC) presented by a group of deputies on the left to the National Assembly in 1992, and for a contract of civil and social union (CUCS) submitted to the National Assembly in 1997. A third possibility grouped together any cohabiting intimate partners (gay or straight), extending to them some of the economic and social rights enjoyed previously only by married couples. This was the suggestion of gay groups such as AIDES, which proposed in 1995 a contract of social life (CVS). According to the proposal, the law would recognize gay and lesbian partnerships under the general rubric of cohabitation. Endorsed by some socialist deputies, the plan was soon referred to as the contract of social union (CUS) and then—taking up the word "pact" from the recommendation for a pact of common interest (PIC) offered by a special commission on the reform of cohabitation law—as the pact of civil solidarity (PaCS) in 1998.[4] A fourth possibility (seen by some as the logical consequence of the third) was to open marriage to gay couples. As the discussion evolved, this became the position of AIDES, Act Up, the Gay and Lesbian Center, and many of their supporters.[5]

These possibilities were discussed throughout the 1990s, but with the left out of power after 1993, there was little hope that any legislation would be enacted. (The minister of justice, Jacques Toubon, rejected a proposal for the CUC in 1995 in stridently pronatalist terms: "It is not a question of creating a contract of civil union; on the contrary, it is a question of encouraging marriages and births in this country so that France can become stronger.")[6] Nonetheless, bills were offered by individual deputies and senators, and pressure was applied within the PS. At the same postdefeat Estates General that heard loud demands for parité in 1993, there were calls, in the party's platform, for including recognition of gay partnerships. At this point, such calls came from minority voices in an overwhelmingly homophobic environment. (As late as 1996, the first secretary of the PS, Henri Emanuelli, could dismiss advocates for homosexual rights crudely: "You are a damned nuisance with your stories about faggots; that doesn't interest the people.")[7] In 1994, the European Parliament endorsed equal rights for gays and lesbians, which added weight to the ongoing campaign. In 1995, the organization AIDES, the Collectif pour le CUCS, and other groups rallied several hundred mayors who agreed to provide certificates of *vie commune* regardless of the sex of the partners—here was the first "official" recognition of the "homosexual bond." In 1996, an article in *Le Monde* signed by leading intellectuals (Pierre Bourdieu, Jacques Derrida, Didier Eribon, Michelle Perrot, Paul Veyne, and Pierre Vidal-Naquet) cited repeated instances of unequal treatment and called for "legal recognition of the homosexual couple."[8] There was growing support, too, within the Socialist Party. In January 1997, some socialist deputies proposed a law for the CUS, and they were backed by a lone voice on the right, Roselyne Bachelot, RPR deputy and head of the Observatoire de la parité, as well as by organizations that sought to mobilize support from jurists, family organizations, and the like. The conservative government had been sufficiently worried about the practical difficulties faced by gay partners to commission a study, headed by jurist Jean Hauser, of the way in which the civil code might be reformed to address these issues. (The Hauser commission proposed that a gay couple be allowed to conclude a contract dealing with certain financial and material aspects of life together, but it did not recommend granting symbolic recognition of the fact that the contracting parties were a couple.) When the National Assembly was dissolved in the spring and the left came back to power, there was renewed hope that the CUS would be enacted, but it took a year for the prime minister to agree to support a law.

At the end of June 1997, some 250,000 people marched in the Gay Pride parade in Paris, including members of Jospin's cabinet (notably the women who had been appointed to fulfill the prime minister's commitment to parité—Elisabeth Guigou, Martine Aubry, and Catherine Trautmann). The recognition of gay unions was a major theme. Dominique Voynet, minister of the environment, depicted the CUS as a regularization of the situation of all unmarried couples: "The CUS is one of the elements in a struggle against exclusion that affects hundreds of thousands of people."[9] In the following months, various proposals were introduced. Guigou, minister of justice, set up a working group (headed by family sociologist Irène Théry) to study the proposals. It had become clear that some kind of law would be enacted in the coming months. In

June 1998, Jospin gave the go-ahead for what was now called the PaCS. Support and opposition intensified. Twelve thousand mayors from small cities all over France—encouraged by the Roman Catholic Church—announced that they would refuse to preside over the signing of such a contract; the conference of bishops condemned it.[10] The UDF pro-life deputy Christine Boutin organized an anti-PaCS demonstration in Paris in January 1999 that drew a hundred thousand people. The Gay Pride parade in Paris in June swelled with two hundred thousand supporters of the proposed law.[11] Day after day, articles appeared in the major newspapers analyzing the implications and predicting the effects such a law would have. The parliamentary debate eventually absorbed some 120 hours, many of them tumultuous.[12] From the spring of 1998 until passage of the law the following year (and even afterwards), a huge and heated public discussion took place about what it meant to treat same-sex partners as couples.

WHICH UNIVERSALISM?

The movement for the legal recognition of homosexual partnerships invoked the rhetoric, not surprisingly, of universalism; it sought equality for—not special treatment of—an interest group. As in discussions of immigrants and women, the rejection of a "communitarian" solution *à l'américaine* was a first premise, one to which all sides felt compelled to appeal. Presenting the PaCS to the National Assembly on October 9, 1998, Socialist Party spokesperson Catherine Tasca echoed a claim that had been made by proponents of such a law since the early 1990s: "The spirit of the Republic requires that we inscribe in the legal structure a recognition open to all cohabiting couples, regardless of their sex, and not only to homosexual couples. We don't want a communitarian solution."[13] And when Patrick Bloche, long an advocate for the law, endorsed the PaCS in March 1999 in his capacity as rapporteur for the assembly's commission on cultural, familial and social affairs, he too underscored its universalist aspect: "It is again and again necessary to remember the republican character of our approach, which seeks to create a global and unified framework for couples of different sexes or of the same sex. It is the universalist principle of rights that leads us to reject all communitarian tendencies of the Anglo-Saxon type and so not to have a statute only for homosexual couples."[14] Speaking (with great emotion) in support of the PaCS during debate in the assembly, RPR deputy Roselyne Bachelot complimented the groups that had long agitated for its passage: "The virtue of these associations was that they rejected communitarian solutions, which are necessarily stigmatizing, in order to construct a project that has room for each and every one of us, male or female, together with our children and our parents, at one moment or another of our lives; for in the end we recognize only one community: the Republic."[15]

The congratulatory tone of these speeches glossed over the evident contradictions the law contained and belied the difficulties (logical and practical) that advocates had encountered as they sought to reconcile the recognition of social differences with the standard of sameness demanded by universalism. On what terms were same-sex couples to be welcomed as such into the singular community of the Republic?

An early suggestion, by gay advocates Jean-Pierre Pouliquen, Gérard Bach-Ignace, and others associated with MDC (Mouvement des citoyens, a splinter socialist group led by Jean-Pierre Chevènement), which remained in play until the final formulations of the PaCS but was not incorporated in the law that passed, was to place homosexual partners under the general rubric of "duos." This, its proponents argued, satisfied the requirements of universalist neutrality (homosexual partnerships were simply a variety of cohabitation) and offered something other than marriage as a way to envisage the life of a couple. Pouliquen, president of the Collectif pour le CUCS, explained that his group did not seek legal recognition of homosexual couples as a goal in itself; rather, "it's two people who have a common project of life together who concern us." Homosexuals did not want to be designated a third category of partnership (in a hierarchy of married and unmarried heterosexuals). "We are convinced . . . that it is always preferable to opt for what is common to individuals rather than to separate them out. Of course, from a *social* point of view . . . differences exist. Just as a man is not a woman and a brunette is not a redhead, a homosexual or a lesbian is not a heterosexual. But these men and women have something in common: they are citizens. . . . It's a question of defending a universalist concept."[16] Critics on the left of the debates accused Pouliquen and his associates of a certain opportunism, downplaying homosexuality in order not to alienate deputies who might vote for the law. (But Frédéric Martel suggests that there was a more subversive, promiscuous goal: "not to reduce sex to a couple.")[17] For these critics, the "duo" strategy effaced exactly what had to be acknowledged—that these were sexual unions, basically no different from heterosexual ones.[18] If the practical problems of gay couples were to be addressed, then they needed to be assimilated to a more comprehensive universal category, either to cohabitation or to marriage. Critics on the right accused supporters of the law of deviously trying to cloak a communitarian wish in universalist garb. The charge of dissimulation carried a homophobic connotation since it relied on general characterizations of homosexual behavior as closeted, subversive, deceptive, abject. According to Théry, who used the pages of the journal *L'Esprit* and then an interview in *Le Monde* to denounce the movement, "disregarding its primary concern, this contract shrouds—for tactical reasons and a bit contemptibly—the fundamental question of homosexuality in an improbable 'social union.'"[19] Some also saw an implicit sexualizing of all two-person households, objecting to intimations of polygamy, incest, and other perversions that seemed to attach (phantasmatically) to anything associated with homosexuality.[20] Pouliquen expressed exasperation with these criticisms in an open letter to Théry. There seemed to be no way to get the balance right between sameness and difference, he said. "When homosexuals and lesbians march in the streets, they are reproached for displaying themselves. When they support a proposition that concerns all of society, they are criticized for being hypocrites. In short, they are never politically correct."[21] Put in other terms, we might say that Pouliquen's comments illustrate the difficulty of arguing for the recognition of the needs of socially different groups in the terms provided by republican universalism: demands for equal recognition in the name of difference reinforce the particularity of the group, while claims for equal recognition in the name of sameness raise the objection of difference.

The problem was no different when the universal group was limited to sexually intimate cohabiting couples, as it was in the law that eventually passed. Here the idea was to eliminate discrimination between unmarried heterosexuals and their homosexual counterparts. Since it was claimed that marriage was fast becoming deinstitutionalized (evidenced by the increase in divorce and the numbers of heterosexual couples who chose not to marry), the law now needed to address the realities faced by all of those who lived together outside its customary boundaries. From this perspective, gay couples could be assimilated to the category of cohabitants. Here the sexual tie was explicit and the commonality between heterosexual and homosexual couples was their unmarried status. Some advocates of this approach pointed out that the numbers of cohabiting straight couples had increased dramatically and that this, as much as the special difficulties faced by homosexual couples, justified a law; there was indeed a "universal" category in which gay couples could fit. Others maintained that love, not practicality, was the common denominator for gay and straight couples. This was the argument of Bertrand Delanoë, then a socialist deputy (and later mayor of Paris), at the Senate hearings on the PaCS in 1999. "There is a bond of love, the right to tenderness, and, quite simply, the dignity of each person. . . . The PaCS recognizes that bonds of love are universal. It creates rights and duties between two people who accept them conscientiously. In so doing it becomes the symbol of a more open and developed society."[22] Loving relations need not be sanctified by marriage—an institution that was anyway losing its status, and whose patriarchal associations led many feminists (among them lesbians) to denounce it.

The equality of heterosexual and homosexual cohabitants rested on their unmarried status, but there was a significant difference between them. The option of marriage was open to heterosexuals as was access to reproductive technology, but neither was available to homosexuals.[23] If legal recognition (that is state sanction) were granted to cohabiting partners as a group, then how could any members of that group be denied the rights to reproduction enjoyed by other members? And if gay and lesbian partnerships were equivalent to heterosexual unmarried relationships, by what logic could they be prohibited the right to choose marriage? These questions (which exposed the limits of a law narrowly confined to the shared circumstances of being an unmarried, cohabiting, sexually intimate couple) were asked by both opponents and supporters of the PaCS. On the one side, conservative opponents of the law denounced it as "an almost marriage"; on the other, radicals dismissed it as "a failed marriage."

The conservative senator Bernard Seillier exposed what he considered to be the dangerous logic of the proposed law this way:

> Cohabitation is, in effect, really marriage, even if it voluntarily foregoes the formalities of marriage. The evolutionary consequences of this for the law have already been sufficiently proved in the past. By inscribing cohabitation in the civil code, we distinguish it from marriage only by the intervention of a representative of the state. In a way, it's only a difference of the luxuriousness of the ceremony. At the same time, since cohabitation is not defined according to sex, we create indirectly what we say we don't want—homosexual marriage.[24]

From the other side, activists in favor of the rights of gay and lesbian couples (many removed from the parliamentary arena and thus less concerned about winning over skeptical or hostile politicians) made the case for logical consistency in the application of universalist arguments. For example, the jurist Marcella Iacub and the sociologist Jean-Marc Weller pointed out that sexual preference was precisely the issue that needed to be addressed and then dismissed as a ground for discriminatory treatment: "No one has challenged the idea that the liberty to marry whomever one chooses constitutes one of our most fundamental rights. . . . If some politician imagined that he could prevent the application of this right by proposing to forbid the union of two people of different skin colors or religions, for example, there's no question that a large number of voices would be raised loudly against him, because there are excellent reasons to want to guarantee civil equality for all. But this consideration seems curiously eclipsed when the question of the right to marriage of two men or two women is raised."[25] And jurist Daniel Borrillo and his coauthor Pierre Lascoumes concluded a book on the PaCS by maintaining that "the PaCS won't constitute real progress until the day that marriage becomes a possibility for couples of the same sex."[26] Many of those who shared Borrillo's and Lascoumes's position insisted that it wasn't marriage per se they were interested in, but a coherent universalism. "Equality of rights is a necessary condition: so it matters that marriage and kinship are open to couples of the same sex."[27]

The law that finally passed did not resolve these issues.[28] The PaCS is a legally sanctified relationship between two partners of whatever sex who share the same bed and who can establish the fact of, and a future commitment to, a life in common. Celebrated before an employee of a lower court, the Tribunal d'instance (to symbolically distinguish it from a marriage which is performed in the city hall by a mayor), the PaCS establishes rules for inheritance, as well as various other fiscal and social protections, which are not, however, as favorable as those offered in a marriage. It does not entitle foreign partners to visas or naturalization. And it is explicitly not a marriage. When justice minister Elisabeth Guigou introduced the law to the National Assembly in October 1998, and again when she presented it to the Senate in March 1999, she firmly stated that the PaCS was not a marriage. To hostile interruptions—"It's a sub-marriage"; "It's a pseudo-marriage"—she simply repeated that the law was not about marriage: "The PaCS only concerns the couple. . . . The PaCS is not a marriage. . . . The government of which I'm a member will never support adoption or medically assisted reproduction for homosexual partners."[29] Catherine Tasca echoed these statements in an article in *Le Monde:* "The PaCS doesn't deal with adoption or with reform of parental authority. It cannot be a possible step toward adoption or medically assisted procreation for homosexual couples. We have chosen to exclude these possibilities. Our choice is clear. It is without ulterior motivation."[30] That a law which enabled heterosexual but not homosexual cohabitants to form families could be offered "without ulterior motivation" came from the fact that this exclusion (this inequity in a law that in the name of universalism was supposed to eliminate discrimination against homosexual couples) was justified in terms of another universal, one that took priority—that of sexual difference. Marriage, Guigou told the assembled deputies, "is the union of a man and a woman: it is the institution that articulates the difference of the sexes."[31]

THE HETEROSEXUAL COUPLE

In the debates over the PaCS, the principle of universalism was applied not to individuals but to couples. Just as race or religion or sex was taken to be irrelevant for considerations of citizenship—abstraction from social characteristics guaranteed equality before the law for individuals—so the sex of the partners was to be irrelevant for couples recognized by the PaCS. This was meant to end discrimination against homosexual partners, guaranteeing them equality before the law. But just as historically the difference of sex had become a sticking point for the citizenship of women (delaying for more than a century their right to vote and for another fifty years their access to elected office), so differences of sex distinguished among the couples that had access to the PaCS. Women's exclusion from political participation was long explained as a consequence of nature: the universal phenomenon of sexual difference. The exclusion of homosexuals from "alliance"—anything that pertained to children, family, and kinship—was now explained as a consequence of the universal phenomenon of sexual difference. "The symbolism of gender, of masculine and feminine, exists in all human societies," wrote Théry, a fierce opponent of the PaCS; "It is the way culture makes sense of the sexed nature of the living species."[32] If human-made law had to abstract people from particular social categories, Théry suggested, gay couples could be absorbed into the category of cohabitants. But this law could not override the law of the difference of the sexes, which was prepolitical—not biological but cultural and for that reason fundamental for human self-understanding. As such it was a difference that could not admit of abstraction for political purposes. By this, Théry meant a challenge not only to PaCS but to parité.[33] The differences of sex (which had always been encumbered with cultural meaning) could not be reduced by law to mere anatomy. But if there was no abstraction possible for differences of sex, could there be equality?

In the campaign for parité, anatomical duality was granted as a "natural fact," but sexual difference was seen as a mutable social concept, the use and meaning of which had to be changed if discrimination against women were to end. To treat women as fully equal required asserting not that women were individuals (like men), but that individuals were women and men, that anatomical duality was part of the definition of abstract individuals. In the debates about the PaCS, where the couple was the unit in question, those who invoked sexual difference assumed a fixed relationship between women and men: complementarity of traits, roles, and functions, as well as attraction rooted in the enduring imperatives of species reproduction. For the paritaristes, the question of nature was said to be without necessary social consequence; individuals simply came in one of two sexes. In the discourse of the couple associated with the PaCS, the fact that there were two sexes in nature became the foundation for the unquestionable truth of normative heterosexuality. Critics of the PaCS warned of the dangers of ignoring essential differences in the name of a spurious equality. "We reject discrimination that channels hatred; but difference can't be neutralized by the requirements of equality."[34] Or, "Ought we to find it normal that all difference is treated as discrimination, and that those who choose to live their difference demand at the same time that it be neutralized in the name of equality?"[35]

The consensus that emerged among those who opposed and many of those who supported the PaCS as a limited domestic-partnership contract was that the full equation of homosexual and heterosexual couples would deny the foundational role of sexual difference in the constitution of individual psyches and social solidarity. The idea of social solidarity, in turn, rested on an organic definition of society, one in which individuals were inextricably linked to one another and in which their practices—however isolated—inevitably affected the whole. There was, of course, a minority position that challenged the essentializing of the heterosexual couple and denounced as homophobic those who sought to prevent gay couples from forming families.[36] But it had a hard time countering the force of expert testimony offered by prominent sociologists, anthropologists, psychiatrists, and priests. As the furor over the PaCS raged, sexual difference became figured exclusively as a heterosexual couple, and the analogy between couples and individuals that lay at the heart of gay advocacy (and of any claim for equal rights) faltered. No abstraction was possible, said the experts, when sexual difference was the key to life itself.

It was the family sociologist Irène Théry who first raised fundamental objections to the PaCS (then still called the CUS) in these terms, in an article published in *L'Esprit* in 1997. While Théry noted with great sympathy the discrimination faced by homosexuals and the difficulties they faced as the AIDS epidemic brought not only encounters with premature death but injustices that must be addressed, she also warned that equating homosexual couples in any way with heterosexual couples was a grave mistake. Opposing discrimination was one thing, she argued, but denying all distinctions was another. Herself an advocate of the reform of family law, of the need to recognize the real existence of a plurality of family forms (she referred often to blended families, and also to the problems faced by single-parent households), Théry drew the line at homosexual families because the very idea violated the symbolics of sexual difference. "The passion for desymbolization," "one of the most disturbing passions of our time," was dangerous, not only to the idea of civil marriage, "the hidden glory of the French Revolution," but to the entire "symbolic order," which rested on the difference of sex.[37] In another article she warned that "the question of the homosexual couple" posed "major anthropological questions."[38] The practical problems of various kinds of domestic arrangements (among them the real existence of large numbers of single-parent households) ought not to be confused, she went on, with the cultural form that preserves and transmits the very meaning of identity: the heterosexual couple, which embodies the masculine/feminine difference that is the primary difference. It is "the fundamental opposition," as anthropologist Françoise Héritier put it a year later in an interview in the Catholic magazine *La Croix*, "that allows us to think. Because to think is first of all to classify, to classify is first of all to differentiate, and the fundamental differentiation is based on the difference of the sexes." According to Héritier, "our way of thinking and our social organization are based on the perception of the difference of the sexes. And we can't reasonably argue that this difference can be displaced onto the homosexual couple."[39] Despite Claude Lévi-Strauss's refusal to endorse these arguments (he suggested that the issue was not the enduring facts of culture but a political struggle about social organization),[40] what sociologist Eric Fassin has labeled "the anthropological illusion" persisted.[41]

The argument from anthropology linked families and sexuality in a way described by Michel Foucault in the first volume of his *History of Sexuality*. "The family," he writes, "is the interchange of sexuality and alliance: it conveys the law and the juridical dimension in the deployment of sexuality; and it conveys the economy of pleasure and the intensity of sensations in the regime of alliance."[42] The intertwining of family (defined as *alliance*—lineage and kinship) with sexuality (the location of sex within the family) at once protected society against the excesses of sexual desire (represented in these debates by homosexuality) and guaranteed the stability, if not of every family, then at least of the heterosexual nuclear-family norm. Opponents of gay families insisted they were driven not by homophobia but by a cultural imperative. The idea of a cultural imperative became the cornerstone both of attacks on the PaCS and of justifications by its supporters for the law's exclusions. Sexual difference, embodied by the heterosexual couple, was taken to be the symbolic mastercode of humankind—immutable, "primordial," not natural but "cultural," a reality "objective" and "universal."[43]

Sexual difference served many related functions in the depictions offered of the heterosexual couple. It was, for one thing, the guarantee of species and social reproduction. For this reason the couple, when equated with family and marriage, was not simply a private arrangement the way homosexual partnerships were; it was a socially useful institution—the key unit of social solidarity in a Durkheimian vision. The mayor of the town of Felletin, Michel Pinton, a devout Catholic who organized the mayors' protest against the PaCS, refused even to refer to homosexuals as couples. Better, he said, to think of them as "pairs." "These pairs have no social utility whatsoever; they are sterile by definition."[44] Senator Anne Heinis repeated this idea: homosexuality was a life choice, an affective relationship, "implying no function in society."[45] And Théry referred to "the finiteness" of the "homosexual bond," by which she implied not only its inability to reproduce but its association (through AIDS) with death.[46] Tony Anatrella, a priest at the Jesuit Faculties of Paris and a practicing psychoanalyst (who also served as a consultant to the Pontifical Council for the Family), refused, like Pinton, to regard homosexual partners as couples, since a couple, for him, represented the possibility, if not the actuality, of becoming parents. Homosexuals had a right to the expression of their private desire, but "the homosexual relation symbolizes nothing on the social plane and cannot be a subject of rights without manipulating reality and deceiving society in the name of good feelings."[47] Homosexual partnerships were characterized as private, fueled by a desire that many deemed unnatural or perverse, and ultimately selfish, while heterosexual couples were foundational social institutions, characterized by selfless love. The one signaled destructive self-indulgence ("a fatal behavior for society"),[48] the other the commitment to another person, to life, and to the future. For its own self-interest, the state must opt for life. "The PaCS," the Académie des sciences morales et politiques (a quasi-official governmental advisory body) opined, "is a project that will lead to deformation of inheritance, of nationality, of taxation."[49]

Those who were willing to grant that homosexuals could be designated couples in a limited sort of way and, as such, subjects of law nonetheless shared the view that the law must not consider them families, for as Françoise Dekenwer-Defossez, an adviser to Elisabeth Guigou (and a supporter of the PaCS law), put it, "the very structure of society . . . would be threatened by families that were too abnormal, and by kinship arrangements that were too atypical."[50] In this organic view of society, in which all parts, all social facts, are indissolubly linked to one another, the fear of contagion is rampant. Théry suggested that marriage was not about couples but about generational continuity; marriage, she said, is "the institution that ties the difference of the sexes to the difference of the generations."[51] These statements from experts in the service of the secular state reiterated a view of the family pronounced by any number of Catholic organizations. The Conference of Bishops and the Association of Catholic Families, for example, each stressed the fact that the nuclear family (consisting of father, mother, and children) was the "germ cell of society," that which permitted "the renewal of generations" and constituted "one of the fundamental structures of society, whose coherence it maintains."[52]

Beyond the literal fact of reproduction, the heterosexual couple was said to incarnate the fact of sexual difference itself. It was not only, Théry announced, "a sexual relation"; it was also "a sexual bond," the institutionalization of the masculine/feminine difference, the difference that not only organizes social life but also humanizes individual beings. (It was precisely this humanization, she said, that made sexual difference cultural, not simply or crudely biological.)[53] Indeed, the symbolic significance of the couple overshadowed its literal reproductive functions in the discourse in these years—in no small part because the facts of family organization (divorced and recombined families, single-parent families, and families in which one parent had changed sexual preference) belied any attempt to point to a single form that was typical or normal. References to the symbolic often gestured to Lacanian psychoanalysis (without much knowledge of its intricacies), although some Lacanian analysts too suggested that all sorts of deformations of individual psychic development would occur if the primary difference were denied.[54] Here again, the idea of social contagion informed the debate—no social fact could take place without affecting all others. Homosexuality was said to be the emblem of the negation of sexual difference; its recognition in law thus an erasure of this primary distinction. It was as if, once the law recognized homosexual couples and families, all other forms would disappear. The boundaries of sexual difference were declared immutable, but the anxiety, indeed the near hysteria, about maintaining them revealed a deep sense of their vulnerability in the eyes of their most ardent defenders.

Some psychiatrists talked as if the legal recognition of homosexual couples would deny the very existence of heterosexuality and of the physical distinction between women and men. Without the masculine/feminine distinction, individuals would remain in an infantile state since their "construction as subjects depends on their inscription in this institution."[55] Homosexuality was a denial of alterity and therefore of the possibility of relation to someone other.[56] Moreover, according to Anatrella, the "psychic structure of love" was not comparable for homosexuals and heterosexuals, since homosexual love—if it could be called that—was narcissistic, a love of self. Anatrella preferred to speak of "the desires, the inclinations, or the subjective intrigues" of homosexuals, reserving the notions of the couple, marriage, and love for heterosexuals.[57] Homosexuality was represented as a form of narcissicism, or even, one child psychiatrist suggested in a Senate hearing, of vampirism. "The vampiric identification is an identification with one's likeness that, at the same time, pushes one to destroy it. The question before us is to know if, in the case of a system very close to cloning, where there are two parents and a child all of the same sex, we wouldn't find ourselves confronting this same vampiric configuration."[58] This pathology could not be confined to homosexual partnerships themselves; there was something contagious for all of society about considering them families: "That risks the complete destabilization of family and social relations and could, in the end, damage the psychological constitution of all children, even those born into normal families."[59]

The narcissism of homosexual attraction, defined as the inability to recognize the demands of the other, was taken as a threat to social cohesion. Pierre Legendre, a jurist and psychoanalyst, formerly a member of Lacan's Ecole freudienne, deemed it "a hedonistic logic, the legacy of Nazism."[60] Others maintained that the model of political authority required by democracy would be negated if homosexuals were to be considered families.[61] Théry invoked "republican values" and democratic law, insisting that these ultimately rested on the symbolics of sexual difference.[62] Historian Emmanuel LeRoy Ladurie considered the PaCS a defiance of the entire Judeo-Christian tradition.[63] There were also those who denounced any legalization of homosexual partnerships as an open invitation to "illicit immigration," making a metonymic link between one "illicit situation" and another, and so suggesting that the boundaries of sexual difference were somehow vital to the national boundaries of France.[64]

Commentators have noted how frantic were the attempts in this discussion to naturalize, anthropologize, and universalize the difference of sex embodied in the heterosexual couple. Eric Fassin has taken tautology to be symptomatic—"Sociology defined the difference of the sexes as heterosexuality after having justified heterosexuality by reference to the difference of the sexes"—a sure sign, he says, that politics and ideology, not science or reason, drove the arguments.[65] Whether ultimately a symptom of homophobia or of tremendous unease about the instability of what Daniel Borrillo calls "the mythic model of the family," or both, the discourse of the couple had a profound impact on political thought.[66] (It should be noted that the family, mythologized as stable and immutable, had undergone a series of changes since the 1960s, which among other things liberalized divorce, ended distinctions between legitimate and illegitimate children, dropped the notion that the father was *chef de famille,* and granted unmarried couples access to medically assisted procreation.)[67] The myth of the family reintroduced irreducible (or incommensurable) sexual difference into discussions of equality—a difference that could not be dissolved by abstraction or altered by law, a difference so self-evident that its recognition needed no justification. As Théry put it,

> the juridical institution of difference amounts to this, the immense importance of which we haven't finished assessing: *to recognize the finiteness of each sex, which needs the other so that the human race can live and reproduce.* That is why at the heart of the symbolic difference of the sexes we find the institutions of marriage and kinship. Through them, law fashions the genealogical order, which inscribes each human being in a double paternal and maternal image. It is there that the difference between masculine and feminine is rooted; this difference is not natural (what *is* natural is the difference between male and female) but cultural.[68]

The heterosexual couple, in this view, was independent of power dynamics between men and women; incommensurable difference did not necessarily mean inequality. But the heterosexual couple was (depending on who was writing) a source of stability, continuity, cohesion, authority, and democracy; it was a guiding principle of social order, the universal foundation of politics in general and French politics in particular. Indeed, an appreciation of sexual difference (of complementarity, of seduction, of "the happy exchanges between the sexes") was said to be a distinctive feature of French (as opposed especially to puritanical American) national character.[69] Already in 1995, as a criticism of parité and of feminism, historian Mona Ozouf had offered a genealogy for this national sexiness and had dubbed it "the French singularity." In the debates about the PaCS, the theme was reiterated. Sexual difference, in the shape of the heterosexual couple, became a way of figuring national identity; protecting this couple then meant defending the values of the republic, maintaining the integrity of France.[70] At stake was the very notion of French national character, one in which republicanism and sexual difference were inextricably intertwined.

In retrospect, there was an easy line to be drawn from the heterosexual couple to the national representation. If sexual difference as embodied in the *couple* were foundational, why not insist that it be reflected as such in representative bodies, the elected assemblies that were the expression of the nation? This is exactly what Sylviane Agacinski did, building on the reasoning used to justify unequal treatment of homosexuals in regard to family formation in the PaCS to argue for equal treatment of women through passage of a law on parité.

POLITIQUE DES SEXES

Sylviane Agacinski had long been an advocate of parité. In 1996, she wrote an opinion piece in *Le Monde* replying to Elisabeth Badinter's criticisms of the movement.[71] In it, she argued for voluntary actions by political parties to gradually implement 50/50 representation so that republican institutions would reflect the complementarity of "the whole human species." There was nothing "communitarian" about such a demand, she pointed out. Rather, it corrected the false universalism of an abstract individualism that had privileged men's power by holding up a single (male) model of the human. A true universalism would recognize that individuals came in two sexes, that "humanity is universally sexed." The translation of this universalism in politics was parité—the inclusion of equal numbers of women in all instances of political decision-making. Like the original paritaristes, Agacinski insisted that no claim was being made for the representation of a separate women's interest; the point was to grant equal value to women's contributions. Although she talked a great deal about *mixité,* by which she meant something like coeducation (or the equal standing of the different sexes), there was no mention in her article of the relations between the sexes, except in terms of unequal access to political power. Neither was there any discussion of heterosexuality or of couples, as there would be in her book *Politique des sexes,* published in 1998. That book shows the influence on her thinking of the PaCS debates and especially of the discourse of the couple. "To think of complementarity," she wrote in 1998, "is to consider that there are two versions of man and to represent humanity as a couple."[72]

Politique des sexes presented itself as a brief for parité; it was also a very strong argument against homosexual families. Although Agacinski was all for fair treatment of minorities (it was she, according to one account, who in 1997 persuaded her husband, Lionel Jospin, then prime minister, to agree to some kind of domestic partnership legislation),[73] she was nonetheless resolutely opposed to the idea that marriage and family could be reconciled with homosexuality. The idea of the couple served to join her two concerns: she could oppose homosexual families and support political equality for women in the name of the *mixité* of the heterosexual couple. The standard for equality became marital complementarity, in families as well as in politics. Same-sex institutions—whether parliaments or marriages—were simply not acceptable because they could not incarnate this equality.

Citing Françoise Héritier, Agacinski argued that the difference of the sexes "is a formative model for all societies," even if there were cultural variations on the theme.[74] This didn't mean that gender was a "cultural construction"; rather, culture gave meaning to the imperative of nature. "The difference of the sexes, even before playing an essential role in all social organization, is the principle of love, of death, and of reproduction" (pp. 31–32). The demands of reproduction meant that humans were naturally heterosexual. "Exclusive interest in the same sex is accidental, it's a kind of exception—even if frequent—that proves the rule" (p. 108). Indeed, sexual identity, Agacinski continued, is established through the experience of reproduction. "There is a kind of 'sex consciousness,' like 'class consciousness,' that accompanies the experience of reproduction and is different from sexuality" (p. 105). Children develop this sex consciousness in families, where they learn they are the products of a male/female coupling. As men and women, they realize their identities as parents. Agacinski rejected the feminist logic she associated with Simone de Beauvoir that "absurdly" denied that maternity was a defining characteristic of women. It may have been true that maternity was devalued in times past, she admitted, but now it ought to be recognized for what it was—a source of women's power (pp. 59, 80).

Even as she insisted on the impact of the actual experience of reproduction on the formation of gender identity, she also recognized that circumstances might deny individuals that experience. It was all the more important, she insisted, that "the symbolic and legal orders of kinship should always signify the natural order of generations" (p. 132). Test-tube babies, cloning, single-parent households might deprive children of the primary experience they needed, but it was up to the law to protect the natural order of life, children's "right" to know that they were born of a man and a woman (p. 135). Agacinski did not directly entertain the possibility that the law could actually produce that "natural order" rather than reflect it, but the logic of her argument can be read as exactly that: an attempt to preserve the "natural" as it was being eroded by new technologies and new conceptions of what might count as reproduction, what might be understood to be a family. "The family, by institutionalizing the complementary parental couple, offers a symbolic representation of the origin of life. . . . We cannot, in fact, abandon this model of procreation; with the exception of cloning, the biological origin of a child is always dual. . . . Is it desirable to abandon the model of the complementary parental couple in establishing kinship? I don't think so. In principle, it ought to remain undergirded by its natural dual origin" (p. 135). Why recognizing homosexual families would suppress this knowledge of the "natural dual origin" of life was never made clear by Agacinski or by those whose arguments she was incorporating into her own. If biological reasons didn't suffice, there were ethical reasons as well to insist on "the dual origin of man." This had to do with the fact that "the other sex is a fundamental figure for the other," without which social solidarity and human connection would be impossible (p. 136). The heterosexual couple, then, became the basis for *all* human relationships—a model of complementary and what Durkheim had called organic solidarity.

Agacinski admitted—citing the writings of Aristotle, Freud, and Lacan—that notions of the couple historically had not always been based on gender equality, but she maintained that feminists had mistakenly assumed that this must forever be the case (pp. 48–49). Binary systems weren't inevitably hierarchical, she argued (in a curious corruption of Derridean thinking), and difference needn't imply lack or deficiency in one of the binaries. Her notion of *mixité* was difference without hierarchy; in place of presence/absence, fullness/lack, there would be complementarity, the interdependence of the different sexes, the acknowledgment of their need of the other for completion. "Each of the two lacks what the other has or is" (p. 50). This idea was not new in France, where the notion of heterosexual complementarity had a long history. Drawing on Mona Ozouf's book, Agacinski pointed out that French culture was notable for the absence of war between the sexes and was marked, instead, by friendship, love, seduction, and even libertinage. "Men and women, here much more than elsewhere, have always sought to understand and to please one another, and they have not scorned borrowing from one another the qualities that are flaws in their own sex: a man with no grace or a woman without strength of character bothers us" (p. 159). Here the specificities of French cultural history become the best expressions of nature's intentions and France becomes the best embodiment of human cultural achievement.

It was time to bring this notion of complementarity into the political realm, said Agacinski, because it was scandalous not to and because modern democracy required it. Instead of using the difference between the sexes to establish separate spheres of competence, it was time to share power equally, to acknowledge that the sovereign people came in two sexes, to introduce complementarity into the notion of sovereignty. "Parité ought to be the complementarity of the 'national representation' *in its entirety,* in order to represent the humanity of the nation *in its entirety*" (p. 196). This explicitly did not mean that men represented men, and women women. Rather, drawing on the republican theory of representation and on an analogy to the theater, which—according to Aristotle, she claimed—was not a reflection but an imitation of "the people," Agacinski pointed out that the nation was a fiction realized through political representation, and parité was about figuring that representation. "The equitable representation of men and women . . . ought, therefore, to be a *figure relevant* to what the people is, universally, that is to say, a people made up of men and women" (p. 202). To worry that figuring "the people" as dual (man and woman)—instead of in the traditional singular terms—meant challenging the indivisibility of national sovereignty was simply wrong-headed. In this, she was echoing the arguments of the original paritaristes. But her differences with them were fundamental. While parité wanted to *sex* the abstract individual as a means *of unsexing* the political body, Agacinski wanted to *sex* the political body, installing the heterosexual couple as the model of perfect complementarity. In this essentialist view of things, *mixité* was not divisive or fracturing, she insisted, but unity, the unity exemplified by the reproductive couple merging to conceive a child.

The original paritaristes wrestled with the difficulty of inserting women into the category of the abstract individual and concluded that only a law implementing "strict equality" between the sexes would achieve it. The human individual had to be figured as both woman and man. If half the National Assembly—the body that incarnated the nation—consisted of women, then and only then would it be clear that women were citizens (individuals) on the same terms as men. The visibility of women in the body of the nation would then have positive ramifications in many other areas of life. The aim was to make women seen to be individuals and in this way to counter discrimination based on sex. With parité, existing relations of power would be altered by the law— a law that had the ability, in the paritaristes' view, to then change the way the relations between the sexes were lived and symbolized in families as well as elsewhere in society. For Agacinski, in contrast, sexual difference—expressed in the unvarying human traits of complementary gender roles and heterosexual attraction—was a natural foundation that law could only reflect.

In the context of the PaCS debates in 1998–99, it is not surprising that Agacinski's vision of parité became the dominant one. If essentialist possibilities always hovered around the early arguments for parité, they did not drive or define them. It was Agacinski's book that brought them out. In her hands, parité became an endorsement of normative heterosexuality, as well as of the strong homophobic impetus that informed the government's version of the PaCS. It may well be that her book helped to persuade legislators to pass both laws. (That she was the wife of the sitting prime minister didn't hurt; indeed, it is hard to imagine that the book would have gotten the attention it did without that prestigious marital connection.) It is certain that her version of parité became the dominant one in the months and years that followed the book's publication.

IN THE WAKE OF AGACINSKI

On December 2, 1998, the National Assembly heard a report from Catherine Tasca on the proposed constitutional revision.[75] Although the word parité itself had been removed from the text, there was now to be an addition to article 3 stipulating that "the law encourages equality between women and men" in access to political office. On December 15, the deputies (a strikingly small number of them, most of these female) discussed the government's proposal and adopted it on the first reading. Some weeks later, at the end of January, the Senate's commission on laws rejected the proposed constitutional revision. Among the arguments was one that rested on an opposition between women and politics. "Do they really like politics anyway?" asked one senator.[76] There followed several weeks of negotiation about wording (for example, whether the stronger verbs "guarantee" or "establish" should replace the weaker "encourage") and a month of intense media discussion when all the pros and cons of parité and of constitutional revision were rehashed. The National Assembly debated a new version on February 16, 1999. On March 4, the Senate approved this version. And on March 10, the National Assembly unanimously adopted the new text, which had amended article 3 (dealing with national sovereignty) to read, "The law encourages equal access of men and women to elective office," and article 4 (dealing with political parties) to read, "Political parties will contribute to the realization of the principle enumerated in the last line of article three, under conditions determined by law." Then both houses met in an extraordinary session at Versailles on May 31 to definitively adopt these amendments.

In the course of the debates leading to passage of the revisions a great many views were aired. The reform was defended as a form of positive discrimination, as a means of granting women full citizenship, and as a way of narrowing the gap between the political class and civil society. There were serious disagreements about the need for constitutional reform rather than a simple law. The reform was also hailed as a way of making France more modern and more democratic. What I want to focus on now, however, was the way in which Agacinski's arguments had come to inform the justification offered for demanding full and equal access for women to elective office and the way in which Agacinski herself became the spokesperson for parité. It was not that earlier arguments or their proponents had disappeared; the repetition of the point that women constituted half of humanity, along with a rejection of the idea that normative views of gender were eternal and natural, echoed a decade of claims by paritaristes. But those arguments were increasingly joined, if not overshadowed, by images of the couple, so strongly endorsed in the controversy over the PaCS.

Before the debate began in December 1998, Tasca called on a number of expert witnesses, whose comments she included at the end of her report. The jurist Danièle Lochak insisted on the antidiscrimination aspects of the constitutional revision, pointing out the dangers of essentialism that lurked in any attempt to talk about women and men as the two faces of humanity. Rather, she looked to pragmatic justifications: given the misogyny of French politicians, parité was the best way of arriving at real equality of opportunity for women. Lochak's was a minority voice, however, in an arena where universalist rhetoric held sway. Monique Pelletier, an advocate in 1979 of quotas for municipal elections, emphasized the complementarity of the couple. She was like many women, she said, "who recognize themselves as different and complementary and who, therefore, have a part to play in decision-making, which will be enriched by their complementarity."[77] Gisèle Halimi, another veteran of 1970s and 1980s feminism, endorsed a solution that had earlier been offered for the problem posed by greater numbers of women for men already holding office. To the suggestion that the numbers of representatives in each constituency be doubled, she added the idea that they would form "a couple, I mean, a male deputy and a female deputy."[78] During the Assembly debates, minister of justice Elisabeth Guigou dismissed the criticism that the law was "communitarian" by citing Agacinski as the authority for her claim that women were half of humanity.[79] When a male deputy referred to "women and other minorities," he was greeted with outrage: "Women, a minority?" shouted one female deputy. "We are not a minority, we are half the world," cried another. "Read Sylviane Agacinski!" retorted a third.[80] Whereas once it had been possible to imagine the statement that women were half of humanity as a demographic description, the reference to Agacinski's work was ideological (full of cultural meanings taken as natural fact), and it carried with it the figure of the couple. The notion that national sovereignty (one and indivisible) wouldn't be divided if incarnated in two sexes now depended on thinking of the couple as a foundational unit for citizenship.

Beyond the imagery of the couple, Agacinski's essentialism—the insistence that social understanding of the difference of sex was equivalent to a prepolitical rule of nature or culture—came to characterize parité. The British newspaper *The Guardian* dubbed parité Agacinski's "brainchild," while an (appallingly uninformed) article in the American *New Republic* referred to Agacinski's *Politique des sexes* as "the bible of the movement."[81] For early critics of parité, this essentialism was a fulfillment of their prophecy that a demand for 50% representation of women would necessarily be heard as an endorsement of normative rules of gender. Evelyne Pisier, who had long objected to what she considered parité's emphasis on women (rather than on individuals), in 1998 seemed to blame the campaign for the defeat of the most radical possibilities of the PaCS. "If sexual alterity is a law of nature, what are we to do with 'the same' in the pair?"[82] Philosopher Jacques Derrida, though he supported parité as a way of correcting the persistent underrepresentation of women in politics (it was a "lesser evil" than continued discrimination), nonetheless worried about the effects of reintroducing the difference of sex (he capitalized "the") into the political arena. Any categorical concept homogenized the differences within categories, he warned, thereby reproducing "the game of phallocentrism."[83] (For him, it seemed, there could be no distinction between anatomical duality and sexual difference, or at least he didn't engage that argument—perhaps because it was no longer visible as an aspect of parité's claim.) In addition, Derrida objected to parité's endorsement of the fantasy of sovereignty (whether indivisible or bisexual). For women it could easily be associated with a certain maternalism at odds with genuine equality.[84] Elisabeth Roudinesco (in conversation with Derrida) opposed parité out of the same worry: its presumed "maternalocentrist" conception of femininity.[85] Sociologist Rose-Marie Lagrave took Agacinski's essentialism to be emblematic of the entire parité movement, mischaracterizing it as "differentialist" and denying its originality by describing it as just another chapter in a long history of feminist conflict between equality and difference.[86]

The realignment of forces was perhaps clearest in a set of articles in *Le Nouvel Observateur* in January 1999 devoted to divisions among feminists about the impending constitutional revision.[87] The opposing sides were represented by Elisabeth Badinter, who railed against parité (as she had for years) as a dangerous return to biological determinism and as a threat to the universalism of the Republic, and by Sylviane Agacinski, who insisted that sexual difference was "a universal difference" that must be the basis for "new democratic models."[88] (That these two emerged as the principals in a feminist debate was, to say the least, ironic since both had gained public attention as a function of their husbands' prestige: Agacinski as the wife of the prime minister; Badinter having made her reputation as a writer/philosopher under the name of her husband, Robert, a noted lawyer who had held a number of elected and appointed political posts.) An article about Agacinski and Badinter cited Françoise Gaspard, who "was amused at this very French talent that preferred dogmatic arguments to pragmatism."[89] Gaspard went on to point out that parité was not "a new foundational principle, which must be engraved in the marble of the constitution, but a simple strategy to lead France out of its backwardness." Her comments, as well as her position as onlooker in a debate between universalism and differentialism, signaled her sense of how futile it had become to try, in the midst of a campaign for legal reform, to hold on to those rigorous distinctions between anatomical duality and sexual difference initially set forth in *Au pouvoir citoyennes*. "Pragmatism" was a way of opting out of a debate whose terms Gaspard and her colleagues had unsuccessfully sought to change while at the same time pursuing the political goal they had advanced. But it was really pragmatism, not parité, that constituted "a simple strategy" to maintain the momentum needed to get a law passed. Rather than cede parité to Agacinski's essentialist rewriting of it, Gaspard redefined it as "a necessary step—one that could eventually be gotten beyond—toward equality, a strategy whose objective was to end masculine domination."[90] Without entirely giving up on a new universalism, Gaspard deferred the project: "The demand for parité, a step toward a universalism still in the making, is a more modest and realistic solution."[91]

It would be a mistake to assume (as sociologist Yves Sintomer does)[92] that this had been Gaspard's position from the beginning. That would be to lose sight of the inventive way in which the movement had sought to reconceptualize abstract individualism (within the terms of abstraction), as well as of the fact that ideas have not just an intellectual but also a political history. For the moment, philosophical debate was beside the point, trapped as it was in the egalitarian/differentialist opposition the original paritaristes had sought to displace. Now full attention must be focused not just on amending the constitution but on the passage of laws that would open political representation to women. As Gaspard put it in comments after the constitution had been revised, "now the devil is in the details."[93]

CHAPTER SIX

The Power of the Law

The parité movement believed in the power of law to change social relationships. "By parité in the political sphere, we mean the recognition, by law, of the equal representation of women and men."[1] The rallying cry of *Au pouvoir citoyennes* was unambiguous: "Passing a law is essential."[2] The paritaristes had a sophisticated conception of the way law worked to effect change. Of course, they expected some immediate results; in much the way that the suffrage had extended the vote to women, they assumed a parité law would quickly bring more women into the political world. But they were also pragmatists, aware that it might take time to achieve the complete equality they envisioned. The immediate goal was to make discrimination visible. "The demand for parité," warned Françoise Gaspard on the eve of the passage of the constitutional revision, ". . . will be without immediate effect. It will have raised the question of the inequality of women and men. Undoubtedly the most difficult of the so-called social questions."[3] Gaspard's prediction proved right. In the short term, the law that became known as the parité law challenged but did not overturn men's control of political power. At the same time, it drew increased attention to discrimination against women, and not only in the realm of politics. Whether it will achieve its ultimate goal of making gender irrelevant to the selection of representatives cannot be known so soon; it may take a long time for the effects of legal change to be felt in the mentalities and behavior of political actors.

COMPROMISE IN THE PREPARATION OF THE LAW

The law the authors envisaged was based on the principle of equality, but also on a certain realism; unless the law itself specified a desired outcome, it would not overcome the resistance to change of entrenched interests. For that reason, the text put forward by the paritaristes stipulated that the composition of elected assemblies would be evenly divided between women and men. "Elected assemblies, at the territorial and national levels, will be composed of as many women as men."[4] How such a law would be implemented—by doubling the number of representatives, say, or by splitting electoral districts in two—could be left to legislative deliberation; the point was to bring about the desired result. "Legislators are enormously creative when they want to put principles into their texts."[5] This comment, offered as a rebuttal to those who claimed that such a law could never be made workable, acquires a certain irony in retrospect. What legislative creativity there was went into the formulation and implementation of a constitutional revision and then a law that minimized, if it did not entirely undercut, the goal held out by the parité movement.

Republican theory to the contrary, laws are the product of negotiation and compromise, not the general will's unanimous articulation of pure principle. The wording of the revision of article 3 of the constitution (the law "encourages" equal access of men and women to political office) was a watered-down version of stronger possibilities suggested by feminists, such as "establishes" or "guarantees."[6] "Encourages" merely suggested a tendency or a disposition that might well be slowed or stopped by other factors; despite objections from legislators, it was all that President Chirac and most other politicians were willing to endorse. The revision of article 4 stated that political parties were expected to "contribute" to the realization of this principle in ways that would be spelled out in new electoral laws. "Contribute," like "encourage," was a vague term, carrying none of the force the paritaristes' version had envisioned.

Still, despite their evident disappointment, the leaders of the parité movement pressed for a law that would translate even these weak articulations of principle into a forceful instrument for change. An editorial in Gisèle Halimi's journal *Choisir: La cause des femmes* put it plainly: "The reform of the constitution . . . will not be a 'parité reform' until it is translated into laws and regulations."[7] The government's commitment to some kind of law was evident. At a conference organized by the Socialist Party in September 1999, the prime minister insisted (in opposition to those who urged a gradual imposition of quotas) that for him "parité is 50/50."[8] And in the National Assembly, as the new law was being debated in January 2000, the government's spokespersons brushed aside the concerns of republicanists and talked of an urgent need to end discrimination. Thus Bernard Roman, the rapporteur for the commission on constitutional laws, insisted on the need for "efficacious solutions." "Republican universalism is an essential value, a magnificent abstraction, a formidable hypothesis, a founding incantation. But this fine republican theory remains atemporal on principle. It ignores reality, the weight of norms, and the power of social constraints. Since it is necessary to understand the real in order to move toward the ideal, we face this terrible fact today: there will be no equality if the law doesn't require it!"[9]

Yet the kind of equality the government had in mind was limited both by practical concerns, the need to win the support of male deputies and senators who sought to protect their positions and their power, and by the idea of *mixité* that Agacinski had offered, the complementary roles of the heterosexual couple. The paritaristes' original notion—that women could be abstracted from the cultural understandings of the difference of their sex and thus could be taken as individuals—was, for the time being, occluded.[10] In this way, the connection between republicanism and sexual difference was maintained.

Ironically, given the French animus against affirmative action and antidiscrimination law, the constitutional reforms and the law of June 6, 2000, closely resembled those policies.[11] They designated an excluded group and sought its inclusion without, however, addressing the underlying reasons for exclusion; in this case, the way sexual difference signified the antithesis both of abstraction and national unity. There was, to be sure, new attention to discrimination; the absence of women in elected office (and in other high positions in French society) became visible as never before. But without some way of being redefined as individuals, women would continue to be treated as different, representatives not of the nation as a whole but of a particular constituency and its interests, one, moreover, whose influence—because it was particularistic—must be limited, whose power must be contained. The short-term impact of the law has been exactly this: the admission of increased numbers of women to elective positions (unevenly, depending on the importance of the office), but usually as representatives of women, not of "France."

This, however, is not the end of the story. Even in the short term, the law has been disruptive, exposing (if not overturning) the way male power works and opening the question of the relationship between sex and political representation. The very contradiction that is posed by the emergence of significant numbers of *femmes politiques* and of women who are deemed *hommes politiques*, and some who fit both categories, has destabilized neat correlations between politics and masculinity, making it possible for women to demonstrate something of the competence they had been assumed to lack by virtue of their sex. The extent of this corrosive effect on established power relations cannot be predicted at this early stage, but it seems safe to say that a process of change has been set in motion.

The government introduced its bill in January 2000. On the 25th, it was adopted by the National Assembly with only one opposing vote. The discussion in the assembly focused not on the grand principles that had earlier divided its members (what one deputy referred to as "the false debate on universalism")[12] but on the need to correct discrimination. Even those who opposed the law (arguing that it devalued women or commodified them) endorsed the rightful "cause" of equality. The pressure of public opinion and the Socialist Party's desire to satisfy it led to testimonials from deputies who were also mayors about their sincere efforts to recruit women for municipal office, the difficulty of finding competent female candidates, and the seriousness of the search for them.

On February 29, the Senate rejected the National Assembly's version of the law. Negotiations followed, which produced a bill for a second reading on March 30. On April 27, the bill was adopted by both houses; it was validated by the Constitutional Council on May 20 and proclaimed the law of the land on June 6. In the end, even its most vociferous opponents voted for the bill, boasting when it passed that France was now leading the world in promoting the equality of women and men. Thus RPR deputy Thierry Mariani: "I regret that we have to resort to law; I regret that time is so short. But I will vote for your bill in order to show my support for a better representation of women in politics."[13] A government pamphlet distributed shortly after the law passed hailed France's pathbreaking approach to the question of gender equality. "This law will accelerate the modernization of political life and reinforce democracy."[14]

The triumphal tone of the pamphlet belied the severe limits the law itself placed on the realization of the goal of equal numbers of women and men in elected assemblies. The 50/50 rule applied to candidates for office, not to the results of elections, and although this has had the important effect of opening the political field to more women than ever before, it has also permitted male politicians to protect key aspects of their power.

The law applied to different kinds of elections in different ways. France has two systems of election: proportional representation (*scrutin de liste*) and majority selection of single candidates (*scrutin majoritaire* or *scrutin uninomi-*

nal). Proportionality applies in municipal elections, regional assemblies, and the Corsican assembly, as well as to those departments with three or more Senate seats and to the selection of French delegates to the European Parliament. Parties submit lists and gain a number of seats in proportion to the votes they receive. The place one is assigned on the list thus determines who will actually hold office. Customarily, the person in the top spot (the *chef de file*) of the winning list becomes the mayor in municipal elections. Municipal, regional, and Corsican elections are decided in two rounds of voting; there is only one round for the Senate seats chosen proportionally and for the European Parliament. The remainder of the Senate and all seats in the National Assembly are chosen by *scrutin majoritaire;* here there are two rounds before a final outcome is declared. Under the law of June 6, lists are acceptable only when the candidates for the Senate and the European Parliament are alternated by sex. For municipalities with populations of more than 3500,[15] regional assemblies, and the Corsican assembly, there must be three women in each group of six candidates.[16] This retreat from strict equality was justified in a number of ways: it would make the fusion of lists in the second round of elections easier to accomplish; it was less restrictive of voter choice (though it was never clearly explained how); and it left more discretion to local party leaders, exactly those the law was meant to bring under control. In either case—strict gender alternation or groups of six—the law made it impossible to place all the women at the bottom of a list, below the anticipated cutoff for gaining a seat, but it said nothing about the need to place women at the top of the list, thereby putting them in line for leadership positions. Regarding single candidacies (for the National Assembly and part of the Senate), the law was less forceful. It deprived a portion of government stipends to those parties in which the difference between the total numbers of male and female candidates in the entire nation was more than 2% in the first round. But (as critics pointed out), since there was no penalty for the final outcome of the elections, parties could simply designate female candidates for seats they knew they would lose.[17] The law did not apply at all to cantonal elections (cantons are administrative units responsible for the maintenance of roads, transport, and other infrastructures, as well as certain allocations for schools), which are considered "the breeding ground for all major national elections" and where women are notoriously scarce.[18]

Overall, it can be said that the law of June 6 was most effective for elections where proportional representation prevailed and where power was thought least likely to be threatened. Its provisions did give women greater access to municipal and regional councils and to seats in the European Parliament, positions which, while powerful, were far less so than those in the National Assembly. The assignment of executive roles in municipal and regional councils—where power was thought to reside—was not covered by the law. At the national level, the highest realm of power, where representatives are chosen by majority vote, there was nothing to prevent the parties from running women candidates where they had no chance of winning; and—as we shall see—the financial penalty was not serious enough to force the largest parties to comply with the letter of the law. In addition, the law did not anticipate the inventiveness of politicians who, while seeming to comply with its letter, violated its spirit in order to hold on to their seats. As one set of elections followed another—municipal, senatorial, legislative, regional, and for the European Parliament—the weaknesses of the law became increasingly evident, and the initial euphoria with which many supporters of parité had greeted its passage was replaced by skepticism, if not about the power of law in general, then about the effectiveness of this law in particular.

APPLICATIONS OF THE LAW OF JUNE 6

The elections held since passage of the law show a clear distinction between the systems of proportional and majority election, but even where proportional representation prevails and women fare better, lines of power have been clearly drawn.

Municipal Elections, March 2001

As early as January 2001, newspapers began reporting on preparations for the March municipal elections—the first test of the new law. The machinations of party leaders, the jockeying for position by women, the calculations of politicians, and the small dramas enacted locally all provided readers with a steady diet of information about women's experience in politics. *Le Monde* ran a regular column called "Place aux femmes," filled with details of this kind; other newspapers offered periodic features about the new generation of aspirants to positions as municipal councilors.

Officially, party leaders accepted the need to comply with the law. In a poll conducted by the Observatoire de la parité, 76% of those heading lists for the municipal elections in communes of over 3500 inhabitants said they approved of the law.[19] Contrary to the prediction of skeptics, there was no shortage of women available to run for office.[20] Indeed, women expressed a great deal of enthusiasm for the possibilities the law opened to them, and many acknowledged their previous hostility. "I was opposed to parité, I found the law to be misogynist and protectionist; but now I understand it," reported Hélène Fraisse-Colcombet, who credited the new law with her position as number two on a UDF list in Lyon's second arrondissement.[21] PS candidate Martine Bonvicini, fifth on a list (Gauche plurielle) in the department of the Aisne, confessed that she once thought the law "devalued" women. Now she believed otherwise: "I realize that the reform speeds things up. Would I have run without this law? I'm not sure."[22]

It was not simply that the law invited them to present themselves for office, but that it forced the hand of recalcitrant local leaders who had long opposed women's participation. The existence of the law emboldened women to press for inclusion on party lists and to volunteer themselves when leaders announced they could not find any female candidates. Among women in conservative parties who had long struggled with the reticence of their leadership even to endorse the principle of equality, one political scientist noted that "the activists 'appropriated' the concept of parité in order to take a kind of revenge on their own party apparatus."[23] Dinners were held by party women to plan strategy; classes were proposed to prepare women for public speaking; and those with some experience gave advice about how women could best market themselves as candidates.[24] In some cities, there were ugly fights about placement on party lists because men who had been previously guaranteed seats on municipal councils were furious about women gaining priority over them. A group of young men in the PS protested in May 2001 that priority given to women would prevent a whole new cohort (of men) from advancing in the party. Positing gender against generation, they argued that "the historic exclusion women were subject to for so many years doesn't justify supplanting . . . new generations of men. We won't accept a system that pits women against the younger generation."[25] Negotiations were tense, but the party leadership held to the rules.[26] Men displaced by women threatened to quit politics altogether, but they were a minority; most sought other local offices or joined dissident lists, thereby fracturing party unity in particular localities.[27]

The determination of women to benefit from the law was evident even in tiny villages, where the law did not apply. A report from Blésignac, a village of 250 in the Gironde, told of a woman who had long struggled with the presiding mayor. Twice she had quit the municipal council because of difficulties with him. When he announced in 2001 that he could not find any women for his list, she offered herself. He declined her offer, so she joined with five other women and filed an all-female list in opposition to his.[28] In Chamarande (population 1026) in the Essone, there was also an all-female list, not because of "exclusively women's demands," but because the women felt that men tended to monopolize affairs and never took seriously the women's solutions to pressing economic problems.[29]

In the midst of these expressions of women's determination to take advantage of the new law were equally strong expressions of men's determination to minimize its impact. As the struggle over positions on lists developed, sitting mayors made it clear that they would allow women to go only so far: women might be chosen as municipal councillors but not as mayors or deputy mayors. Customarily, the head of the winning list automatically became the mayor (by a vote of the new municipal council), and those just below him his deputies, but nothing in the law required that this custom be followed. And some reigning mayors, displaced from first position on a list, announced their intention to violate customary practice. This was the case in the thirteenth arrondissement in Paris, where a coalition of right-wing parties decided that the incumbent mayor, Jacques Toubon, a former minister of justice, would be listed second to Françoise Forette. Forette, a professor of medicine, was not a card-carrying party member; she was dubbed a representative of "civil society" by the leadership—a concession to the general mood as well as to the law. According to the press account, Toubon vehemently protested his demotion and accepted second place only on condition that, if the slate won, he'd be mayor again. "I will direct [*dirigerai*] the united list, which will be headed [*conduite*] by Françoise Forette in first position. . . . If the results of the election are favorable, I will once again be the mayor of the thirteenth arrondissement." The reporter noted wryly that "one heads, the other directs." But Forette said she did not object to this arrangement; Toubon was the experienced politician, after all. In many other towns, women were rarely placed at the head of a list; indeed, many were in the bottom three positions of each group of six, ensuring that few could even aspire to the position of mayor. On the eve of the election, women of both right and left agreed that women mayors were an unlikely outcome. Colette Cauvigné-Bourland, affiliated with the local UDF in Chartres, told a reporter she doubted that many women would be chosen as mayors. And Colette Bonnet of the feminist group Elles aussi predicted, "The number of deputy mayors and first deputies will increase. But women mayors? That will come later."[30] This despite a poll (taken in January 2001) that showed that 66% of women and 63% of men had no objection to female mayors.[31] As the outcome of the elections would demonstrate (women constituted 47.5% of municipal councillors and only 6.9% of mayors in towns of 3500 or more), the choice of mayors— and, it turned out, contrary to Bonnet's prediction, deputy mayors as well— was not up to the general electorate but to the men who ran local party affairs.[32]

These men had other ways of maintaining control as well. Some used women as bargaining chips with groups who sought inclusion on a party list, in this way protecting the positions of male party stalwarts. One example of this came from the eleventh arrondissement in Paris, where the united left parties (the Gauche plurielle) wanted to include a representative from an organization of North Africans. In negotiations they made it clear they hoped to kill two birds with one stone. The leader of the North African group was told, "It's fine if your group is represented on our list, but we need a woman. Don't you have a *beurette?*"[33] In Auxerre, a candidate attributed her inclusion on the list to the many bases her presence could cover. "I arrived at an opportune time . . . , as a woman, . . . as a member of the PS, and as a black of African origin. . . . Instead of having several people, they had one and that cost fewer places."[34] In some towns, the leadership turned to women who would be proxies for them: wives, lovers, widows of local notables (what one critic of the practice called "conjugal parité"); in some cases these women ran under their maiden names to disguise their connection to powerful men.[35] Other party leaders preferred novices to experienced political women because they would be dependent on the men's expertise. On the one hand, they were a sign of the party's commitment to modernity, on the other, they were thought to be malleable and dependent—not politicians but just women in political office. A PS leader told a team of sociologists following the election in Auxerre: "It's I who enlist them, and no one challenges me, at least not those people from 'civil society.' Since they don't have political experience, they have a personal attachment to me, which means I'm their reference in the political realm. There's an immediate understanding established between them and me."[36] The research on Auxerre showed that while the newcomers enjoyed a great deal of public attention and were used for such things as door-to-door campaigning (the difference of sex here was a resource, drawing curiosity and interest from voters, and it could be used to signal a party's openness to civil society), they had little access to the backroom meetings, where strategies were mapped and favors exchanged. A seasoned politician explained to an interviewer: "On the practical level, for the last six months now, I've sort of initiated and trained them, but not for the game of politics, that's something else."[37]

Media coverage of the election campaign, although it reported some of the local conflicts, provided a far rosier picture of what was going on, emphasizing the sheer novelty of women's presence and its implications for the future. Newspapers ran whole pages with pictures of the candidates, noting the diversity among them and their relative youth—signs of hope for a rejuvenated politics. The cover of the business weekly, *Le Point,* heralded "the flood of women." On an inside page, a reporter cited Jospin's characterization of the imminent arrival of thousands of women municipal councillors as "a gentle and democratic revolution" and went on to announce the dawn of a new era in French politics.[38] (It's hard not to hear, in words like "gentle," an allusion to the difference of femininity.) Once denounced as a foreign (American) import, parité had become, for the media, a new feature of a uniquely French way of doing politics.[39]

The campaign generated great interest and even excitement when the outcome of the elections on March 11 and 18 was announced. When the vote was counted, some 38,000 women held 47.5% of all municipal council seats in towns with more than 3500 residents, nearly doubling their previous representation. In 1995, women had made up only 25.7% of the municipal councillors in these towns. The effects of the law were also evident in municipalities with fewer than 3500 inhabitants, where the law did not apply; now 30.5% of the municipal councillors in these towns were women, as opposed to 21% in 1995. As predicted, there was scant increase in the number selected as mayors; only 6.9% of towns of more than 3500 named women as mayors. In towns with populations under 3500, the increase was greater: 11.2% in 2001 as compared to 7.8% in 1995.[40] If the need for a parité law was in doubt, the cantonal elections, held at the same time, proved its importance. In those elections (where half the assembly is chosen every three years), parité did not apply, and there was little change in the number of women elected. Although a greater number of women ran for these seats than in the past (20.1% as opposed to 15.1% in 1998), the proportion elected increased only slightly, from 8.3% in 1998 to 9.4% in 2001.[41]

The greater success of right-wing parties in the municipal election led some on the left to conclude that the promised reform of politics was a failure. But for other commentators the profiles of the new councillors suggested otherwise: an opening to a new constituency, new blood in an old system. The women elected were, on average, younger than the men and not already cogs in the party machinery; many had no formal party affiliation. Housewives or women "sans profession" accounted for some 15% of the newly elected; 13% were teachers; and of students elected, twice as many were female as male. The head of the Observatoire de la parité noted that the gender outcome of the election varied little from town to town, a sign that the rules for drawing up lists had been respected by the party leadership. The secretary of state for the rights of women declared victory: "The fact that a large portion of the women elected have no party affiliation is a sign of renewal."[42]

But sheer numbers did not necessarily mean renewal, and lack of party affiliation could be a sign of weakness as well as strength. Executive power remained in male hands. With only a few exceptions (Paris, Rennes, and Strasbourg) the new mayors chose men as their deputies. "The distribution of deputy mayor positions" commented Gaspard, "is far from *paritaire*."[43] Moreover, the new

councillors received assignments that tended to correspond to gender stereotypes—women were put in charge of more "domestic" concerns: education,
the aged, public health, and cultural affairs; while men dealt with such matters
as finance, sports, construction, and roads.[44] The presence of large numbers of
"new" women was undoubtedly an achievement, but the division of labor resembled that of a couple; men were still *chefs de famille.*

Regional Elections, March 2004, and Elections
to the European Parliament, June 2004

The regional elections and those for the European Parliament, the last elections of any kind to be held until 2007, confirm the pattern for proportional
elections under the parité law: an important increase in female candidates and
in their election to council seats, accompanied by determined and successful
efforts by men to preserve the most powerful places for themselves. In the case
of the European elections, a new law that chooses deputies on a regional rather
than a national basis increases the probability that men will be elected, even
when the lists for each region are *paritaire.*

There was more access for women to seats on regional councils than there
had been for municipal councils, the result of a law passed in April 2003 that
required strict alternation of men and women on electoral lists for regional elections.[45] The lists are drawn up by department, but each party designates one
head of the list for the entire region; it is that person's face that adorns campaign
posters, that person's name that voters identify with a list. Seats on the regional
council are allotted proportionally according to the totals received by the parties. For these contests in 2004, as in the municipal elections of 2001, there was
a sharp distinction between council seats and positions of power. Even though,
after the election of March 2004, the regional councils were hailed as "the most
feminized assemblies in France," the leadership of the councils remained overwhelmingly male.[46] The proportion of women had nearly doubled, from 27.5%
in 1998 to 47.6%, but the presidencies of these councils—allotted to whoever
was at the head of the list—showed no similar evolution. Vice-presidencies too
were chosen among the (typically male) heads of department lists. The two
leading parties—the UMP (the umbrella party for the right) and the PS—designated only one woman on their lists as *chef de file;* other parties did somewhat
better. Women were heads of lists for 4 of 21 regions for the UDF and 4 of 18
for the National Front. Only the joint list of two small left-wing parties, Lutte
ouvrière and la Ligue communiste, achieved parité for heads of lists.[47] After
the election, in all of France just one woman presided over a regional council,

the socialist Ségolène Royal. The fact that she triumphed over the party of the sitting prime minister, Jean-Pierre Raffarin, led to talk among socialists of her possible candidacy for the presidency.[48]

Cantonal elections were held at the same time as the regionals, but in 2004 they were not governed by the parité law. The positive effects of the law, however, though attenuated, were evident when the results of these elections were compared to the regionals. In the cantonal races only 21.5% of the candidates and a mere 10.9% of those elected were women. Only three out of a hundred general councils are presided over by women. Arlette Arnaud-Landau, who had managed, as a socialist, to become mayor in the conservative town of Puy-en-Velay in 2001, and who headed her department's list in the regional elections and so became vice-president of her regional council, attributed her success to the parité law. In contrast, she said, the cantonal elections had yielded only one woman—and this for the first time—on the Conseil général of the Haute-Loire. "We might regret it, but we need tools like the parité law to put women in politics," she noted.[49]

As elections for the European Parliament approached in the spring of 2004, feminists warned that a new way of voting would weaken the potential impact of the parité law. Until 2004, each party had presented one list that was voted on by all of France. In 2004, however, the nation was divided into eight electoral districts, each of which was allocated a certain number of deputies to elect. The decentralization and the multiplication of districts increased the number of lists presented and hence the likelihood that only the top names on a list would win seats. With men likely to head most lists and an uneven number of deputies to be selected, the outcome would favor men, one women's group argued, leading to a decreased percentage of women in the French delegation. In fact, the results turned out to be better than anticipated, though not as good as they would have been had the single national district been retained. In 2004, about one-third of the heads of party lists were women. After the voting, of the 78 seats to be filled, 34 are now held by women, representing 43.5% of the delegation—a small gain over the 40.3% held by women in 1999 before passage of the parité law.[50] In these elections, the splitting of electoral districts certainly helped reduce the impact of parité.

Senate Elections, September 2001

The Senate elections, conducted by *scrutin de liste* as well as *scrutin majoritaire,* offer confirmation that while proportional representation (when following the rules of the parité law) favors women, it offers no guarantee of equality.

There are two methods of voting for the Senate. In 2001, contests in districts with three or more senate seats at stake were decided proportionally (*scrutin de liste*); parties had to present lists that were strictly *paritaire* (alternating men and women). In the remaining districts, candidates ran as individuals; whoever gained a majority of votes was the winner (*scrutin majoritaire*). Parité's effect on the outcome of these different systems of voting was not as great as it should have been for the 102 seats at issue. At its best, the law had an incremental effect, raising the percentage of women in the Senate from 5.9 to 10.9%[51]—a significant increase, to be sure, but not the kind of result the parité movement had hoped for. Among those whose seats were up for reelection, only 7 were women (6.9% of the total); among those elected, 22 were women (or 21.6% of the total of 102). So women were definitely added to the Senate. In districts with *scrutin majoritaire*, the showing of women was, predictably, far less impressive than in those with *scrutin de liste*, demonstrating the differential effect of the parité law—it worked better for proportional than for majority elections. Of the 28 senators elected by *scrutin majoritaire*, only 2 were women (7.14%); of the 74 elected by *scrutin de liste*, 20, or 27.03%, were women. In the latter case, however, the proportion should have been far higher, closer to 50/50 if the rules had been observed. What went wrong?

Local party leaders took advantage of a law designed by the PS to increase its own representation in the Senate, where it had not had a majority since 1958. This law extended proportional representation to districts with three or more Senate seats so as to undermine the application of the parité law (which required that every other candidate on a list be a woman).[52] Clearly, the most desirable position when few seats are at stake is to be first on the list; women were rarely in first place in Senate elections. Those men who might lose a seat by being third or fifth on a list (when women were second and fourth) formed their own lists, placing themselves in the number one position. *Le Monde* offered the department of La Manche as a good example of the subterfuge. There were three incumbents on the right in La Manche, two men and a woman, who—when they had run as single candidates—had supported one another's efforts and won, though the men were members of the RPR and the woman UDF. Proportional elections changed the picture, however, and each man formed his own list. On one of them, the incumbent woman was in the number two position, but because of the second list (and the fact that seats would be allocated proportionally, opening the way for the left to gain at least one of them), she risked losing her seat. "Until now, the three of us worked together. This time, changes in the method of voting and the parité law forced us to make separate lists," she complained, placing the blame—a reporter noted—on the laws passed by the socialists instead of on the behavior of her male colleagues.[53] The result of these maneuvers in La Manche was that the two men were re-elected, while the woman was not. On the left, too, women were rarely placed at the head of a list. François Autain, then a member of the PS, declared that "few women are credible at the head of a list." Incumbent senators refused to accept second place on the official party lists when they conformed to parité, forming new dissident lists with themselves on top. This was notably the case in the Haute-Loire, where Autain himself organized a dissident list with the Greens. In that way they defeated socialist Marie-Madeleine Dieulangard, who was in second place on the Gauche plurielle list.[54]

Commentators condemned the hypocrisy of the politicians who had voted for the parité law and then violated it in practice, but they had few concrete remedies to propose.[55] The Senate was not only a more powerful institution than a municipal council, but the relatively smaller number of seats at stake made the creation of separate lists a plausible strategy for men who wanted to protect their positions, and there was nothing in the parité law to prevent such action. Women too, of course, could put themselves at the head of a list of their own making, but they usually lacked the clout and the visibility to act inde-pendently.[56] Without some kind of party support, most often controlled by men, such a strategy would be both difficult and futile. The Senate election of 2001 thus demonstrated that proportional representation alone could not guarantee equality for women. It also showed that the parité law could go only so far with entrenched party leaders.

Legislative Elections, June 2002

The parité law was least effective in elections in which candidates were chosen by majority vote, not coincidentally those elections in which the most power-ful offices were at stake. This was demonstrated clearly in the legislative elec-tions of June 2002. The extraordinary circumstances created by the presiden-tial elections in April of that year provided a convenient rationalization for the decision of the major parties to forgo financial support for their campaigns rather than abide by the law on parité. But rationalizations aside, the election demonstrated the weakness of the law as it applied to the *scrutin majoritaire.* In these elections, in which the law stipulated that half of all candidates should be women, parties lost government funds—there were no other sanctions—if they did not comply.

The presidential election of April 2002 was characterized by a certain bore-dom on the part of the electorate: everyone assumed that the contest was be-

tween Jacques Chirac, the incumbent on the right, and Lionel Jospin, the socialist prime minister. Among the fifteen candidates in the first round were
Jean-Pierre Chevènement, who had long represented a dissenting voice within
the PS, and Jean-Marie Le Pen, the perennial candidate for the National Front.
Other candidates represented various left- and right-wing groups, and there
was much talk, especially on the left, of casting protest votes for one of the
small left-wing parties instead of voting for Jospin in the first round. On the day
of the first round of voting (April 21), abstentions hit a record high of 27.6%.[57]
Although polls had been predicting that Le Pen might attain a higher-than-
expected score, no one seemed prepared for his coming in second. But he did,
displacing Jospin as the candidate to beat in the second round, where only the
top two candidates compete. When the first-round votes were tallied, Chirac
had 19.8%, Le Pen 17.2%, and Jospin 16.3% of the votes cast.[58]

Political scientists explained Jospin's poor showing as a result of a weak
campaign, which, among other things, failed to consolidate the support of
women voters. The polls showed clearly that Jospin had lost support among
the women who had helped carry the party to victory in 1997. True, these commentators said, Jospin claimed credit for parité, but he allowed himself to be
pulled into discussions about national "insecurity"—anxieties about terrorists
and immigrants heightened by the September 11 attacks in New York City and
Washington. These were typically the issues of the right and, moreover, allowed Le Pen to set the agenda. Jospin would have been better off, some feminists insisted, if he had taken up the theme of domestic insecurity as it applied
to economic and social issues, especially those affecting women: unemployment, unequal wages, low-paying part-time jobs, and family violence.

Whether Le Pen's success was taken as an aberration or a warning about the
growing appeal of the extreme right, the sense of crisis was palpable. Journalists declared that France had been hit by "an earthquake"; students took to the
streets in huge numbers to rally support for the democratic Republic; socialists
gathered to pick up the pieces, resisting the diagnosis that this election meant
the definitive collapse of the left. Since Chirac was under investigation for corruption (and might end up convicted if not protected by presidential immu-
nity), the weekly satirical paper *Le Canard enchaîné* remarked that France had
a pitiful choice in the second round "between a crook and a fascist."[59]

As the nation prepared for the second round of elections, there was no
doubt that Chirac would receive the overwhelming number of votes. Despite
some hesitation by those living in the wreckage of the PS and some attempts
by politicians on the left to bargain for influence in exchange for support, there

was little question that the way to defeat Le Pen was to elect Chirac. That happened on May 5. Chirac's landslide of nearly 80% was a relief and taken as a confirmation of the strength of republicanism, but the fact that Le Pen won over 20% nationally (with greater strength in certain localities) was a nagging reminder of his growing populist appeal. Chirac's cabinet, named shortly after his victory, was for feminists a sign of things to come: in a government of twenty-eight there were only six women and no position dedicated to the rights or concerns of women. Moreover, the man appointed as minister of health and family, Jean-François Mattéi, was considered by the Collectif national pour les droits des femmes someone likely to put in place "a particularly moralistic and reactionary policy" on issues such as abortion.[60] So much for the spirit of parité reaching beyond the requirements of the law!

Almost as soon as the presidential election was decided, campaigns began for the legislative elections in June. The parties on the right were determined to take back the National Assembly from the socialists, their desire fanned by Chirac's overwhelming victory. The fight for the legislature between the major parties (the socialists and their allies, on the one hand, and the coalition of conservative parties—the RPR, the UDF, and others constituting the UMP, l'Union pour la majorité présidentielle, on the other) led them all to refuse to comply with the law on parité. The PS, the party most responsible for voting in the parité law, had announced in January, well before the presidential election, that it would run only 40% women among its candidates. After the disaster of the presidential election, the leadership lowered the number to 36%. The right was even more cautious: the UMP ran 19.9% women in the first round. (Among the smaller parties, which could ill afford to lose government funds, the law on parité was respected: the communists ran 44% women, while 48.9% of the candidates sponsored by the National Front were women.)[61]

Party leaders on both the left and the right tended to regard men as "natural candidates."[62] For some this meant simply that particular candidates were well-known figures, with name recognition and wide appeal. But even among newcomers, men were still preferred because they were thought more likely to win: they posed "stronger" alternatives to the National Front, they were presumed to be more familiar with the demands of national politics. When "serious" matters were at stake, it was men who must take a stand.[63] "It's more advantageous to have men elected," declared Amaury de Saint-Quentin, financial and administrative director of the RPR, "than to have women defeated."[64] This comment not only indicates that incumbents (most of whom were men) were a safer bet but also equates representation with individuality and masculinity.

The legislative elections, commented political scientist Marion Paoletti, one of the unsuccessful contenders for office, evidenced "a brutal eviction of the theme of women in politics." Both major parties followed the same practice, favoring men in winnable districts and allowing women to run where there was little chance of success. Although feminists argued that 1997 had proved women capable of winning in difficult contests and that women, for unified party slates, might be a better choice than men because they had a lesser history of conflict within political circles, the party leaders paid little heed. Sometimes the discrimination was glaring; perfectly qualified women were discounted, as happened in the UMP in the seventeenth arrondissement in Paris. There the presumptive candidacy of Françoise de Panafieu—the mayor, a former minister (one of the fired "juppettes") and deputy, and the daughter of a prominent Gaullist family—was denied in favor of Bernard Pons, the seventy-five-year-old incumbent who according to party rules ought to have retired. "If you want the reason why so few women are allowed to run, look at the committees that appoint the candidates," said Panafieu; "They are all men."[65] Some party leaders professed not to be able to "find women at the right level." Others suggested that women themselves chose not to run because "they are less interested in national politics, where the discussion is about concepts and policy."[66] It might be acceptable for women to work at the municipal level, but the big questions, the heavy work, required not just men but *hommes politiques.*

A very few women were designated candidates in recognition of their service to a party. Here the municipal elections became a stepping-stone to higher office. In Caen, for instance, the new mayor Brigitte Lebrethon, a member of the RPR, was put up for a legislative seat in recognition of the work she had done to rally votes for Chirac during the presidential campaign.[67] For those who took the long view of the effects of the law, her example was encouraging. In the short run, however, the outcome of the legislative elections was a great disappointment. The UMP trounced the socialists, and the proportion of women in the Assembly barely increased, from 10.92% in 1997 to 12.2% in 2002.

An analysis of the results by the Observatoire de la parité concluded that "it is difficult to rejoice at such weak progress," but went on to call for new measures to encourage the cooperation of party leaders.[68] To this end, the report presented figures to challenge the hypothesis that women weren't electable. Although a larger number of male than female incumbents had been reelected (68.6% as opposed to 49.1%), part of the reason was the overall loss of socialist seats, since many of the defeated women had been elected in the socialist sweep of 1997. More telling, women turned out to be more successful candidates than men in districts that shifted from right to left or from left to right. Women (perhaps perceived as agents of change) defeated men in 35.2% of such upsets, whereas men defeated women in only 26.3%. But the report also concluded that facts alone would not convince unwilling politicians to change their minds. These men justified their desire to maintain power by alleging the lesser capacity of women to represent the nation. Although proportional elections clearly favored women, it was politically impossible to adopt this system for legislative elections. Instead, the Observatoire recommended strengthening the law by increasing financial penalties to the point where they would be punitive for the major parties. The Observatoire suggested as well that the system by which each deputy had a substitute in the assembly might be changed to require that the substitute be of the opposite sex to that of the deputy, thus increasing the visible presence of women on electoral lists but—I would add— also running the risk of confirming the "couple" image of women and men in political office.[69] And there was a call to promote a "culture of parité," not only within the parties (where "a more equitable distribution of leadership positions in political parties is desirable" and where adjustment of meeting times and the provision of child care might take the demands of "daily life" into account), but in the society at large. If the economic and social inequalities between the sexes were addressed (differential rates of unemployment, unequal wages, glass ceilings in the corporate and professional worlds), more women might contemplate holding political office at some point in their lives. Here was an implicit recognition that the law alone—this law at least—could not alter the gender balance of power as its proponents had predicted it would.[70]

The immediate lesson of the legislative elections was that the law of June 2000 had not gone very far in solving the "crisis of representation" that it was meant to address. The profile of women candidates revealed greater social diversity than that of the men; women were teachers, professionals, and private-sector employees, whereas men were public-sector employees or worked in commerce, industry, and agriculture. Men were twice as likely as women to already hold some other elective office; they were, on average, older than the women. The failure of most of the "new women" to gain office confirmed that the rule of the *hommes politiques* remained in place.[71] Both as representatives of civil society and as women, the female candidates had been blocked. At the highest levels of political officeholding, the parties continued to operate as closed systems, run by a caste of powerful men. France still ranks very low (sixty-eighth, when compared with other nations) in terms of women's presence in national elective bodies.

PROPOSALS TO STRENGTHEN THE LAW OF JUNE 6

As election after election unfolded and the limits of the law became clear, the government body charged with its surveillance sought suggestions for improvements. In the interest of making practice come closer to principle, of encouraging political parties to respect the constitution and act in "the spirit of the law," the Observatoire de la parité solicited recommendations and comments from a number of groups in France, including the various party leaderships during 2003. The discussion was far-ranging and often self-interested, as when Jean-Marie Le Pen recommended, in the name of parité, that legislative elections be decided proportionally.[72] (His aim, of course, was to win seats for his party, not to promote the equality of women.) There were suggestions for improving the working of the law: for example, including requiring that the mayor and executive committees in municipalities be chosen according to their place on the ballot; extending the law to cantonal elections; resisting any changes that adversely affected women's chances of being elected; and adding a financial incentive for those parties that did comply with parité in the legislative elections. The jurist Guy Carcassonne proposed taking the money forfeited by parties that did not offer 50% women candidates and giving it to those parties that did. "In our experience, while political parties are, in the end, not touched by financial penalties, especially modest ones, they will react very negatively to the idea that the money they lost has gone to their competitors."[73] He and others also proposed a financial reward to those parties whose election results came close to parité. Some of the speakers offered specific plans for the recruitment and training of women politicians.

The overwhelming sense one gets from reading the Observatoire's report is that the process of full implementation will be slow and will demand the commitment of at least some politicians. Attention to procedures, to the implications of proposed changes in electoral laws, and to winning—or forcing—cooperation from recalcitrant politicians is not exciting, and a monitoring institution like the Observatoire de la parité can only recommend, but not require, reforms. If the parité law is to achieve its full impact, it must be used as a tool to gradually extract concessions from the politically powerful. This means ongoing attention to the details of its enforcement—from "inside" organs like the Observatoire and from feminists on the "outside" who can bring pressure to bear by mobilizing public opinion when equality is threatened or too slowly achieved. The obvious leadership for such an effort would be the new political women, those who have directly benefited from the law. But their situation is difficult because playing the "woman" card could undermine what legitimacy they have, compromising their need to demonstrate that they are not mere women but politicians just as much as the men.

IDENTITY AS A WOMAN: ASSET OR LIABILITY?

If the goal of the paritaristes was to remove considerations of sex from the choice of representatives, the initial effect of the parité law—inevitably—was to emphasize it. In this, the law operated as does any antidiscrimination or affirmative-action law, drawing positive attention to those whose difference has previously led to their exclusion. The election campaigns that followed passage of the law demonstrated all the difficulties of correcting discrimination: there is no way to do it that avoids calling attention to difference and so reproducing the very terms one wants to displace. Were female candidates women or politicians? Could women be politicians? Were they different or the same as *hommes politiques?* Questions of this kind were raised implicitly (and sometimes explicitly) in the course of the campaigns.

Women who were candidates found themselves facing a double bind—one incisively described by political scientist and PS member Marion Paoletti, who ran unsuccessfully in the legislative elections of 2002. Invoking her identity as a woman (and a mother) was a definite asset for campaigning under the parité law, she reported, but not for establishing one's seriousness within party circles. Unlike her male colleagues, who seemed under no pressure to declare their masculinity, "women candidates in the context of 2002 were enjoined, tacitly and collectively, to be women." Yet "if one has to be a woman, it's at the risk of not being political."[74] The old problem of the nonabstractablity of women's sexual difference remained. On the campaign trail, femininity was a strategic resource. Often Paoletti was advised to wear makeup and cultivate a more feminine look. "Your body is a weapon," one (female) colleague told her. Within the party, however, such behavior could become a liability. Charm (a female attribute) had nothing to do with charisma (ascribed to men), and the line was thin between exploiting one's gender and using sex to advance a political career, "as if only women engaged in seduction."[75] The attention called to her identity as a woman, Paoletti thought, could serve to naturalize that identity, reinforcing social stereotypes and casting her as dependent on more powerful men. The figure of the political woman, she noted, was at best "ambiguous" but, I would add, for that reason potentially disruptive of the very stereotypes she sought to avoid.

Roselyne Bachelot's campaign during these same legislative elections exemplifies the ambiguity of the political woman, but in a different way. A long-

standing member of the RPR, a deputy since 1988, with an impressive political pedigree, Bachelot did not "play the gender card" directly in the 2002 legislative campaign, as Paoletti did.[76] Instead, like any male candidate, Bachelot
dwelled on issues of concern to her constituents. Although she was known nationally for her dissenting positions within her party (in support of the PaCS,
for example, and of feminist goals as the first head of the Observatoire), she did
not capitalize on them when she spoke at local meetings. But those positions did
contribute to the image of her as a person of courage and integrity. She was atypical, not a party hack, and there may have been some implicit resonance here
with the fact that she was a woman; she turned her difference into a matter of
actions and positions, not of sex. In the election of 2002, say two political scientists who followed her campaign, Bachelot simply had more political and
cultural capital than her eleven rivals, of whom five were women. Indeed, the
fact of so many women running (a direct result of the parité law) had the effect
of "banalizing" any appeal to her identity as a woman; it wasn't as a woman that
she was distinctive, it was by virtue of her deep knowledge of local issues and
her long national experience.[77] Still, Pierre Leroux and Philippe Teillet note
the complexity of Bachelot's strategy, which, they say, oscillated between eclips-
ing the relevance of her identity as a woman and exploiting it, if only indirectly.
The risk she apparently wanted to avoid is, they conclude, a "permanent" one
for women: "to be reminded of their illegitimacy in the political sphere."[78]

The question is, how permanent? Is Bachelot's need constantly to prove
her legitimacy? Is Paoletti's evident discomfort at the traps of claiming identity as a woman the fate of political women? Only if one assumes that male mo-
nopolies of power are eternal; only if one assumes that masculinity will forever
remain a defining feature of political space. Leroux and Teillet point out that
it would be premature to come to those conclusions: "The entry of women
into politics cannot lead to a total and immediate transformation of the values
of a world that continues to be strongly marked by the practical and cultural
consequences of a long history of masculine monopoly."[79] Paoletti attributes
some of the problem to the parité law itself—"It's at best a fragile resource"—
but no law could instantly transform a situation in which gender and power
have for so long been intertwined.[80]

At this point, it is the unraveling of the connection between masculinity and
politics that is interesting to watch. The parité law has introduced confusion
and consternation into the political field. There are the defensive reactions of
men to an unprecedented invasion of women, reactions that rely upon the deployment of stereotypes, insults, and—as we have seen in this chapter—established power in order to alter the law or hinder its application. There are, in

contrast (rarer, but still important) politicians' endorsements of women's capability that reflect exactly the desymbolization the paritaristes had in mind. The mayor of Rennes, for example, insisted in an interview that men and women shared many problems and outlooks. "Personally, I'm very committed to listening [to my constituents]. A woman isn't the only one who does that. She's a citizen, she ought to be interested in everyone. I'm against instrumentalization. One does politics as a citizen and that's it."[81] There are also the confused responses of political women, who face new and complex strategic decisions and whose choices vary. If being identified as a woman runs the risk of being thought of solely in essentialist terms, practical involvement in politics fractures any sense of a singular, coherent identity for *femmes politiques.* Paoletti describes, for example, the ambivalence of younger women, new to the PS, toward the intervention of feminist women's committees on their behalf (and her own ambivalence to their rejection of feminism). While some welcomed the support as a sign of women's solidarity, others refused any such collective identification. "I don't agree with the story that women do a different kind of politics. That's not it. We do politics the same way," commented a twenty-four-year-old candidate for the cantonal elections in 2001. Another, an elected municipal councillor, echoed this view. "I don't see it. A women's commission bothers me. There's no men's commission."[82] In Rennes, a woman running for a municipal council seat on the Lutte ouvrière ticket (she was a long-time political militant) insisted that in all her years in politics, she'd seen more similarities than differences between women and men. "In my political milieu I see women and men, and they're exactly the same. I see as much aggression on the part of women as of men; I don't see a difference. . . . There aren't a whole lot of different ways of doing politics."[83] There is, too, a shared concern on the part of some women about the difficulties of contesting established power. Commented one woman, who had served on both regional and municipal councils, "On a municipal council there are relations of power; relations with male colleagues are so difficult! I couldn't have imagined it before. . . . Things are in the process of changing because of parité, but it's still very hard. You have to prove you're not necessarily stupid. . . . It's a power relationship, and women don't much like those relationships."[84] But there is also evidence of a renewed determination to learn the ropes, an aspiration to a certain "professionalization." "I want to say that women are different at the outset. But I'm not sure that at the end of three terms we'll still be taking the floor only when we have something to say. I'm not sure. Because the parties will see to it that we're integrated into the world of influence and alliances."[85]

In sharp contrast to the perturbation of the political field is the surprising ease with which voters have accepted the law, despite media coverage that plays on and appeals to gender stereotypes. In a poll in March 2004, for example, fully 70% of respondents thought that the numbers of women in politics ought to increase.[86] This kind of popular support is, in itself, a remarkable testament to the impact of the parité movement on popular opinion beyond the political field. There is, too, a new self-consciousness about the underrepresentation of women in sports, business, academia, and elsewhere. A committee consisting overwhelmingly of men is often criticized by a member of the group itself, and the presence of equal numbers of women and men is a reason for congratulation. The media tend now to give more time to women in sports and politics than in the past. Gender equality has become—because of the law—a principled position. And even if sometimes contravened in practice, the principle of equal access to elective office remains in place, providing the reference point for years of political struggle that lie ahead. For all its limitations, the parité law has achieved something of what its proponents hoped for: the exposure of the injustices of discrimination and a long-term potential for the renewal of political life.

There was considerable distance between the original conception of parité and the law that was passed in its name. The distance had to do both with meaning and time. The paritaristes wanted to make the difference of sex susceptible to abstraction as a way of insisting that women, like men, were individuals. The point was to rid political representation of the symbols of sexual difference and so to fully include women in the figure of the universal. Maintaining the distinction between anatomical duality and sexual difference proved extremely difficult, however, because references to abstract sexed bodies could not be fully detached from the concrete social and historical meanings attributed to them; individuals with female bodies were, it seemed, always "women," always had been, and always would be.[1] To add to this difficulty, history intervened: the theoretical ground for parité was preempted during the debates over the PaCS. In the hands of Sylviane Agacinski, abstraction was abandoned, and the heterosexual couple was substituted for the abstract individual as the universal unit of political representation. The constitutional reforms of 1999 and the law implementing them in June 2000 reflected her reasoning. As a result, they resembled the kinds of antidiscrimination measures that the founders of the parité movement had hoped to improve on. Women were granted access to elective office not as individuals but as women; their access was uneven, decreasing as the power of the office increased; those politicians who subverted or resisted application of the law did so by reasserting the inevitability of prevailing gender arrangements. So is this the end of the story?

Some of the reflection on parité suggests that it is. For an early supporter, Monique Dental, the law does nothing to achieve equality in the composition of elective assemblies; therefore it is insufficient as "a real stimulus to a social transformation that will lead to a redefinition of the relations between private and public life."[2] Even if large numbers of women are eventually admitted, political scientist Mariette Sineau adds, it will only be after the "devaluation of the sphere of politics and its desertion by men."[3] Real power, in this view, will always elude women. If they gain it at the level of the National Assembly, it will be because that body has lost its standing, and power has come to reside in the office of the president. The law is also faulted for having neglected social and economic inequalities between women and men. According to two political scientists, "at each stage of the decade-long mobilization, the larger politics of representation worked to narrow the meaning of equality to the political and to silence claims seeking redress of other types of discrimination and other forms of inequality, whether social or economic."[4] In addition, parité has been accused, if not of racism, then of "failing to take differences among women into account."[5] "The voices of immigrant women," one commentator notes, "were almost entirely absent from the public debates leading to the parity law."[6] For some of its critics, the movement's conscious refusal to substitute pluralist visions of democracy for French republicanism's insistence on unity represented a lost opportunity, a concession to the very terms that had for so long marginalized women in politics. Instead of contributing to the fall of a republic in crisis, parité "became an instrument for rescuing the liberal democratic institutions of France."[7]

These critiques are doubly ahistorical. They neglect the history of the movement itself, the complexities of which I have tried to delineate in these pages. And they fail to take into account the way events such as the adoption of laws achieve their effects. The law, as the first paritaristes insisted, is an instrument for change; as such, its long-term impact cannot be deduced from its short-term applications. Similarly, there is no neat correlation between strategic interventions and their outcomes. That the parité movement operated within the principles of French republicanism does not mean it simply reproduced them; iteration, as philosophers have told us and political activists constantly demonstrate, need not be conservative, it can also be transformative.[8]

The call for parité was a strategic intervention at a moment of crisis for the French republic, a moment that has by no means ended. In response to challenges from organized groups (of North African "immigrants," of homosexuals, and others) who wanted their differences to be not assimilated but recognized, and to the pressures of globalization and Europeanization, government spokesmen and public intellectuals forcefully reasserted the universalist principles of abstract individualism, insisting that they were not only the hallmark of French republicanism but vital to the preservation of the integrity of the nation. The founders of the parité movement accepted these principles and at the same time challenged them, by insisting that difference—the difference of sex—was compatible with abstraction. Their effort combined appeals to political theory with pragmatic efforts to pass a law that would impose new rules on politicians and political parties. To the extent that they were successful, the paritaristes showed that the notion of the abstract individual was compatible with a difference until then considered irreducible. To the extent that they failed, they exposed the inadequacies (indeed the particularities) of French universalism and the centuries-old bond between national sovereignty and established understandings of sexual difference.

But it is too soon to say whether they have succeeded or failed, for conceptions such as the universal abstract individual are more likely to be changed by practical experience than by theoretical pronouncement. The slow entry of women into the political system, from the bottom up, may eventually have a desymbolizing effect, making sexual difference an irrelevant consideration for politics, and so alter the political field of force in ways we cannot yet foresee. (This was the premise of affirmative action in the United States and the experience in politics in the Scandinavian countries.)[9] The influx of large numbers of women into regional and municipal councils will surely spark the imaginations of a new generation of girls who, as Gaspard suggests, can now dream of becoming mayors of their towns.[10] (Example alone is, of course, not necessary for sparking aspiration, as, among others, Gaspard's own career—she became a mayor and a deputy long before parité—makes plain.) More important, perhaps, is that the presence of a critical mass of women has already begun to alter some of the practices associated with party cultures of masculinity. The women on the Paris municipal council, for example, pressed for different meeting hours so that all elected officials could combine their political work with household responsibilities. Some sociologists have speculated that the large numbers of newcomers may alter politics even more, substituting a certain amateurism—and thus a voice for "civil society"—for the caste of professional politicians who have long dominated French political life.

> What's at stake here is not to celebrate a return to amateurist values, the primal vector of which would be the influence of the feminine. We know how the opposition between professional and amateur has been used, historically and socially, in struggles for the devolution and legitimation of political power. It's rather a matter of floating the hypothesis of a sexually differentiated understanding of political temporality. To the extent

that women introduce the possibility for a new amateurism in politics, one that doesn't turn a term in office into a political career, they might introduce . . . friction into the fragile mechanism of the professionalization of politics.[11]

There are other possibilities as well: local councils can become the first step in national political careers for women whose ambition is now aided by the parité law. The law is effective in this way both in its actual provisions and because it has forced gender discrimination out into the open, where it can be tracked and publicized by government oversight commissions and political activists. In the long term, the presence of large numbers of women at all levels of politics (most analysts agree that 30% should be the minimum) may indeed make considerations of their sex less relevant; at that point, politicians will be regarded as individuals, male or female, whose differences are ideological and programmatic, not sexual. If this prediction is too utopian, it can at least be said that although tensions between abstraction and embodiment are bound to persist in some way, they will diminish significantly in the arena of politics—not because sexual difference has disappeared as an object of social identification, but because sex will have been thoroughly desymbolized for purposes of politics. To put it simply, stereotypes of gender will no longer matter in the selection of representatives.[12]

The paritaristes viewed the law as a tool that could do the work of desymbolization. It would take time for a new order to come into being, for change initiated by a law was a slow and often imperceptible process. Nevertheless, whatever its form, once the transformation had occurred it would seem inevitable, a reflection of the nature of things. Claude Servan-Schreiber put it eloquently in an address to a gathering of women in 1994.

> I will end by recalling that the rights of women, all the rights obtained in the course of history, have arisen from struggles that ended with the inscription of these rights into law. Today, those rights seem to us to be self-evident: we have forgotten, fifty years after the institution of universal suffrage, that for many, many generations, women's right to vote did not seem so self-evident, not at all. I am convinced that one day it will be said that parité was instituted by law precisely because it too was "self-evident."[13]

Should Servan-Schreiber be right, then women will someday be treated, at least in the realm of political representation, as equally susceptible to abstraction as men are, as universal individuals capable of representing the nation. When that occurs, universalism might be said to prevail. Of course, this will not be the end of exclusions, for it is as likely that something other than the difference of sex will come to incarnate universalism's antithesis, its "obscene underside."[14] Universalism gains its meaning by contrast to particularism, to some category that is said to permanently resist abstraction. (Islam is already in that position—as the struggle over girls' head scarves in public schools indicates—and much more powerfully so now than in the past.)

To project this outcome, of course, requires thinking that universalism, as mythologized in the 1990s, will remain in place indefinitely, defined as the very essence of French republicanism, and so set the rules of political engagement. It is not at all clear that this will be the case. The battle for parité, as for the PaCS and for the rights of North Africans to be accepted as fully French, can also be seen as a set of pressures for the democratization of French political life. This democratization would involve not the abstraction of difference but its recognition, thus a more pluralistic vision in which the universal would be figured as a mosaic. Some supporters of the parité movement predicted that it would open a Pandora's box in relation to minority representation because it addressed concrete issues of social injustice. Law professors Eric Millard and Laure Ortiz, for example, argued that parité's goals of restructuring relations of power moved the issue from the abstract political to the concrete cause of real social actors. "In placing itself on this terrain, parité becomes totally corrosive for the republican model of representation. It forces consideration of the real social position of political protagonists and of the logic of the social relations that undergirds their position."[15]

The architects of the parité movement saw no contradiction between the concrete goal of social justice and their insistence on abstraction. They were firmly committed to universalism and to the idea that abstraction was the key to equality; they believed that women could become part of the universal rather than remain antithetical to it. The possibilities for democracy, they believed, were best realized through their version of abstract individualism. But the questions for the long term are whether the implementation of parité will affect the workings of democracy in any way beyond the gradual increase in access for women to public office, and how that increase will be achieved. These questions can only be answered in the years to come. I end, then, on an inconclusive note, for the story of parité awaits its conclusion not in the speculations of philosophers but in the contingencies of history.

NOTES

INTRODUCTION

1. Belgium also had a law that imposed quotas but now has raised them to 50%, and Italy had a parity law briefly, until it was annulled. For comprehensive information, see "Electoral Quotas for Women" on International IDEA and Stockholm University's Department of Political Science Web site, www.quotaproject.org or www.idea.int/quota.

2. *La parité entre les femmes et les hommes à portée de main* (Observatoire de la parité entre les femmes et les hommes, September 2000).

3. "Frenchwomen Say it's Time to be 'a bit Utopian,'" *New York Times,* December 31, 1993.

4. Joan W. Scott, *Only Paradoxes to Offer: French Feminists and the Rights of Man* (Cambridge: Harvard University Press, 1996).

5. For a particularly astute discussion of US/French contrasts see Eric Fassin, "L'épouvantail américain: Penser la discrimination française," *Vacarme,* nos. 4 and 5 (September–November 1997); "The Purloined Gender: American Feminism in a French Mirror," *French Historical Studies* 22 (Winter 1999): 113–38; and "Du multiculturalisme à la discrimination," *Le Débat,* no. 97 (November–December 1997): 131–36.

6. Naomi Schor, "French Feminism is a Universalism," in Schor, *Bad Objects: Essays Popular and Unpopular* (Durham: Duke University Press, 1995), p. 17.

7. Clifford Geertz, "The World in Pieces: Culture and Politics at the End of the Century," in Geertz, *Available Light* (Princeton: Princeton University Press, 2000), pp. 218–64; and "What Is a State If It Is Not a Sovereign? Reflections on Politics in Complicated Places," *Current Anthropology* 45 (December 2004): 584.

CHAPTER ONE

1. Hubertine Auclert, "Programme électoral des femmes," *La citoyenne,* August 1885, cited in *Hubertine Auclert: La citoyenne 1848–1914,* ed. Edith Taïeb (Paris: Syros 1982), p. 41.

2. Cited in William Guéraiche, *Les femmes et la république: Essai sur la répartition du pouvoir de 1943 à 1979* (Paris: Les Editions de l'Atelier/Editions Ouvrières, 1999), p. 43. See also the deliberations of the provisional assembly: *Débats de l'Assemblée consultative provisoire, 3* vols. (Paris: Imprimerie des journaux officiels, 1943–45).

3. In the National Assembly, the figure fell from a high of 6.8% in 1946 to 1.5% in 1958—the first Assembly of the Fifth Republic. It rose to 3.7% in 1978 and then, with the election of Mitterrand in 1981, above 5%, reaching 6% in 1993. See Jane Jenson and Mariette Sineau, *Mitterrand et les Françaises: Un rendez-vous manqué* (Paris: Presses de la Fondation nationale des sciences politiques, 1995), apps. 7 and 8, pp. 368–70.

4. Paul Friedland, *Political Actors: Representative Bodies and Theatricality in the Age of the French Revolution* (Ithaca: Cornell University Press, 2002).

5. Cited in Pierre Rosanvallon. *Le peuple introuvable: Histoire de la représentation démocratique en France* (Paris: Gallimard, 1998) pp. 48–49.

6. Maximilien Robespierre, "Sur le gouvernement représentatif," in *Robespierre: Textes choisis* (Paris: Editions Sociales, 1957), 2:142.

7. Cited by Alain Juppé in "Ouverture du débat sur la place des femmes dans la vie publique" (Assemblée nationale, March 11, 1997). Typescript of the full speech (in the personal papers of Françoise Gaspard), p. 6.

8. Chap. 1, sec. 3, art. 7 of the Constitution of 1791.

9. See Keith Michael Baker, "Representation Redefined," in *Inventing the French Revolution: Essays on French Political Culture in the Eighteenth Century,* ed. Baker (Cambridge: Cambridge University Press, 1990).

10. Cited in Eric Millard and Laure Ortiz, "Parité et representántions politiques," in *La Parité—Enjeux et mise en œvre,* ed. Jacqueline Martin (Toulouse: Presses universitaires du Mirail, 1998), p. 192.

11. Maximilien Robespierre, "Lettres à ses commettants," no. 2 (Spring 1973), in *Oeuvres complètes,* vol. 5 (Paris: Société des Etudes Robespierristes, 1962), p. 209.

12. Friedland, *Political Actors,* p. 12.

13. Etienne Balibar, "Ambiguous Universality," *Differences* 7 (Spring 1995): 58.

14. Jacques Rancière, "Post-Democracy, Politics and Philosophy," *Angelaki* 1, no. 3 (1994): 171–78.

15. Cited in Pierre Birnbaum, *Jewish Destinies: Citizenship, State, and Community in Modern France,* trans. Arthur Goldhammer (New York: Hill and Wang, 2000), p. 19.

16. Jean-Jacques Rousseau, *Emile, ou De l'éducation,* in *Oeuvres complètes,* vol. 4 (Paris: Gallimard 1969), book 5, p. 697.

17. Jean-Jacques Rousseau, *Lettre à d'Alembert* (Paris: Garnier-Flammarion, 1967), pp. 195–96.

18. Cited in Pierre Rosanvallon, *Le modèle politique français: La société civile contre le jacobinisme de 1789 à nos jours* (Paris: Seuil, 2004) p. 54. Rosanvallon is both historian and political theorist. His work seeks an accommodation of liberal theory to present conditions.

19. Ibid., pp. 52 and 53.

20. Rosanvallon rejects feminist analyses of the reasons for the exclusion of women because he is in fundamental agreement with the revolutionaries about the self-evident meaning of the difference of sex. For him sex is either "socially constructed" (an impossible thought for the men of 1789 and for Rosanvallon) or natural. The idea that meaning is imputed to the natural—that sexed bodies have no self-evident meaning— seems absent from his thinking on this question. Ibid., pp. 47–55.

21. Condorcet, "Sur l'admission des femmes au droit de cité" (1790), in *Oeuvres de Condorcet* (Paris: Firmin Didot Frères, 1874), 10:122.

22. Cited in Darlene Gay Levy, Harriet Branson Applewhite, and Mary Durham Johnson, *Women in Revolutionary Paris, 1789–1795* (Urbana: University of Illinois Press, 1979), pp. 220–221.

23. Jules Tixerant, *Le féminisme à l'époque de 1848 dans l'ordre politique et dans l'ordre économique* (Paris: Girard & Brière, 1908), p. 86.

24. Astonishingly, Rosanvallon ignores the history of feminist movements in the nineteenth and twentieth centuries (though there is ample evidence available in published form). He treats the identity that parité claimed for women as political subjects as "previously nonexistent or, at least, unexpressed." Rosanvallon, *Le peuple introuvable*, p. 448.

25. Ibid., pp. 118–29.

26. Hubertine Auclert, *Le vote des femmes* (Paris, 1908), p. 20.

27. Cited in Rosanvallon, *Le peuple introuvable*, p. 108.

28. Hubertine Auclert, *Le vote des femmes*, p. 13.

29. Rosanvallon, *Le peuple introuvable*, pp. 266–83.

30. It is the argument of Pierre Rosanvallon in *Le Modèle politique français* that these conflicts have been overlooked or ignored in characterizations of French political thought. His project is to expose them by bringing to bear the findings of social history on the history of ideas and so to create new understanding of the French political model. See also Rosanvallon, *Pour une histoire conceptuelle du politique* (Paris: Seuil, 2003).

31. The record on minorities is not as consistent as republicanists now maintain. There was, in effect, an affirmative action program for North Africans in the 1950s. See Todd Shepard, "Integrating France: Rethinking Equality during the Algerian Revolution," unpublished paper (in author's possession), June 2004.

32. There is a great deal of debate among demographers on this question. See, for example, François Héran, "La fausse querelle des catégories 'ethniques' dans la statistique publique," *Débat: Démographie et catégories ethniques* 12 (November 1998).

33. Cited in Hafid Gafati, "Nationalism, Colonialism, and Ethnic Discourse in the

Construction of French Identity," in Tyler Stoval and Georges Van den Abbeele, p. 198; see also Herrick Chapman and Laura Frader, eds. *Race in France: Interdisciplinary Perspectives on the Politics of Difference* (New York: Berghahn, 2004).

34. See Joan W. Scott, "Symptomatic Politics: Banning Islamic Head Scarves in French Public Schools," *French Politics, Culture, and Society* 23, no. 3 (Fall 2005).

35. Riva Kastoryano, *La France, l'Allemagne et leurs immigrés: Négocier l'identité* (Paris: Armand Colin, 1996), pp. 15–40.

36. Françoise Gaspard and Claude Servan-Schreiber, *La fin des immigrés* (Paris: Seuil, 1984), p. 92; Adrian Favell, *Philosophies of Integration: Immigration and the Idea of Citizenship in France and Britain,* 2nd ed. (Basingstoke, UK: Palgrave, 2001), p. 40.

37. Gérard Noiriel, *Le creuset français: Histoire de l'immigration XIXe–XXe siècle* (Paris: Broché, 1988).

38. Kastoryano, *La France, l'Allemagne et leurs immigrés,* p. 132.

39. An unanticipated consequence of this practice of having states of origin send teachers to France was the arrival of three to four thousand Islamic scholars and activists, considered undesirable in Morocco or Algeria, and who taught French-based North African students by using the Koran as a language textbook in their courses.

40. Patrick Weil. *La France et ses étrangers: L'aventure d'une politique de l'immigration 1938–1991* (Paris: Calmann-Lévy, 1991), p. 90.

41. Henri Giordan, *Démocratie culturelle et droit à la différence* (Paris: La Documentation française, 1982), p. 48; see also William Safran, "The Mitterrand Regime and Its Policies of Ethnocultural Accommodation," *Comparative Politics* 18 (October 1985): 41–63.

42. Cited in Gaspard and Servan-Schreiber, *La fin des immigrés,* p. 70.

43. This was the case in Dreux. See Françoise Gaspard, *A Small City in France,* trans. Arthur Goldhammer (Cambridge, MA: Harvard University Press, 1995).

44. Schor, "French Feminism Is a Universalism," in *Bad Objects,* pp. 3–27; Pierre Bourdieu, "Pour un corporatisme de l'universel," in Bourdieu, *Les règles de l'art: Genèse et structure du champ littéraire* (Paris: Seuil, 1992); and Bourdieu, "Deux impérialismes de l'universel," in *L'Amérique des Français,* ed. Christine Fauré and Tom Bishop (Paris: Bourin, 1992).

45. Françoise Gaspard and Farhad Khosrokhavar. *Le foulard et la République* (Paris: La Découverte, 1995); Gaspard and Servan-Schreiber, *La fin des immigrés;* and Gilbert Chaitin, "'France is my Mother': The Subject of Universal Education in the French Third Republic," *Nineteenth-Century Prose* 32 (Spring 2005): 129–59.

46. See Ernest Renan, "Qu'est-ce qu'une nation?" (1882), in *Oeuvres Complètes* (Paris: Calman-Lévy, 1947), 1:905–6. See also Herman Lebovics, *True France: The Wars over Cultural Identity, 1900–1945* (Ithaca: Cornell University Press, 1992).

47. Cited in Gaspard and Servan-Schreiber, *La fin des immigrés,* p. 77.

48. Le Pen, writing in the first issue of his journal *Identité* in 1991, cited in P. Birnbaum, *The Idea of France,* trans. M. B. De Bevoise (New York: Hill and Wang, 2001), pp. 241–42.

49. Gaspard and Servan-Schreiber, *La fin des immigrés,* p. 181.

50. On the general question of immigration and integration, see also John Crowley, "Immigration, racism and *intégration:* Recent French Writing on Immigration and Race Relations," *New Community* 19 (October 1992): 165–73; Jean Leca, "Welfare State, Cultural Pluralism, and the Ethics of Nationality," *Political Studies* 39 (1991): 568–74; Martin A. Schain, "Policy-making and Defining Ethnic Minorities: The Case of Immigration in France," *New Community* 20 (October 1993): 59–78.

51. Here I can only cite a few of the many outpourings of opinion on this question in 2003–4: Charlotte Nordmann, ed. *Le foulard islamique en questions* (Paris: Amsterdam, 2004); the special issue of the journal *Prochoix* on "le voile," no. 25 (Summer 2003); Etienne Balibar, Said Bouamama, Françoise Gaspard, Cathérine Lévy, and Pierre Tévanian, "Oui au foulard à l'école laïque," *Libération,* May 20, 2003; Etienne Balibar, "Dissonances dans la laïcité," *Mouvements: sociétés, politique, culture,* nos. 33–34 (May, June, July, August 2004); and "Le voile, la laïcité et la loi," *Le Nouvel Observateur,* November 20–26, 2003, pp. 54–63. See also Scott, "Symptomatic Politics."

52. *Le Monde,* October 28, 1993.

53. Elisabeth Badinter, Régis Debray, Alain Finkielkraut, Elisabeth de Fontenay, Catherine Kintzler, "Profs, ne capitulons pas!" *Le Nouvel Observateur,* November 2, 1989, pp. 58–59.

54. Régis Debray, "Êtes-vous démocrate ou républicain?" *Le Nouvel Observateur,* November 30, 1989, p. 51.

55. Jacques Le Goff, "Derrière le foulard, l'histoire," *Le Débat,* no. 58 (January–February 1990): 31. An entire section of this journal, pp. 21–76, was devoted to a discussion of the head scarf.

56. Cited in Favell, *Philosophies of Integration,* p. 155.

57. Ibid., p. 68.

58. Ibid., p. 70.

59. Ibid., pp. 78–82. See also Rogers Brubaker, "The Return of Assimilation? Changing Perspectives on Immigration and Its Sequels in France, Germany, and the United States," *Ethnic and Racial Studies* 24 (July 2001): 531–48.

60. Favell, *Philosophies of Integration,* p. 85. Birnbaum, extolling the new religious tolerance in France, links such tolerance to *political* assimilation: "Given the disfavor with which France looks upon multiple and partial allegiances, the acceptance by these [Muslim] immigrants of full and complete French citizenship, carrying with it all the attributes of nationality, remains the only alternative consistent with traditional French conceptions." *The Idea of France,* p. 251. (Birnbaum here contributes to the mythologizing of conceptions whose history is far more complex than the notion of "traditional" allows.)

61. Harlem Désir, "Pour l'intégration: Conditions et instruments." In *Face au racisme,* pt. 1: *Les moyens d'agir,* ed. Pierre-André Taguieff (Paris: La Découverte, 1991), p. 107.

62. Ibid., p. 108.

63. Ibid., p. 109.

64. Favell, *Philosophies of Integration,* p. 85.

65. The heading of this section, "Malaise dans la représentation," is the title of an article by Pierre Rosanvallon in François Furet et al., *La République du centre* (Paris: Calman-Lévy, 1989), pp. 133–82.

66. H. Portelli, "La crise de la représentation politique," *Regards sur l'actualité* 164 (October 1990): 4.

67. Ibid., p. 7.

68. Bernard Lacroix, "La crise de la démocratie représentative en France: Eléments pour une discussion sociologique du problème," *Scalpel* 1 (1994): 6–29.

69. Rosanvallon, "Malaise dans la représentation," p. 139.

70. Ibid., p. 135.

71. Ibid., p. 151.

72. Ibid., p. 142.

73. Marcel Gauchet, "Pacification démocratique, désertion civique," *Le Débat,* May–August 1990, p. 92.

74. Lacroix, "La crise de la démocratie représentative en France." There seems to be some merit to this argument when one considers, for example, Rosanvallon's suggestion that a new body of experts be created to deliberate questions of social policy as an intermediary between politicians and "civil society." "The question is not that of the social legitimacy of political power but that of the relationship between concrete populations and policy," Rosanvallon, "Malaise," pp. 181–82. Here is the justification for the Fondation Saint-Simon, founded in 1982, which Rosanvallon headed until its closing in 1999. See Pierre Rosanvallon, "La Fondation Saint-Simon, une histoire accomplie," *Le Monde,* June 23, 1999.

75. Lacroix, "La crise de la démocratie représentative en France," p. 27.

CHAPTER TWO

1. Jenson and Sineau, *Mitterrand et les Françaises;* Eric Fassin and Michel Feher, "Parité et PaCS: Anatomie politique d'un rapport," in Daniel Borrillo, Eric Fassin, and Marcela Iacub, *Au-delà du PaCS: L'expertise familiale à l'épreuve de l'homosexualité* (Paris: Presses universitaires de France, 1999), pp. 13–44.

2. Mitterrand's party was what is now the Socialist Party (PS), but it underwent several name changes in this period. From its founding in 1905 until 1969 it was the Section française de l'internationale ouvrière (SFIO); from 1969 to 1971, it was called the NPS (Nouveau parti socialiste); since 1971, it has been called le Parti socialiste (PS).

3. Jenson and Sineau, *Mitterrand et les Françaises,* p. 38.

4. This group, founded in 1961, was "a subgroup within the Convention of Republican Institutions directed by François Mitterrand." It was led by a close associate of Mitterrand's, Marie-Thérèse Eyquem, from 1966 to 1970. See the account by Denise Cacheux in *Projets féministes* 4–5 (1996): 191. This special issue of the journal

contained the transcript of a year-long seminar. Since there are no individual articles, I simply cite page numbers.

5. "Interview de François Mitterrand," *La Femme du 20ieme siècle* 3 (June–July 1965).

6. Gauchet, "Pacification démocratique, désertion civique," p. 93.

7. Mariette Sineau, "Pouvoir, modernité, et monopole masculin de la politique: Le cas français," *Nouvelles questions féministes* 13, no. 1 (1992): 57.

8. Jenson and Sineau point out that although the organization of the Fifth Republic put a temporary halt to the political advancement of women, their electoral participation increased. Politicians were aware, too, that young educated women no longer espoused the conservative tendencies long attributed to them. *Mitterrand et les Françaises,* p. 51. On other changes in the female electorate, see ibid., pp. 37–38. See also Janine Mossuz-Lavau, "Le vote des femmes en France (1945–1993)," *Revue française de science politique,* August 1993, pp. 673–82.

9. A secretary of state is a lesser position than a minister in the French government.

10. The law of January 1975 legalizing abortion is referred to as the Veil law (*la loi Veil*).

11. Cited in Guéraiche, *Les femmes et la république,* p. 229. See also his discussion of presidential appointments, p. 232.

12. Cited in Guéraiche, *Les femmes et la république,* p. 224.

13. Jean Mauduit, *La révolte des femmes: Après les Etats généraux de Elle* (Paris: Fayard, 1971), p. 184.

14. Jenson and Sineau, *Mitterrand et les Françaises,* p. 197.

15. The United States has yet to ratify this measure.

16. Françoise Gaspard, "Les enjeux de la parité," *Parité-Infos,* supplement to no. 10 (1995); and Gaspard, in *Projets féministes* 4–5 (1996), p. 226.

17. Eliane Vogel-Polsky, "Les impasses de l'égalité, ou pourquoi les outils juridiques visant à l'égalité des femmes et des hommes doivent être repensés en termes de parité," *Parité-Infos,* special issue 1 (May 1994): 9.

18. This willingness to entertain the possibility of women's participation in municipal elections only, based on an association between the feminine and the local, is a long-standing one that predates the granting of suffrage in 1944.

19. Laurent Zecchini, *Le Monde,* November 23, 1980, cited in Danièle Lochak, "Les hommes politiques, les 'sages'(?) et les femmes (à propos de la decision du Conseil constitutionnel du 18 Novembre 1982)," *Droit social,* no. 2 (February 1983): 132.

20. Françoise Gaspard and Philippe Bataille, *Comment les femmes changent la politique et pourqoui les hommes résistent* (Paris: La Découverte, 1999), p. 73.

21. Cacheux, in *Projets féministes* 4–5 (1996): 196.

22. Gaspard, in ibid., p. 230. On the *courant 3* see Gueraiche, *Les femmes et la république,* pp. 242–47; Marie-Odile Fargier, "Le temps des femmes . . . peut-être," *F Magazine,* no. 6 (June 1978): 28.

23. Guéraiche, *Les femmes et la république,* p. 245.

24. Bataille and Gaspard, *Comment les femmes changent la politique,* p. 77.

25. This did represent a significant increase. During de Gaulle's reign—when proportional representation (*scrutin de liste*) was replaced by individual candidates (*scrutin majoritaire*)—women constituted between 1.5 and 2% of deputies. In 1978, the figure was 3.7%. Still, the numbers came nowhere near the promises that had been held out. Ibid., pp. 187 and 190.

26. Bérengère Marques-Pereira, *La citoyenneté politique des femmes* (Paris: Armand Colin, 2003), p. 157–58; see also Gisèle Halimi, *La nouvelle cause des femmes* (Paris: Seuil, 1997), pp. 107–21; and Georges Vedel, "Le 'quota' aux élections municipales: Les 20% de femmes et la Constitution," *Le Monde,* February 3, 1979.

27. For the full account of the debates, see *Journal officiel,* Assemblée nationale, 1st sess., July 26, 1982, pp. 4841–43; 2nd sess., July 26, 1982, pp. 4860–61; 3rd sess., July 27, 1982, pp. 4899–4918.

28. The Constitutional Council was brought into being in 1958 by the constitution of the Fifth Republic. It is the appointive judicial body charged with evaluating the constitutionality of laws and referenda. (The much older Council of State—a Napoleonic invention—adjudicates disputes between individuals or administrators and the state.) Of its nine members, drawn largely from the world of party politics, three are chosen by the president of the Senate, three by the president of the Chamber of Deputies, and three by the president of the Republic. (*Code administratif,* Constitution et pouvoirs publiques, Constitution, 1958, Titre VII, p. 10.) In 1974, during the presidency of Giscard d'Estaing, a law was passed that permitted 60 deputies or senators to appeal to the council for a ruling on constitutionality before final publication of a law. Analysts of French political life often point to this law (and to the council itself) as one of the instruments that strengthened the executive and administrative branches of government at the expense of the parliamentary system. The council has also been referred to as less a court and more a "third legislative chamber." Indeed, the use of the nonelected Constitutional Council to overturn laws passed by a majority of the legislature was taken to be one of the causes of the "crisis of representation" that preoccupied commentators after 1988. See, for example, Portelli, "La crise de la représentation politique," p. 7.

29. *Journal officiel,* July 27, 1982, p. 4914; and Clarisse Fabre, ed. *Les femmes et la politique: Du droit du vote à la parité* (Paris: Librio, 2001), p. 68 (a very useful collection of articles from *Le Monde*).

30. Interview with Gaspard. See also Lochak, "Les homme politiques, les 'sages'(?) et les femmes," pp. 131–37.

31. *Journal officiel,* July 1982, p. 4917; see also article from *Le Monde* in Fabre, *Les femmes et la politique,* pp. 67–68.

32. Code administratif, Constitution 1958, p. 16.

33. Fabre, *Les femmes et la politique,* p. 70.

34. Yvette Roudy, "La part qui revient à chacun," *Le Monde,* November 24, 1982. Other critics included Andre Laignel, "Le gouvernement des juges," *Le Monde,* Janu-

ary 27, 1983; and Lochak, "Les hommes politiques, les 'sages'(?) et les femmes," pp. 132–33.

35. As jurist Georges Vedel argued, à propos of the Pelletier proposal in 1979, "our legal system indeed proclaims the equality of the sexes, but it recognizes it as legitimate. It prohibits racial discrimination, but denies 'legitimacy' to the notion of race. A census of Frenchmen of color, even if its goal were to strengthen their ability to exercise their rights, would be unconstitutional as well as intolerable." Vedel, *Le Monde,* February 3, 1979.

36. Lochak, "Les hommes politiques, les 'sages'(?) et les femmes," p. 135.

37. *Journal officiel,* July 27, 1982, p. 4917.

38. For a study of the various ministries for women, see Siân Reynolds, "The French Ministry of Women's Rights 1981–86: Modernisation or Marginalisation?" in *France and Modernisation,* ed. John Gaffney (Brookfield, VT: Avebury, 1988), pp. 149–68.

39. Jenson and Sineau, *Mitterrand et les Françaises,* pp. 360–66, for a list of laws by year.

40. Instead of running as an individual and being elected by a majority vote, candidates ran on party lists, and the number of seats assigned corresponded to the proportion of votes the party received. The ability of any candidate to win a seat depended, in this system, on where they were placed on the list (as well as on how successful the party was in winning votes).

41. Gaspard and Bataille, *Comment les femmes changent la politique,* pp. 187, 190.

42. Jenson and Sineau, *Mitterrand et les Françaises,* p. 315.

43. Favell, *Philosophies of Integration,* p. 53.

44. Cited in Jenson and Sineau, *Mitterrand et les Françaises,* p. 315.

45. Ibid., p. 355.

46. "How does this serve these leaders, if not to mask the oppression of other [women]?" asked Eliane Viennot, "Femmes et partis politiques: Une greffe impossible," *Nouvelles questions féministes,* October 1981, p. 37.

47. Mariette Sineau, "Les femmes politiques sous la Ve République: A la recherche d'une légitimité électorale," *Pouvoirs* 82 (1997): 49, 54–55.

48. See the account by Gaspard, "De la parité: Genèse d'un concept, naissance d'un mouvement," *Nouvelles questions féministes* 15, no. 4 (1994): 35. The Athens declaration was signed by female ministers of European Union member states in Athens at the first European summit on "women and decision-making," on November 3, 1992.

49. It was true that France sent more women to the European Parliament than to the National Assembly, but this was a measure of the low esteem politicians had for the EP; it wasn't a locus for power—the kind of power, at least, that party leaders sought. In fact, seats in the EP often provided a kind of consolation, a temporary place for men who had been defeated in national elections to bide their time until they were reelected. On the European Commission see Agnès Huber, *L'Europe et les femmes: Identités en mouvement* (Rennes: Apogée, 1998); and Gaspard and Bataille, *Comment les femmes changent la politique,* p. 188.

50. See Laure Bereni, "Le mouvement français pour la parité et l'Europe," in *Les usages de l'Europe: Acteurs et transformations européennes,* ed. Sophie Jacquot and Cornelia Woll (Paris: L'Harmattan, 2004). See also the European community conferences: "Premier sommet européen, Femmes au pouvoir," Athens, 1992; conferences in Brussels (1993) and Dublin (1995); and the Rome summit (1996). See also Réseau européen d'expertes, "Les femmes dans la prise de décision," *Panorama: Données statistiques sur la participation des femmes à la prise de décision* (Luxembourg: Communautés européennes, 1992).

51. Cited in Mariette Sineau, "Pouvoir, modernité, et monopole masculin," *Nouvelles questions féministes* 13, no. 1 (1992): 47.

52. Ibid., p. 46.

53. "Dialogue de femmes, 18 octobre 1992," typescript, p. 3. (Dialogue de femmes was a feminist group that held periodic meetings which were recorded and transcribed by Alice Colanis, who then distributed the typescript to participants. I used a copy of the minutes of the meeting of October 18, 1992, that was in the personal papers of Françoise Gaspard.)

54. Daniel Gaxie wrote about this in 1980: "The inevitable outcome of unregulated political competition will be that agents privileged by social hierarchies (not only hierarchies between social groups considered in terms of economic or cultural capital, but also hierarchies founded upon ethnic origin, age, or sex) will monopolize positions of political power and thereby reinforce their social supremacy at the same time as the political authority that sanctions it." "Les logiques du recrutement politique," *Revue française de science politique,* no. 1 (1980): 6, cited in Frédéric Besnier, "La parité hommes-femmes en politique: Histoire d'une revendication," Mémoire de diplôme approfondie, Université de Paris I, September 1996, p. 48.

CHAPTER THREE

1. The same "diagnosis" was made again after the first round of the presidential elections of 2002, though this time it sounded formulaic.

2. *Le Monde,* February 25, 1999.

3. "Le Manifeste des dix pour la parité," *L'Express,* June 6–12, 1996, pp. 32–33.

4. Françoise Gaspard, Claude Servan-Schreiber, and Anne Le Gall, *Au pouvoir citoyennes: Liberté, égalité, parité* (Paris: Seuil, 1992), p. 10.

5. Such a law, modeled on the 1972 law against racial discrimination, was proposed first by the Ligue des droits des femmes (the organization associated with Simone de Beauvoir) in 1975. After his election, François Mitterrand endorsed the idea—in the name of tolerance—in 1982. Efforts to pass an antidiscrimination law continued with no results until about 1986, when it became clear that most legislators still endorsed the 1980 comment of Valéry Giscard d'Estaing: "L'avenir de la condition féminine est dans les esprits plutôt que dans les textes." See Alice Colanis's account, "La loi antisexiste," *Dialogue de Femmes,* January 31, 1988, pp. 6–8; and Laure Bereni and

Eléonore Lépinard, "Les stratégies de légitimation de la parité en France," *Revue française de science politique* 54 (February 2004): 71–98.

6. E. Vogel-Polsky, "Les tares génétiques du droit de l'égalité des sexes" (unpublished paper [1995–96?], in the personal papers of Françoise Gaspard).

7. Eliane Viennot, in *Projets féministes* 4–5 (1996): 142.

8. Jean Vogel, in ibid., pp. 127–139.

9. Françoise Gaspard, "La parité, pourquoi pas?" *Pouvoirs*, June 1997, p. 13.

10. Elisabeth G. Sledziewski, "Report," in *The Democratic Principle of Equal Representation: Forty Years of Council of Europe Activity: Proceedings of the Seminar at Strasbourg, November 6 and 7, 1989* (Strasbourg: Council of Europe Press, 1992), p. 23.

11. American writing on sex/gender includes (the list is by no means exhaustive) Gayle Rubin, "The Traffic in Women: Notes on the 'Political Economy' of Sex," in *Toward an Anthropology of Women*, ed. Rayna R. Reiter (New York: Monthly Review Press, 1975), pp. 157–210; Donna Haraway, *Simians, Cyborgs, and Women: The Reinvention of Nature* (New York: Routledge, 1991); Sherry B. Ortner and Harriet Whitehead, *Sexual Meanings: The Cultural Construction of Gender and Sexuality* (Cambridge: Cambridge University Press, 1981); Elizabeth Wilson, *Neural Geographies: Feminism and the Microstructure of Cognition* (New York: Routledge, 1998); Judith Butler, *Gender Trouble: Feminism and the Subversion of Identity* (New York: Routledge, 1990), and *Undoing Gender* (New York: Routledge, 2004).

12. Eliane Vogel-Polsky, "Les impasses de l'égalité, ou pourquoi les outils juridiques visant à l'égalité des femmes et des hommes doivent être repensés en terms de parité," *Parité-Infos*, special issue 1 (May 1994): 11. Vogel-Polsky cites Kuhn for her conceptualization of a paradigm shift.

13. Giselle Donnard, "Se réapproprier la politique par la parité," *Parité-Infos*, supplement to no. 8 (December 1994): 3; see also Gaspard et al., *Au pouvoir citoyennes*, p. 126.

14. Etienne Balibar, "Ambiguous Universality," *Differences* 7 (Spring 1995): 64.

15. Ibid., pp. 67–68.

16. Martha Minow, "Learning to Live with the Dilemma of Difference," *Law and Contemporary Problems* 48, no. 2 (1984): 157–211. On the general question of representation and sexual difference, see Philippe Maître, "Différence sexuelle et représentations de la politique dans la France contemporaine" (Mémoire de maîtrise: ethnologie, Université de Paris 8, Vincennes, 1997).

17. Eliane Viennot, "Parité: Les féministes entre défis politiques et révolution culturelle," *Nouvelles questions féministes* 15, no. 4 (1994): 85–86.

18. Jacques Rancière, "Citoyenneté, culture et politique," in *Mondialisation, citoyenneté et multiculturalisme*, ed. M. Elbaz and D. Helly (Paris/Quebec: L'Harmattan / Presses universitaires de l'Université de Laval, 2000), pp. 55–68.

19. Geneviève Fraisse, citing herself. She participated in a discussion of the parity law, the transcript of which is included in Catherine Tasca, *Rapport fait au nom de la commission des lois constitutionnelles, de la législation et de l'administration générale*

de la république sur le projet de loi constitutionnelle (no. 985) relatif à l'égalité entre les femmes et les hommes (Paris: Assemblée nationale, December 2, 1998), p. 48. For an engagement with some of the philosophical issues, see the articles by Christian Lazzeri, Janine Mossuz-Lavau, Evelyne Pisier, Gwénaële Calvès, Françoise Gaspard, and Gisèle Halimi in "Débat sur le principe de parité," *Cités: Philosophie, politique, histoire 3* (2000): 169–94.

20. In his introduction to a special issue of the journal *Politix*, I think Eric Fassin overemphasizes the strategic aspects of parity in an effort to get beyond the philosophical debates about essentialism and universalism it occasioned. He attributes many of the difficulties of articulating a clear theoretical position to the constraint imposed by the need to avoid "American multiculturalism." While there is much to agree with in Fassin's reading of the movement, I would argue that he misses what is most original about it—its undeniably *theoretical* attempt to desymbolize the difference of sex by distinguishing between abstraction and embodiment, duality and difference. See Eric Fassin, "La parité sans théorie: Retour sur un débat," *Politix: Revue des sciences sociales du politique* 15, no. 60 (2002): 19–32.

21. Of course, the book was not the only text to argue for parité; it drew on the writings and discussions of French and other European feminists of the period, providing an important synthesis as well as an original argument of its own.

22. For *courant 3*, see chap. 2, in "Quotas."

23. Interview with Le Gall, Paris, July 4, 1998.

24. Gaspard, "De la parité," p. 42. See also Gaspard, "La parité, pourquoi pas?" p. 13.

25. Gaspard et al., *Au pouvoir citoyennes*, p. 54.

26. Ibid., p. 144

27. Cited in Besnier, "La parité hommes-femmes en politique," p. 49.

28. Ibid., p. 38.

29. See chap. 1, in "The Subject of Representation."

30. Françoise Gaspard, "Le fratriarcat: Une spécificité française," *Après-demain* 380–81 (January–February 1996): 4.

31. Claude Servan-Schreiber, "La fausse-vraie maire de Vitrolles: Une insulte pour toutes les femmes," *Parité-Infos*, no. 17 (March 1997), p. 5.

32. Alain Lipietz, "Parité au masculin," *Nouvelles questions féministes* 15, no. 4 (1994): 62.

33. Viennot, "Parité, p. 70.

34. Françoise Collin, "L'urne est-elle funéraire?" in *Démocratie et représentation*, ed. Michèle Riot-Sarcey (Paris: Kimé, 1995), p. 71.

35. Françoise Collin, in *Projets féministes* 4–5 (1996): 103.

36. Claude Servan-Schreiber, "Dialogue de femmes" (typescript, October 18, 1992), p. 9.

37. Ibid.

38. Gaspard et al., *Au pouvoir citoyennes,* p. 130.

39. French usage of the term "communitarian" is not the same as the American usage. The French refers to a corporate cultural identity, a sense of belonging to an ethnic or religious group that is at odds with individual identity protected by the state. The state in France protects individuals from the claims of "communities."

40. Gaspard et al., *Au pouvoir citoyennes,* p. 166.

41. *Le Monde,* February 17, 1999.

42. Françoise Gaspard, "Des partis et des femmes," in Riot-Sarcey, *Démocratie et représentation,* p. 239.

43. I have used the term "republicanist" to designate those who took their mission to be the defense of the republic and its principles. In France, almost everyone is a republican, so that term would not have been specific enough. Many of those I refer to as republicanist also considered themselves to be on the left, indeed were members of or voted for the Socialist Party.

44. Jean Vogel, in *Projets féministes* 4–5 (1996): 130.

45. Cited in Besnier, "La parité hommes-femmes en politique," p. 133.

46. Ibid.

47. Servan-Schreiber, "Dialogue de femmes," p. 29.

48. Yvette Roudy, "L'autre regard," *Après-demain* 380–81 (January–February 1996): 40.

49. "Election présidentielle—le vote des femmes peut faire la décision: Entretien avec Janine Mossuz-Lavau," *Parité-Infos,* no. 9 (March 1995), p. 2.

50. *L'Express,* June 6, 1996, pp. 32–33.

51. Voynet, cited in Besnier, "La parité hommes-femmes en politique," p. 132.

52. *Le Monde,* March 23, 1999, pp. 1, 16.

53. Sylviane Agacinski, *Politique des sexes* (Paris: Seuil, 1998).

54. Cited in Yves Sintomer, "Délibérer, participer, représenter: Vers une sociologie de la justification politique" (Mémoire d'habilitation, Université de Paris V, 2001), p. 17.

55. Sintomer, ibid., 16–26, mislabels this left-wing critique a "radical deconstructionist" position. None of those associated with it were deconstructionists in any formal philosophical sense. They were, rather, traditional feminists, feminists affiliated with the far left, and social scientists like Pierre Bourdieu, who characterized the emphasis on women in elective office as elitist because it ignored the social and economic conditions that impoverished women who were not bourgeois.

56. Assemblée nationale, 2nd sess., December 15, 1998, p. 10506.

57. Helena Hirata, Danièle Kergoat, Michèle Riot-Sarcey, and Eleni Varikas, "Parité ou mixité?" in *Le piège de la parité: Arguments pour un débat,* ed. Micheline Amar (Paris: Hachette Littérateurs, 1999), p. 12. (This article first appeared in 1993 as "La représentation politique en question: Parité ou mixité?" in *Futur antérieur* and again in 1994 as "Parité ou mixité?" in *Politix.*)

58. See Hirata et al., in *Le piège de la parité,* p. 13. If "men" were substituted for

"women" in these comments, the contradictions of the critics would be revealed; but since men were already synonymous with individuals, the inconsistency was not apparent to them.

59. Eleni Varikas, "Une représentation en tant que femme? Réflexions critiques sur la demande de la parité des sexes," *Nouvelles questions féministes* 16, no. 2 (1995): 81–127.

60. Josette Trat, "La loi pour la parité: Une solution en trompe-l'oeil," ibid., pp. 129–39.

61. Varikas, "Une représentation en tant que femme?" pp. 120–21.

62. Michèle Le Doeuff, "Problèmes d'investiture (De la parité, etc.)," *Nouvelles questions féministes* 16, no. 2 (1996): 14.

63. Pierre Bourdieu, *La domination masculine* (Paris: Seuil, 1998), p. 124.

64. Varikas, "Une représentation en tant que femme?" p. 112.

65. Hirata et al., in *Le piège de la parité*, p. 13.

66. Varikas, "Une représentation en tant que femme?" p. 114.

67. Ibid., p. 121.

68. Elisabeth Badinter, "La parité est une régression: Entretien avec Elisabeth Badinter réalisé par Isabelle Girard et Benoît Rayski," in Amar, *Le piège de la parité*, p. 88. (First published in *L'événement du jeudi*, February 4–10, 1999.)

69. Evelyne Pisier, "Universalité contre parité," in Amar, *Le piège de la parité*, p. 15. (First published in *Le Monde*, February 8, 1995.)

70. Danièle Sallenave, "Le piège de la parité," in Amar, *Le piège de la parité*, p. 24.

71. E. Badinter, "La parité est une regression," in ibid., p. 88.

72. Elisabeth Badinter, "Non aux quotas de femmes," *Le Monde*, June 12, 1996. ENA is the Ecole nationale d'administration, which trains high-level administrators, civil servants, and politicians.

73. Ibid.

74. Ibid.

75. Sallenave, "Le piège de la parité," p. 23.

76. E. Badinter, "Non aux quotas de femmes."

77. Cited in *L'Express*, June 6, 1996, p. 31.

78. E. Badinter, "La parité est une régression," p. 88.

79. Dominique Schnapper, *La communauté des citoyens* (Paris: Gallimard, 1994), p. 49.

80. Robert Badinter, speech in the Senate, January 26, 1999, in Amar, *Le piège de la parité*, p. 36.

81. E. Badinter, "La parité est une régression," p. 89.

82. Pisier, "Universalité contre parité," p. 16.

83. E. Badinter, "La parité est une régression," p. 89.

84. Sallenave, "Le piège de la parité," p. 24. *Beur* refers to someone born in France of North African parents. It does not have racist connotations and is derived from a slang word for Arab.

85. E. Badinter, "La parité est une régression," p. 89.

86. Ibid., p. 88.

87. Lipietz, in *Projets féministes* 4–5 (1996): 114.

CHAPTER FOUR

1. "Manifeste des 577 pour une démocratie paritaire, 2 avril 1993," *Parité-Infos,* supplement to no. 4 (December 1993).

2. Sledziewski, "Report," in *The Democratic Principle of Equal Representation,* p. 26.

3. Françoise Gaspard, "La parité—principe ou stratégie?" *Le Monde diplomatique,* November 1998, pp. 26–27.

4. *Guide pratique en 25 questions et réponses,* published by *Parité-Infos,* 1995.

5. For the chronology see *Parité-Infos,* no. 1 (March 1993): 7; and Bataille and Gaspard, *Comment les femmes changent la politique,* pp. 32–40.

6. Evelyne Pisier, "Parité," in *Dictionnaire du vote,* ed. Pascal Perrineau and Dominique Reynié (Paris: Presses universitaires de France, 2001), p. 720.

7. *Projets féministes,* 4–5 (1996): 217.

8. For example a SOFRES poll on February 23–25, 1993, showed that 62% of respondents expressed "no confidence" in politicians, and 67% "no confidence" in political parties. Cited in Besnier, "La parité hommes-femmes en politique," p. 127.

9. Philippe Petit, "Le grand réveil du deuxième sexe," *Marianne,* May 26–June 1, 1997, p. 62. This issue also had articles for and against parité by Claude Servan-Schreiber and Danièle Sallenave.

10. Bataille and Gaspard, *Comment les femmes changent la politique,* p. 146.

11. "Résultats des élections législatives: Les femmes symboles du renouveau politique?" *Parité-Infos,* no. 18 (June 1997): 5–6.

12. Pisier, "Parité," pp. 720–721; and Hélène Le Doaré, "Parité," in *Dictionnaire critique du féminisme,* ed. Helena Hirata, Françoise Laborie, Hélène Le Doaré, and Danièle Senotier (Paris: Presses universitaires de France, 2002), pp. 136–41.

13. A copy of the Athens declaration is included in an appendix to *Les femmes dans la prise de décision en France et en Europe,* ed. Françoise Gaspard (Paris: Harmattan, 1997) pp. 207–10.

14. "Conseil national des femmes françaises," extrait de *L'historique des conseils nationaux affiliés* (Conseil international, 1938), pp. 121–26. See also Laurence Klejman and Florence Rochefort, *L'égalité en marche* (Paris: Presses de la Fondation nationale des sciences politiques, 1989), pp. 149–58.

15. Three hundred copies of the first issue were xeroxed and sent out free with the help of Senator Monique Ben-Guiga. A year later, with money from the Service des droits des femmes matched by the European Commission, the number had risen to thirty-five hundred. Of these, about three hundred were paid subscriptions. The rest were sent free to politicans, journalists, libraries, and other groups and institutions. In this way, parité achieved wide public visibility.

16. The minutes of the Réseau femmes pour la parité from April to December 1993

and copies of correspondence and contact lists are in the personal papers of Françoise Gaspard.

17. Other groups included Association française des femmes diplômées des universités; Coordination française pour le lobby européen des femmes; Union féminine civique et sociale; Union professionnelle féminine; and Organisation internationale des femmes sionistes. See the listing in Gaspard, *Les femmes dans la prise de décision*, p. 205.

18. Included as an insert in *Parité-Infos*, no. 9 (March 1995).

19. This is the suggestion of Besnier, "La parité hommes-femmes en politique," p. 54.

20. Announcement for the "Table ronde: La Parité hommes/femmes en politique," report on a speech by Françoise Giroud, who chaired the meeting, in the personal papers of Françoise Gaspard.

21. Eliane Viennot, "Pour un front de femmes dans et hors des partis," *Parité-Infos*, no. 3 (September 1993): 6. See also Claude Servan-Schreiber, "La prochaine étape," *Parité-Infos*, no. 6 (June 1994): 1; and Servan-Schreiber and Françoise Gaspard, "Au delà du clivage droite/gauche: Une alliance pour la parité?" *Parité-Infos*, no. 12 (December 1995): 2.

22. *Le Monde*, April 6, 1993.

23. Eliane Viennot, "Le second souffle des femmes pour la parité," *Parité-Infos*, no. 5 (February 1994): 5.

24. The collection of statistics on gender to document women's disadvantaged position was also recommended in the Athens summit plan of action.

25. Renée Lucie (the pseudonym used by Françoise Gaspard), "Législatives 93: Plus ça change, plus c'est pareil," *Parité-Infos*, no. 1 (March 1993): 1–4. Page 3 has the analysis of how women candidates fared in the legislative elections in relation to the size of their parties.

26. *Le Monde*, April 6, 1993.

27. Coco Bonnier, "Choses vues: Devant l'Assemblée natiomâle, la parité en fête," *Parité-Infos*, no. 2 (June 1993): 7.

28. Correspondence in the personal papers of Servan-Schreiber.

29. Gisèle Stievenard, *Projets féministes* 4–5 (1996): 210.

30. Denise Cacheux, ibid., p. 211.

31. Denise Cacheux, "Le Parti socialiste est-il prêt pour une vraie mixité?" *Parité-Infos*, no. 3 (September 1993): 5. (This is the text of the speech Cacheux gave at the meeting of the Estates General. Cacheux, a long-time party activist from the Départment du Nord, had been a deputy.) See also Hanem El Fani, "Les femmes du PS sortent de l'ombre," *Parité-Infos*, no. 3 (September 1993): 4; Claude Servan-Schreiber, "Le coup d'éclat paritaire des socialistes," *Parité-Infos*, no. 4 (December 1993): 1, 2, 4.

32. "J'ai pris cette décision seul," interview with Michel Rocard, *Parité-Infos*, no. 4 (December 1993): 3.

33. Bataille and Gaspard, *Comment les femmes changent la politique*, p. 89; Claude Servan-Schreiber, "La prochaine étape," and Françoise Gaspard, "Formidable progression du nombre de candidates sur les listes françaises," both in *Parité-Infos*, no. 6

(June 1994): 1 and 1–4. This issue of *Parité-Infos* also cited a report from *Le Parisien* (April 21, 1994), which showed that 59% of respondents thought that parité was an effective way of improving women's representation in politics; 82% of both sexes said they were ready to vote for women in municipal elections; and 80% said the same for the legislative elections (p. 5).

34. Besnier, "La parité hommes-femmes en politique," p. 10.

35. See report in *Parité-Infos*, no. 2 (June 1993): 8.

36. Elisabeth Weissman, "La parité et les médias dans l'élection présidentielle," *Parité-Infos*, no. 10 (June 1995): 3–4.

37. Réseau femmes pour la parité, "Compte rendu de la réunion du 11 Novembre 1993," in the personal papers of Servan-Schreiber.

38. The full text and all the signatures were also published in *Parité-Infos*, supplement to no. 14 (December 1993).

39. Eliane Viennot, ed. *La démocratie à la française, ou les femmes indésirables* (Paris: Cahiers du Cedref, 1996).

40. Françoise Gaspard and Claude Servan-Schreiber, "La solitude de Marie Curie," *Libération*, March 22, 1994, p. 6.

41. The transcripts of this year-long seminar were published in *Projets féministes* 4–5 (February 1996) and constitute an invaluable resource for the study of the parité movement.

42. When Gaspard was nominated, only 7.8% of the nominees were women. When she finally accepted in 1998, Lionel Jospin (by then prime minister) had named as many women as men to receive the honor. The entire group, however, was not *paritaire* since only a few other ministers followed his lead. *Parité-Infos*, no. 9 (March 1995): 8.

43. RPR = Rassemblement pour la République, the Rally for the Republic. UDF = Union pour la démocratie française, the Union for French Democracy. Both are parties of the center right dating from the 1970s.

44. Besnier, "La parité hommes-femmes en politique," p. 139.

45. Gaspard, "Formidable progression du nombre de candidates," p. 4.

46. "Elections européennes: Les raisons d'une bonne surprise," *Parité-Infos*, no. 7 (September 1994): 7.

47. A poll by IFOP/Ministère des affaires sociales, 28 mars–11 avril 1994 (1502 personnes) showed that 62% of respondents were for adding parité to the constitution. See "Une femme présidente de la République?" *Parité-Infos*, no. 9 (March 1995): 4, which compares responses to this question from polls in 1974, 1981, 1987, and 1994 to show the evolution of opinion on this matter.

48. *Parité-Infos*, no. 9 (March 1995): 8.

49. Ibid.

50. Shortly after this event, Kreder left the CNFF and devoted herself full-time to Demain la parité.

51. Françoise Gaspard and Claude Servan-Schreiber, "Au delà du clivage droite/gauche: Une alliance pour la parité?" *Parité-Infos*, no. 12 (December 1995): 1.

52. Cited in Besnier, "La parité hommes-femmes en politique," p. 133.

53. Ibid.

54. Ibid., p. 134; interview with Françoise Gaspard, July 2001.

55. *Parité-Infos,* no. 10 (June 1995): 8.

56. Interview with Roselyne Bachelot, *Parité-Infos,* no. 12 (December 1995): 4.

57. "Un comité de vigilance contre l'exclusion des femmes," ibid.

58. "'Juppé II: Un gouvernement qui fait mâle,' propos de Mariette Sineau, recueillis par Andrée Mézières," *Parité-Infos,* no. 12 (December 1995): 3. (Andrée Mézières was a pseudonym used by Claude Servan-Schreiber.)

59. Ibid., p. 2.

60. Besnier, "La parité hommes-femmes en politique," p. 66.

61. *L'Express,* June 6, 1996, p. 31.

62. Gaspard and Servan-Schreiber, "Au delà du clivage droite/gauche," pp. 1–2. For the Gaspard quote, see Besnier, "La parité hommes-femmes en politique," p. 66.

63. The proceedings of the Demain la parité conference were published as *Les femmes et la prise de décision en Europe,* ed. Françoise Gaspard (Paris: Harmattan, 2000).

64. "Les Femmes pour le renouveau de la politique et de la société," European summit, Rome, May 18, 1996. A copy of the charter issued at the end of this meeting appears in *Parité-Infos,* no. 14 (June 1996): 4, and also in Gaspard, *Les femmes dans la prise de décision,* pp. 211–15.

65. *L'Express,* June 6, 1996, p. 32.

66. Ibid., p. 33.

67. IFOP pour *L'Express,* poll conducted May 29 and 30, 1996; results published in *L'Express,* June 6, 1996.

68. Ibid., p. 31.

69. Ibid., p. 36.

70. *L'Express,* September 19, 1996, pp. 34–36. There are different and probably more precise numbers in Bataille and Gaspard, *Comment les femmes changent la politique,* pp. 178–81.

71. "Place des femmes dans la vie publique," Assemblée nationale, *Compte rendu analytique officiel,* 2nd sess., March 11, 1997, pp. 10–51.

72. "Le débat sur la parité hommes-femmes," *Le Monde,* March 8, 1997, pp. 1, 6, 7, 17.

73. Laurent Fabius, "Débat sur la parité," *L'hebdo des socialistes,* March 14, 1997, p. 10 (the text of Fabius's speech to the National Assembly on March 8).

74. A call issued in February 1997 by Gisèle Halimi's group, Choisir: La cause des femmes, for "une juste mixité entre femmes et hommes en politique," brought a scathing critique from Françoise Gaspard, who wrote that she was "floored" by their confusion of "mixité" and "parité." Halimi's spokeswoman replied—terribly offended—with a list of Halimi's and Choisir's actions on behalf of parité, and with the explanation that the call in question was the work of a number of groups and so a kind of compromise document. These documents are in the personal papers of Françoise Gaspard.

75. *La République des Pyrénées,* March 1997. The comment was included in a press review provided by a service engaged by *Parité-Infos.*

76. See chapter 5.

77. Alain Juppé, "Ouverture du débat sur la place des femmes dans la vie publique," (Assemblée nationale, le 11 mars 1997), typescript of the full speech (in the personal papers of Françoise Gaspard), p. 8. A section of this speech is deleted in the *Compte rendu analytique officiel* (see n. 71 above).

78. Assemblée nationale, *Compte rendu analytique officiel,* p. 31.

79. Eric Fassin and Michel Feher, "Parité et PaCS: Anatomie politique d'un rapport," in Daniel Borrillo, Eric Fassin, and Marcela Iacub, *Au delà du PaCS: L'expertise familiale à l'épreuve de l'homosexualité* (Paris: Presses universitaires de France, 1999), pp. 13–44.

80. Assemblée nationale, http://www.assemblée-nat.fr/connaissance/élections-1997.asp.

81. Since only one of these deputies had a female substitute deputy, the numbers of women in the assembly were reduced by these appointments.

82. *Le Figaro,* June 5, 1997, p. 6.

83. *Le Monde,* June 6, 1997, p. 20.

84. *Le Figaro,* June 5, 1997.

85. Georges thought it remained to be seen what effect this promise would have on Jospin's leadership. "Il lui reste maintenant à gouverner," he concluded. Pierre Georges, "Harpes célestes," *Le Monde,* June 6, 1997, p. 36.

86. N. Gautier, "La parité a d'abord été imposée par l'opinion," *Libération,* June 18, 1998, p. 3.

87. Cited in a promotional package ("De l'égalité à la parité; de la parité à la liberté") prepared and distributed in June 1998 by the office of Geneviève Fraisse.

88. See "La Ministre? Over the Immortals' Dead Bodies," *New York Times,* July 1, 1998, p. A4. Among the many other articles published on this debate, see Marc Fumaroli, "La querelle du neutre," *Le Monde,* July 31, 1998, p. 1; Michelle Coquillat, "Académie et misogynie," *Le Monde,* January 20, 1998, p. 15; Geneviève Fraisse, "La double évidence du féminisme," *Le Monde,* January 20, 1998, p. 15. Much earlier, *Parité-Infos* had raised the issue in an interview with Marina Yaguello, who had written a book called *Le sexe des mots* (The gender of words) in 1989. "Le langage de l'égalité au service de la parité," *Parité-Infos,* no. 7 (September 1994): 1–4. In the same issue, see Benoîte Groult, "Cachez ce féminin que je ne saurais voir . . . ," p. 2.

CHAPTER FIVE

1. Hubert Haenel, "Pacte civil de solidarité: Discussion d'une proposition de loi," Sénat, March 17, 1999.

2. An early analysis of the impact of the AIDS epidemic was a report prepared by a working group within the Socialist Party, written by Françoise Gaspard, "Face au

SIDA: Vérité, responsabilité, solidarité," typescript, February 1988, in the personal papers of Françoise Gaspard.

3. Cour de Cassation, July 11, 1989, cited in Gérard Bach-Ignasse, "Le contrat d'union sociale en perspective," *Les Temps Modernes* 53, no. 598 (1998): 164. The court upheld its decision in another case in 1997. See also Daniel Borrillo and Pierre Lascoumes, *Amours égales? Le PaCS, les homosexuels et la gauche* (Paris: La Découverte, 2002), pp. 25–29.

4. "Pact" was offered as a more precise term than "union" and less limited than "contract." A pact is a formal agreement that connotes an alliance, a relationship that preexists its formalization, whereas a contract is only what is established by the document. Borrillo and Lascoumes, *Amours égales?* p. 35.

5. For a chronology of the movement, see Borrillo and Lascoumes, *Amours égales?* pp. 15–16, and Frédéric Martel, *Le rose et le noir: Les homosexuels en France depuis 1968* (Paris: Seuil, 2000), pp. 595–663, 719.

6. Cited in Martel, *Le rose et le noir,* p. 607.

7. Cited in *Libération,* September 23, 1998, p. 12.

8. Pierre Bourdieu, Jacques Derrida, Didier Eribon, Michelle Perrot, Paul Veyne, and Pierre Vidal-Naquet, "Pour une reconnaissance légale du couple homosexuel," *Le Monde,* March 1, 1996.

9. *Journal du dimanche,* June 29, 1997.

10. Caroline Fourest and Fiammetta Venner, *Les anti-PaCS, ou la dernière croisade homophobe* (Paris: ProChoix, 1999). See also "Comment les ultras catholiques menacent le Pacs," *Libération,* August 12, 1998, p. 2.

11. Martel, *Le rose et le noir,* p. 742.

12. Ibid., chap. 18, for a detailed account, as well as Borrillo and Lascoumes, *Amours égales?* pp. 79–90.

13. "Discours de Madame Catherine Tasca, présidente de la Commission des lois, vendredi 9 octobre 1998," typescript of her presentation to the National Assembly (in the personal papers of Françoise Gaspard), p. 5.

14. Assemblée nationale, 2nd sess., March 30, 1999.

15. "Principaux extraits de l'intervention de Madame Roselyne Bachelot-Narquin, députée (RPR) à la tribune de l'Assemblée nationale, le 7 novembre 1998 (3ème Séance)," *Compte rendu analytique officiel.*

16. Collectif pour le contrat d'union civile et sociale, "Lettre ouverte à Madame Irène Théry," Paris, December 5, 1997, signed by Jean-Paul Pouliquen, president; photocopy of typescript in the personal papers of Françoise Gaspard. See also the article "Pour l'égalité sexuelle," *Le Monde,* June 26, 1999, which defends the universalist concept in the same terms: not to claim special rights for homosexuals but to demand "sexual equality, between the sexes and between the sexualities."

17. Martel, *Le rose et le noir,* p. 603.

18. Borrillo and Lascoumes, *Amours égales?* p. 32.

19. Irène Théry, "La fausse bonne idée du contrat d'union sociale, c'est de tout

mélanger," *Le Monde,* November 25, 1997, and Théry, "Le contrat d'union sociale en question," *Esprit* 10 (1997): 159–211. See also Hugues Moutouh, "Controverse sur le PaCS: L'esprit d'une loi," in *Les Temps Modernes,* no. 603 (1999): 205, citing J.-Fr. Mattei, a deputy of the opposition during the 1998 debate: "By presenting your text as universal in order to avoid raising directly the question of homosexuality, you trespass on the fundamental sexual taboos of our society." See also Tony Anatrella, "Une précipitation anxieuse," *Le Monde,* October 10, 1998: "In reality, the PaCS is sustained by a perverse discourse which uses cohabitation to better disguise the institutionalization of the homosexual relationship."

20. Caroline Eliacheff, Antoine Garapon, N. Heinich, Françoise Héritier, A. Nouri, P. Veyne, and H. Wismann, "Ne laissons pas la critique du PaCS à la droite!" *Le Monde,* January 27, 1999. See also Ali Magoudi, "Et la différence des sexes?" *Le Monde,* October 9, 1998.

21. Collectif pour le contrat d'union civile et sociale, "Lettre ouverte à Madame Irène Théry." For comments on these issues see the work of gay-movement leader Didier Eribon, a vociferous critic of Théry. Eribon, *Réflexions sur la question gay* (Paris: Fayard, 1999), and *Papiers d'identité: Interventions sur la question gay* (Paris: Fayard, 2000).

22. Bertrand Delanoë, Sénat, March 17, 1999.

23. Adoption had long been permitted for single individuals but not for unmarried couples. On reproductive technology, see Marcela Iacub, "Homoparentalité et ordre procréatif," in Daniel Borrillo, Eric Fassin, and Marcela Iacub, *Au-delà du PaCS: L'expertise familiale à l'épreuve de l'homosexualité* (Paris: Presses universitaires de France, 1999), pp. 189–204. Iacub points out that the 1994 laws on reproductive technology sought to mask the fact that no sexual act had occurred to produce the pregnancy. "Thus, paradoxically, the sexual act, the great absence in the new procreative techniques, is supported, re-created by the fictions and artifices of law" (pp. 195–96).

24. Bernard Seillier, Sénat, March 17, 1999.

25. Borrillo and Lascoumes, *Amours égales?* p. 115.

26. Ibid., p. 122.

27. Eric Fassin "Pour l'égalité des sexualités," in Sénat, *Auditions publiques du 27 janvier 1999.* Fassin, a sociologist teaching at the Ecole normale supérieure, was an "expert" witness at the Senate hearings on the PaCS. His numerous articles on behalf of full recognition for homosexual partners include "Ouvrir le mariage aux homosexuels," *Le Monde diplomatique,* June 1998, p. 22; "Homosexualité, mariage et famille," *Le Monde,* November 5, 1997, p. 21; "Usages de la science et science des usages: A propos des familles homoparentales," *L'Homme: Revue française d'anthropologie,* special issue, "Question de parenté," nos. 154–55 (April–September 2000): 391–408. Fassin has also written incisively on the differences between the American and French gay movements: "Homosexualité et mariage aux Etats-Unis: Histoire d'une polémique," *Actes de la recherche en sciences sociales,* no. 125 (December 1998): 63–73.

28. Caroline Mécary and Flora Leroy-Forgeot, *Le Pacs* (Paris: Presses universitaires de France, 2001).

29. Cited in Martel, *Le rose et le noir,* p. 634.

30. *Le Monde,* October 9, 1998, p. 5.

31. Elisabeth Guigou, Sénat, March 17, 1999.

32. Théry, "Le contrat d'union sociale," p. 178.

33. As was the case with parité, supporters and opponents of the PaCS did not follow traditional political or ideological lines, although for the PaCS there was a greater concentration of Catholics and conservatives in opposition. But they were joined—unpredictably—by secular republicans, liberal professionals, and others on the left not usually associated with them politically.

34. Jean-Louis Lorain, Sénat, March 17, 1999.

35. Eliacheff et al. "Ne laissons pas la critique . . . ," *Le Monde,* January 27, 1999.

36. Didier Eribon was an especially eloquent voice. His *Réflexions sur la question gay* was written in the heat of the controversy. See his preface to the American edition of the book, *Insult and the Making of the Gay Self,* trans. Michael Lucey (Durham: Duke University Press, 2004).

37. Théry, "Le contrat d'union sociale," pp. 172, 170, 174.

38. Théry, "La fausse bonne idée," *Le Monde,* November 25, 1997.

39. Françoise Héritier, "Aucune société n'admet de parenté homosexuelle," *La Croix,* November 1998.

40. "The gamut of human cultures is so broad and varied (and so easy to manipulate) that arguments in support of almost any proposition can be found there. The ethnologist's role is to catalogue and describe those solutions to the problems of life in society that, in determinate conditions, have shown themselves to be viable. The familiarity this study provides with the most widely varied customs teaches us—at best—a certain wisdom that may turn out to be useful for our contemporaries. But we must never forget that social choices do not belong to the scholar as such, but—and the scholar himself is one—to the citizen." In Borrillo, Fassin, and Iacub, *Au-delà du PaCS,* p. 110.

41. Eric Fassin, "L'illusion anthropologique: Homosexualité et filiation," *Témoin,* no. 12 (May 1998): 43–56; and Fassin, "PaCS socialista: La gauche et le 'juste milieu,'" *Le Banquet,* October 12–13, 1998, p. 9.

42. Michel Foucault, *The History of Sexuality,* vol. 1, trans. Robert Hurley (New York: Random House, 1978), p. 108.

43. Théry, "Le contrat d'union sociale," p. 180; and Tony Anatrella, "Une précipitation," *Le Monde,* October 10, 1998.

44. *Le Monde,* October 10, 1998.

45. Anne Heinis, Sénat, March 17, 1999.

46. Théry, "La fausse bonne idée," *Le Monde,* November 15, 1997.

47. Anatrella, "Une précipitation," *Le Monde,* October 10, 1998.

48. Jean-Luc Auber, "Note sous arrêt Cour de cassation" (December 17, 1997), cited in Borrillo, Fassin, and Iacub, *Au-delà du PaCS,* p. 165.

49. Cited in Borrillo and Lascoumes, *Amours égales?* p. 130.

50. Cited in ibid., pp. 109–10.

51. Théry, "Le contrat d'union sociale," p. 181.

52. On the Association of Catholic Families' petition, see the article in *Le Monde*, (October 10, 1998); for the comments of the spokesman for the bishops, see Hugues Moutouh, "Controverses sur le PaCS: L'esprit d'une loi," *Les Temps Modernes*, no. 603 (1999): 211.

53. Théry, "Le contrat d'union sociale," pp. 173, 177. See also comments of Borrillo and Lascoumes, *Amours égales?* p. 100.

54. The critics of this position argued that psychoanalysis was being misused to protest the PaCS. See Michel Tort, "Homophobies psychanalytiques," *Le Monde*, October 15, 1999; Geneviève Delaisi de Parseval, "La construction de la parentalité dans les couples de même sexe," in Borrillo, Fassin, and Iacub, *Au-delà du PaCS*, pp. 225–44; and Sabine Prokhoris, "L'adoration des majuscules," in ibid., pp. 145–60.

55. Théry, "Le contrat d'union sociale," p. 174. See also Tony Anatrella, "PaCS: Pourquoi l'Etat ne peut pas être neutre," *Le Figaro*, December 1, 1998.

56. See quotes from the Catholic deputy Christine Boutin and from Xavier Thévenot, cited in Borrillo and Lascoumes, *Amours égales?* p. 97.

57. Anatrella, "Une précipitation," *Le Monde*, October 10, 1998.

58. S. Lepastier's testimony to the Senate, March 10, 1999, cited in Borrillo and Lascoumes, *Amours égales?* p. 101, n. 15.

59. Comments of Françoise Dekeuwer-Défossez, cited in Borrillo and Lascoumes, *Amours égales?* p. 109.

60. Pierre Legendre, quoted in *Le Monde*, October 23, 2001, cited in Borrillo and Lascoumes, *Amours égales?* p. 138.

61. Daniel Borrillo, "Fantasmes des juristes *vs. Ratio juris*: La *doxa* des privatistes sur l'union entre personnes de même sexe," in Borrillo, Fassin, and Iacub, *Au-delà du PaCS*, pp. 161–85, esp. p. 184, n. 2. For an insightful discussion of "the logic of conjugality"—the way nineteenth- and early twentieth-century social theorists linked marital complementarity and social order, see Judith Surkis, *Sexing the Citizen: Masculinity and Morality in France, 1870–1920* (Ithaca: Cornell University Press, 2006), forthcoming.

62. Théry, "Le contrat d'union sociale," p. 160.

63. Emmanuel LeRoy Ladurie, "Pourquoi le PaCS contredit l'héritage judéo-chrétien," *Le Figaro*, October 19, 1998.

64. Report on comments of RPR deputy Thierry Mariani in *Le Monde*, September 25, 1998. On October 9, 1998, Patrick Bloche, speaking in the National Assembly for the commission on social affairs, was called an "Islamist" by an opposition deputy in the course of the debate on the PaCS. See Borrillo and Lascoumes, *Amours égales?* p. 77.

65. Eric Fassin, "PaCS socialista," p. 10.

66. Borrillo, "Fantasmes des juristes," p. 183.

67. Ibid., p. 180; see also Irène Théry, *Le démariage: Justice et vie privée* (Paris: Odile Jacob, 1993).

68. Théry, "Le contrat d'union sociale," p. 180.

69. Mona Ozouf, *Les Mots des femmes: Essai sur la singularité française* (Paris:

Gallimard, 1995), p. 395. See also Joan W. Scott, "Vive la différence," *Le Débat* 87 (November–December 1995): 134–39, and Scott, "'La querelle des femmes' in late twentieth-century France," *New Left Review* 26 (November–December 1997): 3–19.

70. In a collection of articles on the juridical idea of the couple, H. Lécuyer stressed the urgency of defining the couple because "Sodom was demanding civil rights." Cited in Borrillo, "Fantasmes des juristes," p. 161.

71. Sylviane Agacinski, "Citoyennes, encore un effort," *Le Monde,* June 18, 1996, pp. 1, 17.

72. Agacinski, *Politique des sexes,* p. 101. See also "Questions autour de la filiation," interview with Agacinski by Eric Lamien and Michel Feher, *Ex Aequo,* July 1998, pp. 22–24.

73. Martel, *Le rose et le noir,* p. 618.

74. Agacinski, *Politique des sexes,* p. 20. Subsequent page references to this book appear in the text.

75. Tasca, *Rapport . . .* (see chap. 3, n. 19).

76. *Le Monde,* March 13, 1999.

77. Cited in Tasca, *Rapport . . . ,* p. 61.

78. Ibid., p. 85.

79. Assemblée nationale, 2nd sess., December 15, 1998, p. 10499.

80. Assemblée nationale, 3rd sess., December 15, 1998, p. 10543.

81. "La parité, ce 'so French' sujet de curiosité internationale," *Le Monde,* March 2, 2001; Judith Warner, "France goes nuts for parity: Same difference," *New Republic,* March 26, 2001, pp. 16–17.

82. Evelyne Pisier, "PaCS et parité: Du même et de l'autre," *Le Monde,* October 30, 1998, p. 18.

83. Jacques Derrida, "Mes 'humanités' du dimanche," *L'Humanité,* March 4, 1999, p. 12.

84. Ibid., p. 13.

85. Jacques Derrida and Elisabeth Roudinesco, *De quoi demain: Dialogue* (Paris: Fayard, 2001), pp. 46–48.

86. Rose-Marie Lagrave, "Une étrange défaite: La loi constitutionnelle sur la parité," *Politix* 13, no. 51 (2000): 113–41.

87. "Vers la République des quotas? Parité, la révolution qui divise," *Le Nouvel Observateur,* January 14–20, 1999, pp. 80–83. There was an outpouring of press coverage in the winter of 1999. Among others see "Oui à l'égalité, non à la parité," *L'Express,* February 11, 1999, pp. 50–55; Sophie Cognard, "La parité: Pour quoi faire?" *Le Point,* February 27, 1999; special issue of *Cultures: Sciences de l'homme et sociétés,* "Les femmes—avenir de la cité: Parité, citoyenneté, pouvoirs," February 1999; and the special issue of *Le Monde diplomatique,* "Femmes, mauvais genre?" March–April 1999.

88. Sylviane Agacinski, "Le droit d'être candidates," *Le Nouvel Observateur,* January 14–20, 1999, p. 82.

89. "Vers la République des quotas?" ibid., p. 81.

90. Françoise Gaspard, "Pourquoi revoir la Constitution?" *Le Monde diplomatique*, March–April 1999, p. 80.

91. Françoise Gaspard, "Ajuster la Constitution à la réalité sociale," *Le Monde des débats*, April 1999, p. 20. This is a good example of the antifoundationalist notion of universality as theorized by Judith Butler in "The End of Sexual Difference?" in her *Undoing Gender*, pp. 189–92.

92. See chap. 3, n. 54.

93. Françoise Gaspard, "La parité n'est pas la fin de l'histoire," *Pour*, no. 54 (March 1999).

CHAPTER SIX

1. Gaspard et al., *Au pouvoir citoyennes*, p. 129. See also Gaspard, "Des élections municipales sous le signe de la parité," *French Politics, Culture and Society*, 20, no. 1 (Spring 2002): 46. "The distinctive aspect of the movement for parity is to propose a method that asks for it to be inscribed in the law."

2. Gaspard et al., *Au pouvoir citoyennes*, p. 173.

3. Gaspard, "De la parité comme révélateur de l'inégalité," *Cultures en mouvement*, no. 14 (February 1999): 31.

4. Gaspard et al., *Au pouvoir citoyennes*, p. 10.

5. Ibid., p. 173.

6. "Parité, es-tu là?" *L'Express*, December 3, 1998, p. 19.

7. *Choisir: La cause des femmes*, no. 83 (December 1999): 6–7.

8. "Intervention du Premier Ministre aux Journées parlementaires du Groupe Socialiste," Strasbourg, September 27, 1999.

9. Assemblée nationale, 2nd sess., January 25, 2000, p. 340.

10. The original goal was not to make the national representation a mirror of society (though there were some politicians on both sides of the debates who maintained that that was the case), but to make access to representation more open (free of its association with men), hence more democratic. See Catherine Achin, "'Représentation miroir' vs. parité: Les débats parlementaires relatifs à la parité revus à la lumière des théories politiques de la représentation," *Droit et société*, no. 47 (2001): 237–56.

11. See Laure Bereni and Elénore Lépinard, "Les femmes ne sont pas une catégorie: Les stratégies de légitimation de la parité en France," *Revue française de science politique* 54, no. 1 (February 2004): 71–98.

12. Mme Martine Lignières-Cassou, Assemblée nationale, 2nd sess., January 25, 2000, p. 358.

13. M. Thierry Mariani, Assemblée nationale, 3rd sess., January 25, 2000, p. 382.

14. *La parité entre les femmes et les hommes à portée de main.*

15. This applied to only about one-third of the 36,000 communes of France, where, however, two-thirds of the French population resided. There were proposals to go below 3500, but these were rejected by the Constitutional Council.

16. In 2003, the requirement for regional lists was changed: there now must be strict alternation of women and men. For the European Parliament, voting is now by region rather than nationally. See later in this chapter, section dealing with regional and European Parliament elections.

17. "Quel avenir pour la parité?" *Choisir: La cause des femmes,* December 1999, pp. 6–7; Testimony of Marie-Jo Zimmermann, Assemblée nationale, 2nd sess., January 25, 2000, pp. 349–51, and of Roselyn Bachelot-Narquin, 3rd sess., January 25, 2000, pp. 369–70.

18. Bachelot-Narquin, ibid.

19. Catherine Achin and Marion Paoletti, "Le 'salto' du stigmate: Genre et construction des listes aux municipales de 2001," *Politix* 15, no. 60 (2002): 37, n. 10.

20. Ibid., p. 36, n. 8 (cites polling results and interviews with candidates).

21. "Les femmes prennent le pouvoir," *Le Point,* March 9, 2001, p. 41.

22. "Place aux femmes: La révolution des municipales," supplement to *Le Monde,* March 9, 2001, p. x.

23. Mariette Sineau, cited in Gaspard, "Des eléctions municipales," p. 54.

24. "Place aux femmes," *Le Monde,* February 22, 2001; March 9, 2001; and February 13, 2001.

25. Marion Paoletti, "L'usage stratégique du genre en campagne électorale," *Travail, genre et sociétés,* no. 11 (2004): 126.

26. Gaspard, "Des eléctions municipales," p. 50.

27. "Place aux femmes," supplement to *Le Monde,* March 9, 2001, p. xi; see also "Place aux femmes," *Le Monde,* February 7, 2001.

28. "A Blésignac, Gisèle et les femmes en colère," *Le Journal du dimanche,* March 11, 2001, p. 7.

29. "Place aux femmes," *Le Monde,* February 3, 2001.

30. "Place aux femmes," *Le Monde,* January 26, 2001; "Place aux femmes," supplement to *Le Monde,* March 9, 2001, p. iv.

31. *Le Monde,* January 9, 2001.

32. There are a number of local studies, with a wealth of detail in "La parité en pratiques," ed. Eric Fassin and Christine Guionnet, special issue of *Politix* 15, no. 60 (2002).

33. "Place aux femmes," *Le Monde,* February 7, 2001. *Beurette,* fem.; for *beur* (masc.) see chap. 3, n. 84.

34. Stéphane Latté, "Cuisine et dépendance: Les logiques pratiques du recrutement politique," *Politix* 15, no. 60 (2002): 69.

35. "Place aux femmes," *Le Monde,* February 24, 2001.

36. Latté, "Cuisine et dépendance," p. 70; Stéphane Latté and Eric Fassin, "La galette des reines: Femmes en campagne," in *Mobilisations électorales: A propos des élections municipales de 2001,* ed. Jacques Lagroye, Patrick Lehingue, and Fréderic Sawicki (Paris: Presses universitaires de France, 2004).

37. Latté and Fassin, "La galette des reines," p. 226.

38. *Le Point,* March 9, 2001, p. 37.

39. "Place aux femmes," *Le Monde,* March 2, 2001.

40. Marie-Jo Zimmermann, *Pourquoi la parité en politique reste-t-elle un enjeu pour la démocratie française,* Rapport à M. le Premier Ministre (Observatoire de la parité entre les femmes et les hommes, March 2003).

41. "Les conseillères municipales sont plus jeunes que leurs collègues hommes," *Le Monde,* April 23, 2001, p. 6; and Zimmermann, *Pourquoi la parité,* part 1.

42. "Les conseillères municipales," p. 6.

43. Gaspard, "Des élections municipales," p. 52.

44. See "La parité en pratique," for the variations.

45. This law superseded the provision for three women in each group of six on electoral lists for the regional elections in the law of June 6, 2000.

46. "Dans les conseils régionaux, les femmes sont mieux représentées mais restent loin du sommet," *Le Monde,* April 3, 2004. See also Mariette Sineau and Vincent Tiberj, "Conseils généraux: Où sont les femmes?" *Libération,* March 24, 2004, p. 37; and L'appel aux femmes de Lepage," *Le Journal du dimanche,* March 7, 2004, p. 1.

47. Http://membres.lycos.fr/sciencepolitiquenet/regionales2004.

48. www.ipsos.com: canal Ipsos, les rendez-vous de l'actualité: Politique et Elections, April 9, 2004. See also "Ségolène, Michèle, les préférées des Français," *Le Journal du dimanche,* March 7, 2004, p. 7. For a detailed analysis of these elections in one locality, see L'Assemblée des femmes du Languedoc et du Roussillon, *'Monsieur d'abord, Madame après': La Parité en Languedoc-Roussillon, Elections régionales et cantonales, 2004: Rapport d'évaluation intermédiare,* March 2004. Ségolène Royal is the companion of PS leader François Hollande. See "Blow to French Patriarchs: Babies May Get her Name," *New York Times,* January 20, 2005.

49. *Le Monde,* April 17, 2004.

50. L'Assemblée des Femmes du Languedoc et du Roussillon, "Communiqué de presse: La fin des Françaises aux avant-postes de la démocratie européenne?" 2004. For a report on the results of the elections, see "Cahier résultats: Elections européennes," *Le Monde,* June 15, 2004, pp. 37–56.

51. Mariette Sineau, "La réforme paritaire en France, ou comment sortir par le haut d'un blocage politico-institutionnel," unpublished paper given at a conference on "L'élection canadienne 2000 et la représentation des femmes: Quels enseignements le Canada peut-il tirer de l'expérience française de la parité?" Ottawa, November 29–30, 2001.

52. Until 2001, proportional representation applied only to districts with five or more seats; in that year, the socialists changed the law to apply to districts with three or more seats; after 2002, when the right regained control of the National Assembly, the number was raised from three to four.

53. "Le Sénat résiste à l'application de la loi sur la parité," *Le Monde,* September 22, 2001, p. 17; Zimmermann, "Rapport," March 2003, part 1; François Maniquet, Massimo Morelli, and Guillaume Frechetter, "Endogenous Affirmative Action: Gender Bias Leads to Gender Quotas," unpublished paper, January 2005 (in the personal papers of Massimo Morelli).

54. "Le Sénat résiste à l'application de la loi sur la parité." The dissident list had Autain at the top and the Green Party's Mireille Ferri (a woman) in second place. Autain promised to give Ferri his seat after three years, something he had not yet done in 2005. In October 2001 the national bureau of the Socialist Party expelled Autain; he is now a member of the Groupe communiste républicain et citoyen.

55. Marie-Jo Zimmermann, *Elections à venir: Faire vivre la parité*, Rapport à M. le Premier Ministre de l'Observatoire de la parité entre les femmes et les hommes, (December 2003), pp. 9–10; and Zimmermann, *Pourquoi la parité*, conclusion.

56. Before passage of the parity law, Gisèle Gautier (UDF) created a dissident list in the regional elections of 1998. Her list won three seats (not a good showing). She did win a seat in the Senate elections of 2001, but ran on the party list. I don't know of any women who established their own list in the Senate election of 2001.

57. This is high for France. In the United States more than half of eligible voters abstained in the presidential election of 2000.

58. Chevènement's 5.4% was widely blamed for Jospin's narrow defeat. Http://www.ipsos.fr.presidentielle.htm "Ipsos soirée présidentielle 2002–1er tour" (consulted May 1, 2002).

59. "Escroc contre facho," *Le Canard enchaîné*, April 24, 2002.

60. "Des féministes réclament un ministère des droits des femmes," *Le Monde,* May 12–13, 2002; "Vingt-sept ministres pour cinq semaines," *Libération,* May 8, 2002; "Le PS pointe le peu de place accordé aux femmes; les Verts dénoncent 'le retour de la Chiraquie,'" *Le Monde,* May 8, 2002; "Jacques Chirac refuse toute concession à la gauche, malgré son soutien," *Le Monde,* May 2, 2002; Michelle Perrot, "AGIR: Femmes, encore un effort," *Le Monde,* May 2, 2002; "In 'hidden vote' for Le Pen, French Bared Growing Discontent," *New York Times,* May 3, 2002, p. A12.

61. As penalty for failing to comply with the law, the UMP lost some 4 million euros, the PS 1.3 million. Zimmermann, *Pourquoi la parité,* March 2003, part 2, "Application de la parité lors des élections législatives de juin 2002. See also "Parité bien votée commence par les autres," *Libération,* July 13, 2002; "L'UMP ne présenterait que 20% de candidates," *Le Monde* May 9, 2002; "Les Verts présentent un projet de réforme de la société," *Le Monde,* May 7, 2002; and testimony of PS head François Hollande to the Observatoire de la parité, in Zimmermann, *Elections à venir,* December 2003, p. 81.

62. Zimmermann, *Pourquoi la parité,* March 2003, part 2.

63. Paoletti, "L'usage stratégique du genre," p. 135.

64. *Le Monde,* May 10, 2002, p. 9.

65. "French Politics Finds Little Room for Women," *New York Times,* June 7, 2002. Displacing Panafieu with Pons was also Chirac's way of settling scores that had less to do with gender than with intraparty politics.

66. Ibid.

67. "Pour les élections legislatives la droite a relégué la parité au second plan," *Le Monde,* May 10, 2002, p. 9.

68. Zimmermann, *Pourquoi la parité,* part 1.

69. Zimmermann, *Pourquoi la parité,* part 3. The substitute (*suppléant*) for an elected deputy usually takes the seat only if the deputy becomes a minister or dies, although in the case of death a new election may be held.

70. Ibid.

71. Ibid.

72. Zimmermann, *Elections à venir,* p. 11.

73. Ibid., p. 131.

74. Paoletti, "L'usage stratégique du genre," p. 126.

75. Ibid., p. 128.

76. Bachelot took over her father's post. Pierre Leroux and Philippe Teillet, "La domestication du féminisme en campagne," *Travail, genre et sociétés,* no. 11 (2004): 143–62.

77. Ibid., p. 153.

78. Ibid., p. 160.

79. Ibid., p. 144.

80. Paoletti, "L'usage stratégique du genre," p. 125.

81. Christine Guionnet, "Entrées de femmes en politique: L'irréductibilité du genre à l'heure de la parité," *Politix* 15, no. 60 (2002): 145.

82. Paoletti, "L'usage stratégique du genre," p. 137.

83. Guionnet, "Entrées de femmes en politique," p. 116.

84. Ibid., pp. 141–42.

85. Ibid., p. 144.

86. *Le Journal du dimanche,* March 7, 2004, p. 7. This percentage represented an increase over previous years: in 2003, 69% agreed that the number of women in politics ought to increase; in 2002, 66%.

CONCLUSION

1. This is the general argument offered by Judith Butler. "Precisely because the transcendental does not and cannot keep its separate place as a more fundamental 'level,' precisely because sexual difference as a transcendental ground must not only take shape within the horizon of intelligibility but structure and limit that horizon as well, it functions actively and normatively to constrain what will and will not count as an intelligible alternative within culture. Thus, as a transcendental claim, sexual difference should be rigorously opposed by anyone who wants to guard against a theory that would prescribe in advance what kind of sexual arrangements will and will not be permitted in intelligible culture. The inevitable vacillation between the transcendental and social functioning of the term makes its prescriptive function inevitable." Butler, "Competing Universalities." In *Contingency, Hegemony, Universality: Contemporary Dialogues on the Left,* ed. Judith Butler, Ernesto Laclau, and Slavoj Žižek (New York: Verso, 2000), p. 148.

2. Cited in Catherine Genisson, *La parité entre les femmes et les hommes: Une*

avancée decisive pour la démocratie, Rapport à M. le Premier Ministre (Observatoire de la parité, March 2002), app. 4, p. 29.

3. Cited in Sylvie Pionchon and Grégory Derville, *Les femmes et la politique* (Grenoble: Presses universitaires de Grenoble, 2004), p. 207.

4. Isabelle Giraud and Jane Jensen, "Constitutionalizing Equal Access: High Hopes, Dashed Hopes?" In *Has Liberalism Failed Women? Assuring Equal Representation in Europe and the United States*, ed. Jytte Klausen and Charles S. Maier (New York: Palgrave, 2001) p. 73.

5. Karen Bird, "Liberté, égalité, fraternité, parité . . . and diversité? The Difficult Question of Ethnic Difference in the French Parity Debate," *Contemporary French Civilization* 25, no. 2 (2001): 278.

6. Ibid., p. 281.

7. Giraud and Jensen, "Constitutionalizing Equal Access," p. 84.

8. See for example, Jacques Derrida, *Writing and Difference*, trans. Alan Bass (Chicago: University of Chicago Press, 1978); Luce Irigaray, *Speculum: Of the Other Woman*, trans. Gillian C. Gill (Ithaca: Cornell University Press, 1985).

9. In Sweden, for example, powerfully organized women's groups within the political parties successfully brought pressure for voluntary quotas. Today, women account for more than 40% of elected officials at local and national levels there. The paritaristes were well aware of the Swedish experience and of the structural differences between Sweden and France. See, for example, Elisabeth Elgán, "La parité dans la vie publique: La différence suédoise," *Parité-Infos*, supplement to no. 16 (December 1996).

10. Gaspard, "Des élections municipales sous le signe de la parité," p. 54.

11. Latté and Fassin, "La galette des reines," p. 239.

12. Parité, in effect, challenged the Lacanian notion of a relentless and inescapable process of symbolization and resymbolization. Here is Slavoj Žižek: "Sexual difference is not a firm set of 'static' symbolic oppositions and inclusions/exclusions, but the name of a deadlock, of a trauma, of an open question, of something that *resists* every attempt at its symbolization. Every translation of sexual difference into a set of symbolic oppositions is doomed to fail, and it is this very 'impossibility' that opens up the terrains of the hegemonic struggle for what 'sexual difference' will mean." Slavoj Žižek, "Class Struggle or Postmodernism? Yes, Please!" in *Contingency, Hegemony, Universality: Contemporary Dialogues on the Left*, ed. Ernesto Laclau and Slavoj Žižek (New York: Verso, 2000), p. 110. Parité was not so much about *re*symbolization as about *de*symbolization, ridding politics, and perhaps eventually all areas of social life, of these symbolic oppositions based on sex.

13. Claude Servan-Schreiber, "Pourquoi la parité est nécessaire et légitime," *Après-demain*, nos. 380–81 (January–February 1996): 34.

14. Žižek, "Class Struggle or Postmodernism?" p. 220.

15. Millard and Ortiz, "Parité et représentations politiques," p. 202.

INDEX

abstract individualism: and aims of parité movement, 151; and campaign for parité, 77, 91, 123; and citizenship, 1, 27, 71; and crisis of representation, 12–15, 19, 21, 22, 27, 32; definition of, 60–61, 109; and democracy, 13; and dilemma of difference, 51–52, 53, 54, 56, 58–62, 68, 71, 72, 73; importance of concept of, 8; and masculinity, 19; and republicanism, 12–15; sexing of, 4, 5, 53, 54, 58–62, 77, 119; and sexual difference, 4, 5; and sovereignty, 44; and universalism, 1, 4, 5, 8, 15
abstract nation, 5, 13, 15, 21, 27, 49, 50, 52
abstraction: and aims of parité movement, 147, 149, 151; and American views of politics, 5; and anatomical duality, 6; and campaign for parité, 5, 77, 91; as essence of French republicanism, 15; and universalism, 1, 4, 5, 8, 15, 17. *See also* abstract individualism; abstract nation
affirmative action, 2, 4–5, 21, 39, 45, 71, 91, 92, 95, 96, 126, 143, 149
Agacinski, Sylviane: and discourse of the couple, 115, 120–23; essentialism of, 65, 119, 121, 122, 123; and heterosexual couple, 66, 115, 147; and

mixité, 116, 118, 119, 126; *Politique des sexes* of, 65, 116–19, 121; as spokesperson for parité, 120
AIDES, 102, 103
AIDs, 100, 101, 110, 112
Alliance des femmes pour la démocratie, 80
Ameline, Nicole, 96
anatomical duality: and abstraction, 6; and campaign for parité, 109–10; and dilemma of difference, 54, 56, 57–58, 60–61, 65, 66, 67, 69, 70, 72; and discourse of the couple, 109–10, 122
Anatrella, Tony, 112, 113
Apprill, Claudette, 76
Arc en ciel, 76
Arnaud-Landau, Arlette, 135
assimilation, 12, 17, 21, 22, 23, 25, 26, 27, 29, 30, 148
Association of Catholic Families, 112–13
Athens conference (1992), 48, 76, 79, 80, 82
Au pouvoir citoyennes (Gaspard, Serban-Schreiber and Le Gall): and campaign for parité, 73, 74, 77, 85, 99; and dilemma of difference, 58–59, 60–61, 63–64, 67, 73; and need for parité law, 60–61, 63–64, 67, 124